Elizabeth Newman

Still makin' history…

Contents

Elizabeth Newman: Abstraction, Simulation, Obscuration[1]

Francis Plagne

Elizabeth Newman's oeuvre is divided in two by a period of nine years in which she essentially ceased to produce and exhibit new work. In this essay I treat the two periods of her art production separately. In my discussion of her work between 1984 and 1992 I focus on her ambiguous relationship to the tradition of modernist abstraction. Arguing that her work can be seen neither as simple revivalism or as knowingly ironic simulation, I show that a tension between her desire to practise modernist abstraction and her consciousness of historical and geographical distance from this tradition is made increasingly explicit in the work leading up to her move away from art production in 1992. I interpret the work Newman has produced since 2001 with reference to her vocal opposition to the conditions and discourses of contemporary capitalism. I find the aesthetic locus of this opposition in the opacity of her recent work, its refusal of communication. Distinguishing her work from both the classic avant-garde paradigm and Minimalism, I demonstrate its investment in the aura and the "traditional" distinction between art and life. A brief detour through Lacan's discussion of "the Thing" allows us to see what alternative her work offers to a contemporary experience that she sees as saturated by representation and the paranoiac need for certainty.

1984–1992

In a survey of "Recent Abstraction in Melbourne" published in 1988, Carolyn Barnes noted the diversity of abstract practices being shown in Melbourne galleries and wrote that this "continual presence of abstraction prompts an investigation of its current uses."[2] In the context of the eclipse of painting as a dominant (or even respectable) mainstream art practice, the proliferation of exhibitions by young artists in the 1980s working in the medium of abstract painting was understood through, broadly speaking, the two opposing paradigms of revivalism and irony. On the one hand, there were artists who were understood (and sometimes understood themselves) as attempting to revive or continue traditions of abstraction developed in the 1960s or earlier (the most important example in Australia being John Nixon's exploration of forms developed by the Russian avant-garde and assertion of a materialist theory of painting). On the other hand, there were abstract practices that, to various degrees and through a variety of techniques, interposed an ironic distance between themselves and the traditions of abstraction to which they referred. Artists such as Ross Bleckner, Philip Taaffe, Peter Halley, and Sherrie Levine developed the dominant example of such ironic abstraction in New York in the mid to late 1980s. As Hal Foster argues, this art "is not properly abstract except in the sense that it sometimes simulates or parodies abstraction."[3] Foster's point is clear in relation to artists such as Jack Goldstein and James Welling who at this time produced seemingly abstract works that were in fact derived from scientific and informational graphics. More importantly, however, it also applies to artists such as Levine, whose ironic distance from her checkerboard and stripe paintings of this period consists less in any specific conceptualist framing than in their refusal of the "immediacy and presence" of modernist abstraction in favour of "conventionalism" in which "painting is produced as the sign of painting,"[4] as "so many conventions and signs."[5] In Foster's reading, Levine's simulated abstraction was intended to demonstrate that the various historical modes of abstraction could no longer claim any fundamental relationship to the materiality of painting or "direct access to unconscious truths"; rather, Levine reduced the history of abstraction to a mere succession of styles.[6]

Writing about Australian abstraction in the 1980s, Barnes noted how often in this work one found a meshing together of abstract styles "in such close proximity that these antithetical systems negated one another."[7] She applied this reading to Elizabeth Newman's 1988 exhibition at City Gallery, *Pictures*, which presented a closely hung group of mainly small-scale geometric abstract paintings, many of them two-colour works, either contrasting a single foreground rectangle to a monochrome background, or dividing the canvas vertically or horizontally into two differently coloured halves. Barnes understood Newman's exhibition to refer to a "range of modernist abstraction from Malevich to Rothko, enlisted as a set of conceptual proposals representing intellect, spirit, subjectivity, transcendence—each in its time invested with truth value by its creator." The juxtaposition of these various models "results in a position of contingency, superseding the belief in absolute positions of the modern."[8] Barnes saw Newman as

1 All otherwise unattributed information comes from conversations between Elizabeth Newman and the author, February 2014.

2 Carolyn Barnes, "Recent Abstraction in Melbourne," *Art & Text* 30 (1988): 82.

3 Hal Foster, "Signs Taken for Wonders" (1986), in *Abstract Art in the Late Twentieth Century*, ed. Frances Colpitt (Cambridge: Cambridge University Press, 2002), 108.

4 Ibid., 111, 116.

5 Ibid., 115.

6 Ibid., 109. Foster asks of this generation of painters: "do they receive abstract painting as so reified, or do they participate in its emptying out?" (ibid.). His later expanded discussion of this issue in *The Return of the Real* makes clear his belief that Neo-Geo actively reified abstraction, reducing it to surface and style. See Foster, *The Return of the Real* (Cambridge, Mass.: MIT Press, 1996), 99–125.

7 Barnes, "Recent Abstraction in Melbourne," 81.

a postmodern artist, unable to continue in good faith the search for essence and finality in painting precisely because the knowledge of the successive and diverging claims to such a mode of painting (Malevich, Mondrian, Reinhardt, Stella) seemed to undermine its possibility. In this reading she would become a kind of *bricoleur* with the history of past styles and theories as the only available tools with which to attempt to negotiate and articulate her own subjective position.

The notion that Newman's work cannot be understood as simple abstraction, but must be understood as in some sense second-order or ironic, even if only through consciously "revisit[ing] influential moments in art history,"[9] is common in the literature on her work.[10] Yet, as Eve Sullivan has argued, while it certainly seems the case that Newman's work in the 1980s participated in her generation's discomfort with "the mystery embedded in the connoisseurship of the mark," it is very difficult to find in her work anything comparable to the "cynical smart contortions" of the "schoolbook approach to postmodernism," or any direct evidence of a critical, "consciousness-raising" intent that would give meaning to such a distance from the high-modernist tradition.[11] That is, while it seems clear that in the 1980s Newman was producing abstract work that was in some sense "second-order," that could be said to *refer to* a tradition of abstraction rather than simply *existing within* one, it is difficult to articulate exactly what this second-order or distanced character consists in.

* * *

Speaking of her time in art school and her work in the 1980s, Newman points to her genuine enthusiasm for the sublime high-modernist abstraction of Mark Rothko and Ad Reinhardt, accompanied, in a familiar pairing, by an interest in romantic landscape painting, most importantly Caspar David Friedrich.[12] The list of artists to whom Newman has dedicated specific pieces in the last few years reads like a connoisseur's collection of important, yet somewhat marginal and idiosyncratic, practitioners of late-modernist abstraction: Ellsworth Kelly, Robert Mangold, Imi Knoebel. And in recent years Newman has written of her work as searching for "a type of 'soul' or subjectivity," a characterisation distanced from a knowingly ironic attitude.[13] What then is it about Newman's painting in the 1980s that seems to stamp it with the quality of somehow not being the "real thing," of demonstrating some sort of reservation in the artist's relationship to her work?

We might begin by looking at Newman's presentation of her paintings in exhibitions such as *Pictures* (City Gallery, 1988). In clear contravention of the conventions of the late-modernist art gallery, distinguished by its uniform eye-level hanging and wide spacing, Newman hung her works in a disorderly salon style reminiscent of, although not as extreme as, the contemporaneous exhibition style of John Nixon. This hanging style complicates the possibility of viewing individual pieces in isolation, and problematises the possibility of any single work being distinguished as a "masterpiece." The paintings thus grouped together display a range of compositional techniques that, as Barnes noted in the comments cited above, seem to refer to several historically distinct precedents. While the paintings are all broadly speaking geometric abstractions, they use their basic elements in ways that are not simply diverse but, in the context of the history of theorisations of abstract painting, contradictory. Many paintings are composed of a single rectangular form set off against a monochrome background: in this adoption of simple foreground/background distinction they refer to compositional practices that were eventually abandoned in the 1960s by artists wishing to suppress the vestigial trace of representational space they contain.[14] Other paintings in the show, however, are structured simply through the symmetrical division of the canvas, either vertically or horizontally, into two halves of different colours. In their refusal to call up any trace of physical illusionism, they seem to exist within the lineage of 1960s hard-edge abstraction and its deductive structures. As Barnes noted, the fact that these paintings are shown alongside those depending on foreground/

8 Ibid., 82.

9 Geraldine Barlow, Max Delany, Francis E. Parker, and Patrice Sharkey, "Proof and Practice," in *Artists' Proof #1* (Melbourne: Monash University Museum of Art, 2012), 79. The authors point to this as a feature of both Newman's and Rose Nolan's work.

10 Damiano Bertoli makes this point eloquently when he calls Newman's work from the 1980s onwards a "reflexive catalogue of meta-paintings: paintings of other painting, paintings about paintings." Bertoli, "Stratified and Gratified: Lizzy Newman's Expanded Feel," in *Elizabeth Newman: More than What There Is* (Melbourne: 3-ply, 2013), 87.

11 Eve Sullivan, "Elizabeth Newman: Interesting Times, the 1980s and 1990s," in *Elizabeth Newman*, 27–29.

12 Robert Rosenblum famously made the link between "sublime abstraction" and the romantic landscape tradition in his *Modern Painting and the Northern Romantic Tradition: Friedrich to Rothko* (London: Thames and Hudson, 1975). The earliest work that Newman chose to reproduce in the recent monograph on her work is a landscape painting copied from an image found in a magazine (*Capri*, 1984), of which she says: "I was interested in the sublime at the time. But I also knew that it was 'second degree.'" Elizabeth Newman, email to the author, March 8, 2014.

13 Elizabeth Newman, "Introduction," in *Elizabeth Newman*, 10.

14 The classic account of this development is Michael Fried, "Three American Painters" (1965), in *Art and Objecthood: Essays and Reviews* (Chicago: University of Chicago Press, 1998), 213–265.

background distinction seems to suggest that Newman does not accept the suppression of this distinction as a form of irreversible progress, with a greater claim to the truth of painting because it has succeeded in purging itself of what Michael Fried calls "material extrinsic to the problems of painting,"[15] namely, the spatial depth which allows one object or plane to exist "in front" or "behind" another.

The sense that what we are looking at are in some sense representations or simulations of particular modes of abstract painting is heightened by the small size of many of the pieces. Grand scale became a distinguishing feature of abstract painting in the American tradition beginning in the late 1940s; far from a simple desire for monumentality, Barnett Newman, for example, felt that the largeness of his paintings was essential for facilitating an immersive experience in the viewer. In this context, and with their clear reference to artists within the abstract expressionist and colour field traditions, Newman's generally small paintings (many around 27 × 20 cm) appear as studies or mock-ups for larger paintings never made; in a different sense to that of postmodern "conventionalism," they appear as "paintings of paintings."

When considered in relation to the art that seems to provide its models, Newman's work, as a number of commentators have noted, appears to "fail."[16] Erich Franz has argued that Richard Tuttle, particularly in his drawings, "often uses the simultaneous presence of geometry and hand-drawing to undermine each other."[17] A similar point can be made about Newman, whose paintings, particularly those created between 1987 and 1989, seem to model themselves insistently on the clean edges and clear geometry of early twentieth-century abstraction and 1960s hard-edged painting while continually, and seemingly deliberately, failing to attain it. Her hand-painted monochrome fields fail to attain the flat, uninflected appearance that so many artists have sought using spray paint and staining techniques, and her central rectangular forms only barely approximate the geometric forms they suggest. But Newman does not insist on this hand-painted nature of her work in order somehow to combine geometric modes with expressionist, gestural abstraction. On the contrary, her paintings are marked by a casual, even desultory style that is the antithesis of the cathartic emotional investment of action painting.[18] The unevenness of the monochrome field is unimportant, as long as it is filled; a form still reads as geometrical despite a few messy edges.

Distanced both historically and geographically from the abstract painting she admired, Newman was influenced by her exposure to Tony Clark's "botched imitations" and her conversations and eventual collaborations with Geoff Lowe to consider her own "failed" attempt at painting in the high-modernist tradition as something interesting and to develop it as an idiosyncratic style.[19] We can see how the "failure" in her work becomes its specific focal point. *Untitled (gold)* (1987), for instance, consists of a blank canvas with a golden rectangle inscribed in crayon on its surface. The simple, linear geometric form on a monochromatic background in some ways recalls the work of Robert Mangold, but the sparseness of the composition puts the focus on its imperfections: the speckled, uneven edges of the crayon line, its slightly off-centre placement, an apparent slip of the hand where a line has veered diagonally away from the intended shape. Even in less obviously messy or "failed" pieces, such as *Untitled* (1989), it is the areas of the canvas containing what appear to be errors that exert the strongest pull on the viewer: specifically, the joins between the sides of the rectangle, where in three cases the horizontal line extends beyond the vertical one, suspending the form between two shapes, one a perfect rectangle, which it only approximates, the other, another irregular shape that it has tentatively begun to trace. The modest, sometimes humorous impression that these "funny abstracts" make is precisely a result of the fact that they suggest but appear to deliberately fail to live up to traditions of high-modernist

15 Michael Fried, "New York Letter: Louis, Chamberlain and Stella, Indiana" (1962), in *Art and Objecthood*, 285.

16 See, for example, Patrice Sharkey's comments (although she is speaking of some of Newman's most recent work): "As examples of the clean non-objective shapes favoured by the minimalist tradition she mines, they willfully fail." Sharkey, "Elizabeth Newman," in *Artists' Proof #1*, 62.

17 Erich Franz, "'One Thing': Unity and Divergences of American Art Concepts," in *Beyond the Picture: Works by Robert Barry, Sol LeWitt, Robert Mangold, Richard Tuttle from the Collection of Dorothy and Herbert Vogel, New York* (Bielefeld: Kunsthalle Bielefeld, 1987), 32.

18 Even her non-geometric abstractions (such as *Abstract* and *Abstract II* [1988]) evacuate the painted mark of its expressive resonance. Unlike the dramatic, singular gestures of Abstract Expressionists such as Franz Kline, in these paintings, Newman repeats her seemingly "expressive" strokes mechanically, like someone doodling absent-mindedly, filling the canvas almost entirely with looping and vertical lines. Although these paintings are consistent with the "all-over" compositional strategy of colour field and monochrome painting, they also demonstrate the importance of Cy Twombly to Newman at this time. As Kirk Varnedoe has remarked, Twombly's work, in opposition to artists such as Kline, is marked by "the apparent mindlessness of a linear activity pursued, both obsessively and indulgently, without concern for the compositional drama of the whole." Kirk Varnedoe, "Inscription in Arcadia," in *Cy Twombly: A Retrospective* (New York: Museum of Modern Art, 1994), 22.

19 Max Delany, "Public and Private Paintings," in *Tony Clark: Public and Private Paintings 1982–1998* (Melbourne: Museum of Modern Art at Heide, 1998), 7.

painting that are consciously bold and powerful, tied to images of heroic subjectivity and historical claims about essence, progress, and perfection.[20]

Far from the theoretically informed concerns of New York postmodernism, which reduced the objects of "simulation" painting to a medium through which to affirm the death of painting, and yet not always radically distinct from the products of this postmodernism, Newman's second-order painting practice developed relatively intuitively from uneasiness and doubt about the possibility of practising high-modernist abstraction in her geographical and historical situation.[21] As we will see, this uneasiness is most clearly voiced in the text paintings Newman made in 1989–1990, but it also informs her earliest surviving work. In 1985, Newman made her most explicitly second-order paintings, a trio of muted and roughly painted representational images showing a blank canvas, a studio with paintings hung and leant against a wall, and, most strikingly, a single gestural abstract painting.[22] She later made a number of drawings that reproduce, in an attractively awkward and amateurish style, magazine images of modernist artworks *in situ* at the Metropolitan Museum of Art. The first pair of drawings (*The Met*, 1987) shows tiny gallery attendees dwarfed by artworks in "The Met's 20th Century Gallery" and "A gallery of works by living artists." The second (*Donald Judd, Agnes Martin*, 1987), this time free of figures, hesitantly reproduces the position of a Donald Judd sculpture in front of a painting by Agnes Martin. It would be easy to see these works as wry, subtle reminders of the enthusiastic embrace of formalist abstraction and Minimalism as a form of cultural capital by corporations and governments (the "corporate lobby decorations" argument against high modernism) or of the importance of the institutional frame within which these works are encountered.[23] Importantly, however, Newman's 1985 paintings depict, if not specific works of her own, then at least the sort of work she was producing at the time; note for instance the similarity between the painting depicted in *Abstract* and a drawing from the same year called *Picture*, both of which are composed of a dense, freely drawn or painted rectangle of knotted black lines, bordered by empty, white space that serves as an inner frame. Rather than affirming an institutional or historical critique, these works stem from Newman's struggle to find a way to continue the practice of modernist abstraction. They suggest that, for Newman, modernist abstraction would only continue to be possible by becoming a representation or sign of itself. Her work of this period is thus deeply marked by a tension: while in its insistently "simulated" quality it draws close to the textbook postmodernism of Neo-Geo, it lacks any reference to a theoretical paradigm that would have allowed her to trumpet this simulated quality as a critique or ironising of modernist abstraction, a tradition in which she continued to be heavily invested. Rather than announcing the transformation of painting into a simulation of itself as a reenactment of the "death of painting" understood as an irreversible historical fact, or instrumentalising this simulation as a tool of critique, Newman's painting was caught in an unresolved contradiction between the "sublime" and the "second degree."[24]

Although she would not continue to "mediate" her abstraction so obviously, most of her work in the 1980s is formed by the insight contained in these early representational paintings. Her titles contribute to the "second-order" effect of her work at this time. In addition to the abstract drawing mentioned above called *Picture*, she produced in the same year a beautiful Twombly-esque pencil and crayon piece called *Abstract*. Although the clear signs of realist representation seen in her paintings of the same year (walls, floors, shadows) are absent, in both of these works the drawn area is contained within a rough rectangle. One could say that, unlike the surface of colour field painting, which asserts itself *as* picture, in these works Newman's surfaces merely *contain* pictures. This inner frame creates an ambiguity about the status of these works: are they abstract works that exist on their terms or crudely drawn representations of other pictures? Newman's titles contribute to this ambiguity: refusing titles that stress the ineffable material specificity of the work (on the model of "Untitled" or "Number 1") or its allusive power (i.e., "Stations of the Cross"), Newman titled many of her pieces and exhibitions in manifestly generic terms: *Abstract, Picture, Paintings* (George Paton Gallery, 1986), *Pictures* (City Gallery, 1988 and 1989), *Art Exhibition* (Roslyn Oxley 9, 1989).

* * *

The changes that Newman introduced into her work in 1989 indicate that she came to believe that this abstract painting at one remove could not be carried on indefinitely without descending into pastiche. Rather than developing an increased comfort with abstract painting that would close the gap between her practice and the formalist traditions she inherited, Newman's work demonstrates precisely the opposite, a dramatisation of her uncertainty about and discomfort with the tradition of abstraction. In 1989, Newman produced a large group of canvases featuring hand-painted

20 Sullivan, "Elizabeth Newman," 30.

21 This reading of simulation painting is suggested by Yve-Alain Bois. See his "Painting: The Task of Mourning," in *Painting as Model* (Cambridge, Mass.: MIT Press, 1990), 242–244.

22 *Blank Canvas; Studio Picture; Abstract*, all 1985.

23 Even by the time Theodor Adorno wrote his *Aesthetic Theory*, posthumously published in 1970, he could refer to the problematic fact that "nonrepresentational art is suitable for decorating the walls of the newly prosperous" as a commonplace of contemporary discourse on the relationship between modernist art and society. Adorno, *Aesthetic Theory*, trans. Robert Hullot-Kentor (London: Continuum, 1997), 300.

24 See the statement cited in n. 12 above.

text over monochrome backgrounds. The texts range from lapidary statements at once truistic and enigmatic ("There are some bad ideas," "People bring their lives to art") to pop-philosophical and personal credos ("I believe in other possible worlds," "I'll see for myself"). Although on a first glance these pieces might seem reminiscent of the ironic, opaque statements of Jenny Holzer's *Truisms* series (1977–79), it is possible to see their continuity with problems that Newman had been dealing with in her previous work.[25]

This series was initially sparked by Newman's reading of an essay by Rosalind Krauss analysing Joan Miró's integration of text into his paintings. For Krauss, Miró's "tense syntheses of the normally separate spaces of looking and reading" set up a series of interactions between painting and the "non-descriptive, non-pictorial carrier of meaning," between "the non-specific space of the page" and "the absolute specificity of the unique picture."[26] In Krauss's interpretation of Miró, the linguistic and the pictorial are only two elements within a complex interplay of different forms of written and painted marks (linguistic, representational, abstract, diagrammatic, ideogrammatic) that Miró uses simultaneously and ambiguously in order to unsettle the distinctions between them. Newman's paintings are more clearly based on a simple opposition between their words and monochrome fields, and it is in this opposition that we can see how the traditions of high-modernist abstraction inform Newman's text paintings. The notion that abstract painting is not only anti-literary but also opposed and inaccessible to language as such is, of course, a commonplace within the discourse of modernist abstraction, particularly in the post-war American variants important to Newman; nobody would have been surprised, for instance, when in 1965 the second-generation abstract expressionist Joan Mitchell distinguished her work from the "intellectual problems" of the post-Duchampian neo-avant-garde by saying "the particular thing I want can't be verbalized."[27] In the context of Newman's interest in the abstract sublime, it is important to understand the monochrome fields of these works not as neutral grounds for the text painted over them, but as ineffable, sensuous expanses of colour that have been interrupted and forced into an encounter with their opposite, language. The piece that most clearly exemplifies the logic of this series features a dark olive-green ground over which is painted "The AUTHORITY of Art rests upon an invisible platform of KNOWLEDGE and POWER." Here traditional views of abstract painting as either ineffable and sublime or derived neutrally from its material characteristics are countered by a sociological critique that points to the ideological and institutional structures that prop up art's perceived "authority."[28]

Miró's interplay of different signifying forms has the effect of destabilising the distinctions between them; Newman's opposition of written word and painted colour, on the other hand, depends on the distinction between its two elements. If in the context of Newman's complex relationship to the heritage of modernist abstraction these works should be seen as in some sense critical of this heritage, or at least as expressing Newman's uneasy relationship to it, it is important to note the ambiguity of this critique. The opposition they pose between mute painting and the written word must in fact affirm (just as an abstract expressionist might) that painting is alien to language in order to confront it with its "other" (language).

The unresolved opposition of Newman's text paintings provided the model for much of the remaining work she would produce before temporarily abandoning art in 1992. A series of paintings made between 1989 and 1991 engages another traditional opposition, that between abstract painting and photographic representation. According to a familiar historical reconstruction, the invention of photography forced painting into a consideration of how it could survive the usurpation of its representational function, setting in motion a process that begins with impressionism and eventually results in abstract or nonrepresentational painting. In *Beautiful* (1989), Newman affixes three magazine images of a rocky coastline to a large monochrome painted in a deep blue. Deliberately failing to achieve any integration between photograph and painted surface, the image forces the viewer to alternate between seeing the blue monochrome as simply the background for the photographs and experiencing the photographs as interruptions in the monochrome field: photograph and monochrome painting are not synthesised but rather negate each other.

Vision (1991) engages the idea of immersion or absorption in modernist abstraction. Michael Fried famously argued for a distinction between the high-modernist abstract art he admired (such as the work of Jules Olitski and Anthony Caro) and Minimalism by distinguishing the "heightened perceptual experience"[29] the latter offered its viewer from the transcendent "presentness" of the former.[30] Fried understood the experience of high-modernist abstract painting and sculpture to be in direct opposition to the "theatrical,"

25 David Pestorius showed keen critical insight when he included one of these works in his 2000–2001 *Monochromes* exhibition. See David Pestorius, 'Monochromes,' in *Monochromes* (Brisbane: University Art Museum, University of Queensland, 2001), 28.
26 See Rosalind Krauss, "Magnetic Fields: The Structure," in *Joan Miró: Magnetic Fields* (New York: Solomon R. Guggenheim Foundation, 1972), 14–19.
27 Cited in John Ashbery, "Joan Mitchell" (1965), in *Reported Sightings: Art Chronicles, 1957–1987* (New York: Alfred A. Knopf, 1989), 101.
28 Newman's discomfort with this "authority" is the subject of another untitled work in the series from the same year, which states, "I'm not an authority on Art."
29 Michael Fried, "An Introduction to My Art Criticism," in *Art and Objecthood*, 40.
30 Fried, "Art and Objecthood" (1968), 166–168.

self-reflexive experience of minimalist art, which occasions in the viewer a heightened awareness of their everyday spatio-temporal experience. Contrary to this self-reflexive awareness, the experience of late modernist abstraction has often been understood as absorptive and immersive, a meditative experience in which one loses awareness of oneself: think for example of the famous photo of Barnett Newman and his assistant demonstrating the ideal position from which to view one of his monumental canvases, standing only a few inches back from the painting.[31] *Vision* is an unpainted piece of stretched linen onto which two plastic eyes have been affixed. It substitutes the immersive experience of high-modernist monochrome expanse for a comical yet uneasy sense of being watched, and thus introduces the self-conscious sense of looking that defines Fried's concept of theatricality. In the context of Newman's text and photo paintings of the same period, it seems again to stage an opposition between painting and its other: this time not in terms of what essentially characterises the modernist painting itself, but rather in terms of what belongs essentially to the experience of looking at a modernist painting.

Looking at *Vision* alongside paintings such as *Untitled (Love)* (1992), which places photographs and texts over a complex "atmospheric" abstraction, allows us hypothetically to reconstruct the problems that led to Newman's temporary exit from art in 1992. Unable to continue in earnest the tradition of modernist painting that inspired her work, she initially developed a remarkable, deliberately failed, "second-order" mode of painting in reference to this tradition. The essentially ironic nature of this position seems to have made it incompatible with her enthusiasm for the modernist tradition, her ambiguous relationship to which she articulated in a highly charged way in the works that follow on from her text paintings. These pieces seem to represent an impasse: in them, the only possibility for the continuation of the modernist tradition seems to be its negation, the irresolvable confrontation between painting and its other.

2001–2014

Since she returned to dedicated artmaking in 2001, Newman's work has taken a variety of distinct yet often clearly related forms: pieces made from sewn, cut, or unaltered fabrics pinned directly to the wall, arranged on canvas, or sometimes displayed on the floor; items of clothing onto which text or found images have been printed; text paintings and posters; polychrome and monochrome abstract paintings, the latter often on unstretched canvas; found objects (vases, wooden logs, pieces of metal or cardboard, blankets, cushions, a clothes rack), sometimes displayed on shelves or plinths; collages, often incorporating material from art magazines. Unlike her work in the 1980s and early 1990s, in which various forms of production followed one another in relatively discrete episodes, most of the forms in which she has worked since she returned to art in 2001 remain part of her current practice. Importantly, she usually exhibits different kinds of objects simultaneously: her exhibit at the National Gallery of Victoria's *Melbourne Now* survey exhibition (2013–14), for example, presented a text painting, a dress produced in collaboration with the fashion designers ffiXXed, two monochromes on unstretched canvas, a found piece of metal, and a wall piece made from chenille fabric. Whereas her work in the 1980s was determined primarily by the necessity of working through a complex and conflicted relationship to her art-historical precedents, her work since 2001 is motivated by an oppositional stance towards the conditions of contemporary life and its dominant discourses (including in the aesthetic sphere), a position she has developed through numerous texts and public presentations. Looking back on her work since 2001, she writes that when she returned to making art in that year she was "addressing the question of art's place in relation to the discourse of capitalism"; more specifically, she sees herself as attempting to articulate a form of artistic "*praxis* that could be an alternative to the dominant discourse."[32] Newman's characterisation of the conditions of contemporary life and its dominant discourse has, I think, three key components. First, the dominant force of contemporary life is capitalism, understood as producing reification, "a type of psychotic discourse that positions human subjects as objects (of consumption)."[33] Secondly, this reduction of subjectivity is compounded by "a growing intolerance for the indeterminacy and polyvalence of representation and language."[34] The languages of bureaucracy, of advertising, of a government that announces that it "says what it means and means what it says" all disavow the fact that the subject is constituted as a relationship to something unknown (the unconscious) that means we can never really say what we mean or mean what we say. The desire to reach definitive agreement on "terms and meanings" can only ever be "a form of coercion and domination" through which subjectivity is repressed.[35] Thirdly, we are faced with a proliferation of

31 He also affirmed this as the ideal viewing position in a statement accompanying an exhibition of his work at Betty Parson Gallery in 1951: "the large pictures in this exhibition are intended to be seen from a short distance." Barnett Newman, *Selected Writings and Interviews* (New York: Knopf, 1990), 178.

32 Newman, "Introduction," 9.

33 Ibid.

34 Elizabeth Newman, "The Distance Between Representation and Domination or... Why We Don't Want a Government that 'Says What it Means, and Means What It Says,'" lecture at Victorian College of the Arts, University of Melbourne, September 2013, now in Elizabeth Newman, *Texts*, ed. David Homewood (Melbourne: Discipline, 2019), 60–61.

35 Ibid.

media and communication technologies that perpetuate this destruction of ambiguity and subjectivity and, in the words of an essay by Australian author and critic Eden Liddelow from which Newman has quoted a number of times, create a situation in which "the fictive and unnecessary occupy our attention much more than the necessary."[36] There is too much communication, "too much representation."[37] She proposes an art that has a "relationship to time and silence, rather than space and sound": silence, because of its opposition to the "noise" of contemporary discourse; time, because time, unlike space, is the form of both inner and outer experience, and thus intimately bound up with subjectivity.[38]

* * *

Although most are untitled, the titles Newman has given to some of her work since 2001 (quite different to the generic titles given to many of her pieces of the 1980s) demonstrate her antipathy to a mode of discourse that would suppress indeterminacy and polysemy by fixing references and tying "words to things."[39] She does not fall into the contradiction of directly addressing this destruction of the indirect: many of Newman's recent works bear titles that are both oblique in their relationship to what they name and quite obscure in themselves. Her 2006 Heide Museum of Modern Art exhibition, titled *You're still making history that no-one even knew how to*, and the 2012 pair of collages called *Immaterial space isn't necessarily ethically superior*, are exemplary in this regard. These titles, which read like fragments cut from longer sentences that might have clarified their meaning, refuse any explanatory role. In their ambiguous relationship to what they name, they strengthen Newman's refusal to accept transparent communication or immediacy, and in so doing they imply (and encourage) a certain kind of spectator: one who will puzzle over whether the "immaterial space" of *Immaterial space isn't necessarily ethically superior* might somehow refer to the images of art galleries that figure prominently in these two collages, one who might ask why Newman would choose to dedicate a found piece of metal *To Bradley Manning* (2013). Importantly, some of these titles are derived from texts written by Geoff Lowe and A Constructed World, and the uncertain, questioning viewer they imply harmonises with the words Newman wrote for A Constructed World's 2007 Australian Centre for Contemporary Art (ACCA) exhibition: "current features of our culture tend ... towards certainty and a fundamental lack of belief in unknown knowledge: towards paranoia. In response to this I say: 'Increase your uncertainty!'"[40]

In the midst of what she sees as a proliferation of coercive and reductive meanings, Newman's oppositional stance is, quite logically, developed as a "capacity of form" rather than content or theme.[41] Her work seems to take Adorno's advice: "in order to resist the all-powerful system of communication [artworks] must rid themselves of any communicative means that would perhaps make them accessible."[42] Writing of Newman's 1990 exhibition of text paintings, Naomi Cass called them "alarming" in their "directness, friendliness."[43] Such a description does not apply to the work that Newman has produced since 2001, much of which does not simply happen to be obscure in its meaning and opaque almost to the point of blankness, but is fundamentally invested in this opacity and structured so as to insist on it. Newman understands her recent collages to "insert and assert the presence of something 'un-representable' into the field of representation."[44]

This occurs through the side-by-side placement of patches of pure colour next to photographic representations, and also through techniques that simply and economically disrupt the signifying potential of word and images: arbitrary cropping of words so that we can no longer literally read them but must speculatively fill them out (as in *Untitled*, 2013 where "Artforum" becomes "rum"), photographs shown upside down (*Collateral Damage*, 2013) or torn. Of course, we can usually work out what these words and images are; and, in fact, part of the pleasure these works give us comes from the simplicity of the means with which they let us see their contents simultaneously as signifying and as reduced to sheer surface.

At other times, Newman's collages stress more directly their interruption of the communicative properties of their source material. *Immaterial space isn't necessarily ethically superior 1* (2012), for instance, simply adds two elements to a full-page advertisement for London's Maureen Paley gallery, obscuring the centre of the image with a roughly cut rectangle of grey paper. Maureen Paley advertisements use a standardised format in which the details of the current exhibition are printed over a generic gallery shot in the central position in which Newman has placed her collaged element; whether or not this particular advertisement features such a text, the effect is that information has been obscured by an opaque surface.

The importance of obscuration in Newman's collages suggests a way of understanding her monochrome painting.

36 Cited in Elizabeth Newman, "No Noise" (2007), in *Elizabeth Newman*, 81.
37 Ibid.
38 Newman, "Introduction," 10.
39 Newman, "The Distance between Representation and Domination," 61.
40 Elizabeth Newman, "Everybody Knows!," in *A Constructed World: Increase Your Uncertainty* (Melbourne: Australian Centre for Contemporary Art, 2007), 135.
41 Adorno, *Aesthetic Theory*, 301.
42 Ibid., 316.
43 Naomi Cass, "Hearsay," in *An Exhibition of Work by Elizabeth Newman* (Melbourne: City Gallery, 1990), n.p.
44 Elizabeth Newman, unpublished artist's statement, 2013.

Any substantial area of colour allows the eye to roam within it in an ambiguously "spatial" way, and this is often at the forefront of our experience of a monochrome painting;[45] but awareness that the surface we are presented with covers over and obscures another surface below is also, in Morgan Thomas' formulation, at the core of this experience. Painting is always a "veiling ... which introduces an opacity, a division, in what presents itself to the eye," and precisely because the opaque surface of the monochrome seems to present its viewer with so little "content," the experience of viewing a monochrome is marked by an awareness of this zero-degree of painting as simply covering a surface.[46] Thus, while the monochrome seems to present nothing (no content, no composition, no "meaning"), this "nothing is not quite nothing" because it "remains opaque" to us.[47] Newman's monochromes appear, as Patrice Sharkey recognises, as a form of painting that is essentially "painting over."[48]

Similarly, *1988* (2008), a brown paper envelope (propped up on a log) on which we can read "Derrida" written upside down on its lower left-hand corner, hinges on our awareness that something is hidden from us. The work teases us by presenting an object so clearly recognisable as a container for contents that remain invisible and which, as Newman has pointed out, in the context of Derrida's position in Anglo-American academia of the 1980s and 1990s as a master-signifier of advanced discourse, seem to hold out the promise of meaning.[49] The hope that something might hide behind these opaque surfaces is also simultaneously dramatised and frustrated in the numerous pieces that Newman has made over the last few years in which three cuts in the centre of a wall-mounted piece of fabric or carpet cause a square of it to hang down, displaying its underside. Of course, just as with the neatly cut logs that have featured in a number of her works, the "inside" is simply another surface, another opacity.[50] The seemingly purely formal motivation behind the cut, entirely unrelated to the carpet's previous function, also engages another register of opacity, in that in its very arbitrariness (with regard to the object's original use) it suggests that nothing will be gained by looking at this object in terms of the significance or symbolism of its everyday context. Thus, in this opacity, vision is blocked in its search for a space to enter into, and interpretation is blocked in its search for a meaningful connection to something outside the work.

* * *

In a text written to accompany her 2007 exhibition at Neon Parc, *No Noise*, Newman explains that her antipathy to the current cultural situation has led her to look again at a certain group of artists from the early 1960s (she mentions Robert Morris, Donald Judd, Yvonne Rainer, Steve Paxton, Trisha Brown, and John Cage), in whom she finds the "negativity and absence that incarnate the avant-garde project."[51] It is easy to find comparable elements across the work of these choreographers, sculptors, and composers in these terms—deskilling, the inclusion of everyday movements, sounds or experiences, silence, stillness, an interest in boredom, an anti-spectacular impulse. In what Newman calls its "promotion of the pedestrian or 'everyday,'" we might relate this avant-garde to the canonical definition of the avant-garde project as the attempt to cancel the distinction between art and life and create a new synthesis of these two terms.[52] Newman's work has also been understood in these terms. Writing of the monochrome paintings and found objects in Newman's exhibition *The true collector looks for the work that is unfinished* of 2012, Shelley McSpedden argues that "their ordinariness collapses distinctions between art and everyday life"[53] and Ulanda Blair, reviewing *No Noise*, in which fluorescent lights and a live plant were attached to rectangular sheets of plywood, wrote that "their indefinite relationship to functionality and the everyday meant that everything was collapsed."[54]

It seems to me that such affirmations miss something of decisive importance in Newman's work, which in many ways insists on its "art character." Damiano Bertoli has formulated the central paradox of her work well: her "objects are only just barely art, yet they couldn't be anything else." He goes on to say that it is not only their context that determines this inescapably aesthetic character but also "the tone of their gesture."[55] I will argue that not only does Newman insist on the distinction between her work and the objects of everyday life, but also that she does so by

45 This optical spatiality is elaborated most famously in Greenberg and Fried, but see also Jeremy Gilbert-Rolfe, "Irreconcilable Similarities: The Idea of Nonrepresentation," in *Beyond Piety: Critical Essays in the Visual Arts, 1986–1993* (Cambridge: Cambridge University Press, 1995), 48–49.

46 Morgan Thomas, "A Minimal Adherence," in *Monochromes*, 64.

47 Ibid., 70.

48 Sharkey, "Elizabeth Newman," 62.

49 Newman, email to the author, March 13, 2014.

50 Damiano Bertoli has also connected Newman's log and fabric pieces. Bertoli, "Stratified and Gratified," 91.

51 Newman, "No Noise," 81.

52 Most clearly formulated by Peter Bürger in his *Theory of the Avant-Garde*, trans. Michael Shaw (Minneapolis: University of Minnesota Press, 1984).

53 Shelley McSpedden, "100% Proof," in *Artists' Proof #1*, 81.

54 Ulanda Blair, "Elizabeth Newman," *Art & Australia* 45, no. 2 (2007): 289.

55 Damiano Bertoli, "Twin Lizzy: Some Observations Relating to Concurrent Exhibitions by Lizzy Newman at Ocular Lab and Neon Parc," in *The Unprecedented Dark Light of the New Letters* (Hobart: CAST, 2008), 12.

adopting modes of presentation and display tied to the "traditional" artwork (primarily painting, but also sculpture). On the surface, this claim is paradoxical because of the prevalence of found objects in her work of the last decade. I will thus first explain how Newman's work can be seen to insist on such distinctions between artworks and everyday objects and between the artwork and the space of its display, before moving on to the rationale for this insistence, which will bring us back to the idea of the specific opacity of Newman's art, touched on already.

Minimalism is often invoked in discussions of Newman's work, both by critics and, as we have seen in her mention of Morris and Judd, in her own writings.[56] The innovations of minimalist sculptural objects—human scale, elimination of surface detail, regular gestalt forms, refusal of the plinth—are intended to remove any element that could distract from the viewer's self-reflexive experience of themselves as a body navigating a space shaped by the objects. Minimalism understands its innovations to consist in a new stress placed on the fact that the sculptural object inhabits a "real" space (and "real" time) shared with the viewer's body. The experience of a traditional sculpture on a plinth, on this view, depends on a distinction between the plinth, which exists in a "real" space shared with the viewer's body, and the sculptural object itself, which, as an aesthetic object in which one may become absorbed and forget oneself, does not exist in "real" space. The antithesis to painting is even clearer because, as Sheldon Nodelman argued a few years after the highpoint of the debates between minimalists and high modernists, a painting, no matter whether it is representational or abstract, occurs on a "posited two-dimensional field." Because the object itself is, of course, three-dimensional, this two-dimensional field can only be an "ideal, i.e., a virtual one."[57] Which is to say that no matter how much a painting might stress its own existence as an object, it is also always a picture, and from the minimalist perspective, this pictorial quality distracts from awareness of one's own bodily experience in "real" space. As Judd wrote, "I finally thought that all painting was spatially illusionistic."[58]

Entirely in opposition to Minimalism, the distinctive form of Newman's work throughout her career has been that of wall-mounted, usually rectangular objects. The dominant form in her work is thus that of painting (what she calls the "painting/self-portrait signifier"),[59] despite the fact that many of these wall-mounted works are not paintings, but instead found, cut, or sewn fabrics.[60] A work such as *Blanket Painting* (2002), which as the title suggests, presents a blanket as a "painting" by hanging it on the wall, is paradigmatic for her recent work. We see in Newman's work an effect that Benjamin H.D. Buchloh, in relation to Kurt Schwitters, has called a "pictorialisation of surfaces and materials."[61] The essentially pictorial structure of Newman's art has two main elements: firstly, her adoption of the painting format means her wall works are read as surfaces or pictures rather than objects; secondly, these surfaces are contained within boundaries, that is, they are in some sense "framed." As David Roberts has noted, the modern concept of the picture is that of a "portable, framed panel"—and this concept of course subsists after the elimination of the literal frame popularised in the Abstract Expressionist era.[62] It is thus significant that the frame itself is a key form within Newman's work: in each of the pair of fabric works dedicated to Knoebel and Mangold,[63] four pieces of fabric frame a central monochrome rectangle, pink in one case and grey in the other; one part of the large plywood construction *Is that a No?* (2007/2011) consists essentially of a three-dimensional frame outlining empty space; the empty clothes rack exhibited at Utopian Slumps in 2012 frames the wall behind it; Newman herself notes

56 See for example, Sharkey, "Elizabeth Newman," 62 and Bertoli, "Stratified and Gratified," 87. Michael Graf questions the relation of Newman's work to Minimalism, but somewhat differently from how I do here. See Michael Graf, "Elizabeth Newman: The true collector looks for the work that is unfinished," in *Elizabeth Newman*, 175.

57 Sheldon Nodelman, "Painting in the Age of Actuality" (1978), in *Abstract Art in the Late Twentieth Century*, 72.

58 Cited in Leo Steinberg, "Reflections on the State of Criticism" (1972), in *Robert Rauschenberg*, ed. Branden W. Joseph (Cambridge, Mass.: MIT Press, 2002), 24.

59 Elizabeth Newman, email to the author, March 13, 2014.

60 The radical distinction drawn by both defenders and critics of Minimalism, between the real space and literal existence of the minimalist object and the illusory space of the painting or sculpture that must "defeat or suspend its own objecthood" (Fried, "Art and Objecthood," 151), is of course exaggerated: Minimalism reminds us that part of our experience of traditional sculpture is our spatial co-existence with it. Many elements of Newman's work stress the status of her paintings as physical objects in addition to optical surfaces: the presentation of her work, in which paintings are exhibited in the same room as other kinds of objects (which are sometimes displayed on the floor or leaning against the wall) has this effect, as do the roughly cut, sometime frayed, edges of her recent unstretched monochrome canvases. But this is less important, and less distinctive of her work, than the separation of her objects, as paintings (and sometimes sculptures), from their surroundings.

61 See Benjamin H.D. Buchloh, "Villeglé: From Fragment to Detail," in *Neo-Avantgarde and Culture Industry* (Cambridge, Mass: MIT Press, 2000), 453.

62 David Roberts, *The Total Work of Art in European Modernism* (Ithaca: Cornell University Press, 2011), 163.

63 *Untitled (For Imi)* and *Untitled (for RM)*, both 2009.

that the form of *1988* (2008) "contains a sort of frame within it."[64] This emphasis on the form of the frame aligns with Newman's general adoption of the pictorial format, which (far from accepting the goal of collapsing the distinction between art and everyday life, even in the reduced form in which this survives in Minimalism as the conflation of aesthetic and "real" space) stresses the demarcation between her works and the space they inhabit. The pictorial format of her work generates an implied or ideal framing effect that, like the real frame in Georg Simmel's description, "excludes all that surrounds it, and thus also the viewer as well, from the work of art, and thereby helps to place it at that distance from which alone it is aesthetically enjoyable."[65] Similarly, the plinths and pedestals she sometimes uses to present her found objects[66] serve to mediate between the "actual site" and the space usually reserved for a "representational sign";[67] the distinctive logic of Newman's work is to occupy this space of representation with something that manifestly refuses to represent.

It is here that we can begin to understand how Newman's art relates to those 1960s artists (Cage, the minimalists, Judson Dance Theatre) who, in her words, "show us that a little structural space has to be made for lack to exist."[68] What interests Newman in this "avant-garde" is exactly what distances it from traditional notions of the avant-garde as the collapse of art into everyday life: the insistence on a "structural space" that allows the usually invisible "everyday" to appear. The example of Cage's *4'33"* (1952) is apposite: the so-called "silent" piece is really a temporal structure that focuses attention on everyday ambience by framing it as a three-movement composition. Similarly, although the Judson Dance works Newman mentions are composed solely of everyday activities (walking and running), the majority of Judson Dance work is notable for its acceptance of the division between performer and audience within a milieu (defined by Happenings and Fluxus) in which this division was being challenged.[69] The structural space that allows the pedestrian movements of Paxton's *Satisfyin' Lover* (1967) and Rainer's *We Shall Run* (1963) to appear and be experienced is the stage, a site distanced from everyday life. In all these cases, as Newman points out, what is remarkable is how little structural space is required for the everyday to be alienated from itself and appear as an object for reflection: a stage on which to perform everyday actions and an audience to watch, durations in which to listen to what one always hears.

Similarly, in Newman's works, the techniques that distance her work from the everyday are minimal: a coat of paint, a cut into a piece of fabric, placement of a found object on a plinth or wall.[70] These minimal actions create the "structural space" that allows the objects in her work to appear. In Newman's words, these minimal actions make a "selection ... out of a temporal continuity" and "seem to stop time for a moment, to cut it in its tracks."[71] Newman considers this "an old fashioned way of being—it is what allowed modernists to think of their work as 'passing into history.'"[72] Here, curiously, but consistent with the opposition to Minimalism I have argued for so far, we might hear an echo of Fried's impassioned defense of high-modernist abstraction against Minimalism (which he called "literalism"). For Fried, it is the perpetual necessity of a realm that transcends the everyday (in which "we are all literalists most or all of our lives") that provides the foundation on which to defend the special temporality of aesthetic experience (an experience that "*has no* duration") against the minimalist reduction of the work of art to everyday spatio-temporal experience.[73]

I would like to take quite seriously Newman's idea that there is something "old- fashioned" about her art. Her work not only insists on its distinction from what is not art (everyday life and the surrounding space); in fact, by presenting itself as painting (and sometimes sculpture), it does so by occupying the position of the "traditional" work of art.[74] Heidegger defined the lived world not primarily as a collection of objects, but as a nexus of relevance and reference of things in relation to one another in terms of their use: "a hammer has to do with hammering, the hammering has to do with fastening something, fastening something has to do with protection against bad weather" and so on.[75] The experience of the traditional artwork, on the other

64 Elizabeth Newman, email to the author, March 13, 2013.

65 Georg Simmel, "The Picture Frame: An Aesthetic Study" (1902), trans. Mark Ritter, *Theory, Culture & Society* 11 (1994): 11.

66 For example: a jug painted white displayed on a plinth (*Untitled*, 2003, shown at TCB Art Inc. in 2005); a dozen pieces of pottery on a shelf (*Untitled*, 2005, shown at CLUBSprojects in 2005); a fragment of sewerage pipe on a low plinth (*The origin of life*, 2012).

67 Rosalind Krauss, "Sculpture in the Expanded Field," in *The Originality of the Avant-Garde and Other Modernist Myths* (Cambridge, Mass.: The MIT Press, 1985), 279.

68 Newman, "No Noise," 81.

69 See Carrie Lambert-Beatty, *Being Watched: Yvonne Rainer and the 1960s* (Cambridge, Mass.: MIT Press, 2008), 19–74.

70 This point has been made by a number of commentators on Newman's work. See Bertoli, "Twin Lizzy," 12 and Kate Briggs, "Vacancies of Being, the Insistent Construct: Elizabeth Newman, Aesthetics and Discontent," in *Elizabeth Newman*, 128.

71 Newman, "Introduction," 10.

72 Ibid.

73 Fried, "Art and Objecthood," 167–168.

74 That is, the characteristic position of the work of art within Western modernity.

75 Martin Heidegger, *Being and Time* (1927), trans. Joan Stambaugh (New York: State University of New York Press, 1996), sec. 18.

hand, is marked by aura, the unbridgeable distance that seems to exist between it and its surroundings and viewers. In this distance the work of art is distinguished from the everyday object, which exists *for* a purpose and thus *with* other objects, and it is this distinction that allows the work of art to take on its traditional qualities: as constituting a unity, as a special site of meaning and emotional investment.[76] What is distinctive about Newman's work in this regard is the fact that it simultaneously occupies the position of the traditional artwork and reduces the structures that allow it to occupy this position to a bare minimum. The blanket or carpet presented as a painting is exemplary here: a few cuts or even just hanging it on the wall are enough to transform the object into a painting, the most dignified art object within modernity. No new content is invested in the object in this transformation (there is no sign that it functions, for example, as a metaphor or symbol); rather what we are presented with is only the auratic distance that has been inserted between the blanket-turned-painting and its everyday context, the negation of its everyday function. The once "transparently" functional carpet or blanket thus becomes radically opaque; and this opacity is intimately bound up with its occupation of the site not simply of "art" (for we know that art can be anything), but of painting, the symbol of a traditional art object to which or *into* which we look for special kinds of content, meaning, and experience.

The opacity that confronts the viewer in Newman's work is thus very different to that of a minimalist sculpture: the opacity of the minimalist sculpture (the fact that it removes symbolism, surface detail, compositional interest—that is, anything we could look at rather than simply be with) is functional, whereas the experience of being confronted with an opaque, resistant object is essential to Newman's practice and her oppositional conception of it. Like Mallarmé's, her work finds the measure of its reality in its resistance.[77]

The role of found objects in her work should also be distinguished not only from the "illustrative" role that such objects often have in contemporary art made on post-conceptual or research-based models, but also from Duchamp. The distance separating Newman from the Duchampian idea of the readymade is obvious from her exhibition *The Unprecedented Dark Light of the New Letters* (2007), which consists of a collection of "things that are ... dark, or black,"[78] grouped together on essentially formal grounds and free from Duchamp's anti-optical bias.[79] More fundamentally, even when her use of found objects is less obviously "aestheticised," it is clear that the Duchampian dialectic, in which the ability for any object to take on the aura of the artwork is accompanied by the destruction of the aura of the traditional artwork through its redefinition as an assisted readymade, is absent from Newman's work.[80] Rather than debunking the aura of the artwork, Newman's work, as I have shown, depends on its aura. Accordingly, her description of the process whereby she nominates what found objects will become part of her work has no relation to the rules for the arbitrary selection of readymades formulated by Duchamp,[81] but rather describes a response to a special quality of the object that somehow distinguishes it from its everyday instrumental context. Newman writes of her attempt to "emphasise the presence of a type of 'soul' or subjectivity" that exists despite the capitalist reduction of the subject: "I knew that 'soul' had existed or occurred when I made work in the past ... but I also found this 'soul' in mass produced fabric ... found objects, found and invented text, cheap day-to-day objects and in some clothes I had made for myself (the *Thingness* of an object)."[82]

* * *

"The *Thingness* of an object": in his seventh seminar, Jacques Lacan discusses at length a fundamental structure of human life that, expanding on an early text of Freud's, he calls "the Thing" (*das Ding*). The Thing is the "absolute Other of the subject, that one is supposed to find again."[83] This search for the Thing "defines the human factor"[84] because desire is the "metonymy of our being";[85] this desire that

76 For a phenomenology of the artwork in these terms see, for example, Simmel, "The Picture Frame."

77 On the relation between resistance and reality in modernism, see Hans Blumenberg, "The Concept of Reality and the Possibility of the Novel," in *New Perspectives in German Literary Criticism: A Collection of Essays*, ed. Richard Amacher and Victor Lange (Princeton: Princeton University Press, 1979), 29–48.

78 Elizabeth Newman, "The Unprecedented Dark Light of the New Letters," in *Elizabeth Newman*, 94.

79 I here assume that visual or formal criteria played no important role in Duchamp's readymade. Although this is the standard view, and accords with his writings on the subject, it has been occasionally challenged: See William Camfield, "Marcel Duchamp's *Fountain:* Aesthetic Object, Icon, or Anti-Art?," in *The Definitively Unfinished Marcel Duchamp*, ed. Thierry de Duve (Cambridge, Mass.: The MIT Press, 1991).

80 See Marcel Duchamp, "Apropos of 'Readymades,'" in *Salt Seller: The Writings of Marcel Duchamp* (New York: Oxford University Press, 1973), 142.

81 See the notes from the *Green Box* in Duchamp, *Salt Seller*, 32.

82 Newman, "Introduction," 10.

83 Jacques Lacan, *The Ethics of Psychoanalysis 1959–1960*, trans. Dennis Porter (New York: W. W. Norton & Company, 1992), 52.

84 Ibid., 124.

85 Ibid., 321.

can never be fulfilled propels the human to leave the realm of the given and enter into signification.[86] The Thing is thus the "beyond-of-the-signified,"[87] the structure that points to "the emptiness at the centre of the real" that defines human life.[88] Because the Thing is determinate for the structure of signification itself rather than any particular signified content, it "presents itself in a form that is completely sealed, blind and enigmatic"[89] and is "characterized by its absence, its strangeness."[90]

Lacan attempts to clarify the concept of the Thing by telling a story about a visit he paid to a friend in the occupation years, during which he discovered that his friend was collecting match boxes. In Lacan's reading, the satisfaction derived from this match box collection is precisely that of demonstrating that the "match box isn't simply something that has a certain utility" but rather "a thing with all its coherence of being." The "quasi absurd character of this collection," its complete lack of conventional value, "pointed to its thingness as match box." The collection ultimately "concerns less the match box than the Thing that subsists in the match box."[91]

Newman is a practising Lacanian psychoanalyst, and often refers to Lacanian concepts in the statements she makes about her art. The relation of Lacan's notion of the Thing to Newman's work is suggestive, particularly because it seems to clarify that her work is not invested in any sort of naive materialism. By stripping objects of the meanings that constitute them within lived experience and presenting them as opaque surfaces, Newman does not intend to stage an encounter between the subject and the pure alterity of the thing-in-itself. Rather than a somehow extra-human experience, Lacan's notion of the Thing allows us to see in Newman's work a reflection on a uniquely human experience. Negating the role that the object plays in everyday systems of meaning is not negating its place in human life; rather, this negation is a structure through which the object is alienated from the "known knowledge" of everyday life and, precisely in its opacity, becomes an object of the desire for "unknown knowledge," a desire which is at the core of subjectivity because the subject cannot be identified with any particular signifiers, any specific meanings, but is rather the "*space between* signifiers."[92]

Of course, the idea of illustrating Lacan's work aesthetically is entirely foreign to Newman: "When I make art I do not consciously choose a topic or theme to illustrate (a more contemporary mode, I believe) but instead rely on my unconscious to direct me, without thinking."[93] Newman's work does not illustrate these ideas but rather enacts them; and the understanding of her work she has developed and put into practice relates as much to the history and problems of modernist abstraction as it does to psychoanalysis. The relation between materiality and meaning has been a key problem in the understanding of abstract or nonrepresentational art throughout its history, and as Georges Didi-Huberman has noted, it has often taken the form of "sterile contradictions" between the "*materiality* inherent in the adventure of abstract art and its notoriously *idealist* reference."[94] Frank Stella complained that viewers of his paintings "always end up asserting that there is something there besides the paint on the canvas," whereas in his view his "painting is based on the fact that only what can be seen there *is* there."[95] Although this was not the whole of Stella's view on the subject, this statement can be taken as typical of a purely materialist view of abstraction that has often been the target of critique by contemporary artists, who have used historical forms of abstraction to question the possibility of any purely nonrepresentational art.[96] We might think here of a work such as *Synecdoche* (1991–93) by the Californian artist Byron Kim, composed of hundreds of small monochrome paintings derived from the skin colour of friends and relatives in order to demonstrate how even the "pure" colour of monochrome painting is bound up with racial discourse: "colour is both specific and always meaningful."[97] The uniqueness and idiosyncrasy of Newman's position can only be grasped if we see that she simultaneously refuses a reductive, purely materialistic understanding of her work while also (unlike artists such as Kim and also in opposition to the ubiquitous idea,

86 "The creation of symbols accomplishes the introduction of a new reality into animal reality"; it thus makes sense for Lacan that the primary symbolic language of psychic experience involves elements that are not derived from reality, and in fact have "nothing whatsoever to do with reality," namely "kinship relation, the master's authority, and life and death." See Lacan, *On the Names-of-the-Father*, trans. Bruce Fink (Cambridge: Polity, 2013), 43–45.

87 Lacan, *Ethics of Psychoanalysis*, 54.

88 Ibid., 121.

89 Ibid., 70.

90 Ibid., 63.

91 Ibid., 114.

92 Newman, "The Distance between Representation and Domination," 70.

93 Newman, "God's Not Dead; He's Upstairs Smoking," in *Elizabeth Newman*, 145.

94 Georges Didi-Huberman, "The Supposition of the Aura: The Now, The Then, and Modernity," in *Walter Benjamin and History*, ed. Andrew Benjamin (London: Continuum, 2005), 9.

95 Bruce Glaser, "Questions to Stella and Judd" (1964), in *Minimal Art: A Critical Anthology*, ed. Gregory Battcock (New York: Dutton, 1968), 157–158.

96 Later in the same interview he expresses his dislike of "things that stress their material qualities." Ibid., 160.

97 See Mark Cheetham, *Abstract Art Against Autonomy: Infection, Resistance, and Cure since the '60s* (New York: Cambridge University Press, 2006), 135–136.

which Newman had approached in some of her earlier work, that abstraction can only be "a representation of abstraction now") taking very seriously the possibilities of a nonrepresentational art.[98] The continuing relevance of abstraction as it appears in Newman's work since 2001 consists in its ability to stage an encounter with a nonrepresentational surface that, because it refuses to become (as in Minimalism) merely a term within an environmental situation, makes manifest its own opacity. Far from a mere negation, this encounter provides us again and again with the seemingly inexhaustible pleasure of being reminded that in every object of human experience there subsists something that is "more than what there is."[99]

98 An opinion voiced by Johanna Burton in "The Painting Factory: A Roundtable Discussion," in *The Painting Factory: Abstraction after Warhol* (New York: Skira Rizzoli, 2012).
99 In this regard, Jeremy Gilbert-Rolfe's critical project, which attempts to think through the meaning and continuing relevance of nonrepresentational art in the contemporary, is instructive for thinking about Newman's work. A comment he makes about James Hayward contains elements of the reading I have been developing here: "The process is one in which exclusion of ideas from the work of art is seen as other than exclusively negative—not as an exclusion of meaning, but as the clearing of a space so that normally excluded kinds of meaning may emerge." Gilbert-Rolfe, "James Hayward: Nonrepresentation which Doesn't Represent," in *Beyond Piety*, 99.

Unknowns
Francis Plagne

One thing that comes immediately to our attention when we look at the art Elizabeth Newman has produced since the mid-1980s is the proliferation of vertically oriented rectangles. This shape provides the format of countless monochrome, abstract, or text paintings on canvas and determines the reductive compositional structures of many of the pictures (often a simple internal "frame" or, in more recent paintings, a set of nested rectangles). It is also frequently encountered in the found objects that Newman enlists into her work. We know from the artist's own commentary that, for her, this form contains a powerful suggestion of subjectivity. Discussing a recent work in grey on a black ground, in which loopy lines are confined to a roughly rendered inner rectangle, she proposes that "the rectangle with the scribbles inside it is like a comic version of the human subject (me)," an image of the formlessness of the unconscious shaped by a socially acceptable identity.[1]

In the tradition of European painting, the vertical rectangle is, of course, the most common format of the portrait. Newman exploits this traditional association in *Untitled (Picasso face)* (1990), in which a reproduction of Picasso's neo-Cézannist *Still Life with Pitcher and Apples* (1919) is affixed upside down to a much larger piece of stretched linen. As the work's subtitle suggests, two apples resting on a table in the reproduced image, roughly centred in the top half of the surface, read goofily yet unmistakably as the eyes of a human face. In *Small Sculpture* (2009), similar connotations are produced in three-dimensional form, the found piece of painted wood (affixed to an amorphous blob of cement by two long nails) reading in unavoidably anthropomorphic terms.

What is most striking about many of Newman's rectangular emblems of subjectivity is their emptiness. They are blank areas of colour devoid of incident, cuts made into fabric, a hole in a found gate (*Untitled*, 2008). In an untitled painting from 2019 that reads as a kind of ghostly inversion of one of Philip Guston's densely built-up mid-1960s "head" paintings, a profile-like form emerges in negative as an area of untouched canvas left at the centre of a loosely brushed expanse of grey. The paintings insistently suggest a subjectivity, but one characterised by absence or negativity. Newman's wonderful 2016 painting that abbreviates Magritte's *Ceci n'est pas une pipe* ("This is not a pipe") to simply *Ceci n'est pas* ("This is not") might serve as our guide here; we might also think of her reminder that the literal translation of Freud's term for the unconscious (*das Unbewusste*) is "the unknown."[2]

In an update on the Renaissance adage that "every painter paints himself," Newman has written that "all works made by an artist are self-portraits, because all works made by an artist involve, intimately, their subjectivity."[3] Looking at an artist's oeuvre would then be a privileged way into this subjectivity, because—to quote again from Newman's writing—"it's the links between signifiers that constitute one's work, one's *lifework*."[4] But the self-portrait constituted by Newman's collected works and the relationships between them is almost as opaque as one of her monochrome painting. Other than a few pieces that refer, with varying degrees of intelligibility, to contemporary political issues—the imprisonment of Chelsea Manning, Wikileaks, Australia's treatment of asylum seekers, the Anonymous movement—the subjectivity embodied in Newman's fields of colour, daubs of paint, and mysteriously imposing found objects is one from which specific traits have been withdrawn, from which the signifiers or representations that contribute to our everyday sense of personality or identity are absent.

Recently, this aspect of Newman's work has been elegantly articulated in Rex Butler's reading of it through the notion of the "cut."[5] Newman's own commentary provides a striking formulation—at once plainspoken and fundamentally mysterious—when she describes the experience of artmaking as "a sort of mythical moment that presents what could be 'the beginning of subjectivity': the bifurcation of experience into something represented, and something that cannot be represented, but nevertheless exists."[6] However, we wouldn't want the depth of philosophical reflection occasioned by Newman's work to mislead us as to its tone, which is often gently comic. The zero-degree of subjectivity is the blankness of the monochrome, of course, but it is also the absurdity of the Picasso face, the fabric on linen torso propped up on the two log legs (*At home with you*, 2010), the plastic eyes staring out from the otherwise blank canvas (*Vision*, 1991). As Newman put it to me in a recent conversation, her work is marked by a "strange combination of lightness and depth."[7]

***

This "strange combination" suggests a way in which we might understand the insistently second-order quality of Newman's work, the sense it gives us of existing at one remove

1 Cited in Naomi Evans, "Elizabeth Newman: Is That a 'No'?" in *Elizabeth Newman: Is That a 'No'?* (Brisbane: Griffith University Art Museum, 2020), 8.

2 Elizabeth Newman, "Un Making" in *Texts*, ed. David Homewood (Melbourne: Discipline, 2019), 138.

3 Newman, "Two Works" in *Texts*, 115

4 Newman, "2008" in *Texts*, 26.

5 See Rex Butler, "Elizabeth Newman: Staging Desire" in *The effect that is propagated is not from the communication of speech but from the displacement of discourse* (Melbourne: Neon Parc, 2016), 13–14

6 Newman, "2008," 26–27.

7 Conversation with the author, August 17, 2021.

from the traditions of modernist abstraction it resembles. This quality is most marked in the artist's earliest surviving works, which include a trio of muted representational images depicting a studio with paintings hung and leant against the wall, a gestural abstract painting, and, in the example included here, a *Blank Canvas* (1985). Viewed alongside these pieces, it can be tempting to read Newman's work as a whole in terms of the contemporaneous discourse of postmodern simulation painting, in which the recognition of distance from the heroic tradition of modernist abstraction meant accepting that painting had become the "sign of itself."[8] Like many other artists working with abstraction in the 1980s, Newman's work seems to embody doubt about the possibility of an authentic continuation of the tradition to which it refers.

However, as Eve Sullivan has recognised, Newman's work is subtly yet profoundly different from textbook postmodernism.[9] Nothing in her work or statements suggests the knowingly ironic stance of many postmodern artists, nor the background presence of a theoretical or critical paradigm for which these works would serve as mere illustration. Rather than irony, the second-order quality of Newman's work comes from her embrace of failure as a kind of working method. Look at how the dripping orange form of *Untitled* (1987) suggests the cleanly articulated geometry of a rectangle while pointedly falling short of it, this discrepancy magnifying the wavering of its lines, the dribbles of paint running down from its top edge.

In *Untitled (after Picasso)* (1988), a similar logic operates in a more complex way, as it also concerns the relationship between the work and its title. In this painting, the format of an internal rectangle placed slightly above the centre of the canvas (familiar from many other works by the artist) is constituted by broken parallel strokes of grey, set off against a lighter grey background. On one level, the work's title simply signals its connection to the repetitively applied daubs found in a similarly monochromatic palette in Picasso's analytic cubist works. But the gesture of tribute takes on another quality when we consider Picasso's role as the preeminent artist of the modernist canon, the enormity of whose pictorial achievements provided the impossible standard by which so many later modernists judged their efforts. (One thinks here particularly of Pollock's oedipal relationship to Picasso.) Viewed in this light, the modesty of Newman's picture takes on a gently self-mocking quality, admitting, in a sense, its failure to live up to the tradition represented by the name of Picasso, while quite unironically drawing its visual inspiration from the master's work in a direct, technical manner that renders irrelevant the critique of Picasso and the modernist tradition unavoidable in the 1980s (as it continues to be today).

Much of the work Newman has produced since the late 1980s can be understood to build on this paradoxical insight: that her failure to produce objects in the heroic and sublime traditions of modernist painting she admires is precisely the way in which she can achieve the qualities of modernist painting in her work. Invested with this deep-seated equivocality (both serious and absurd, earnest and mocking), her objects possess an internality, a sense of subjective animation that distances them from the tendency evident in much postmodern art for the physical work to become an illustration of a theoretical proposition. Equally, it refuses the contemporary mode theorised by David Joselit in which paintings are conceived as nodes in a wider network.[10] Rather, Newman's work develops an ever-evolving set of techniques to generate within her objects that fragile, mysterious quality that—taking up the artist's suggestion that she is "a 'product' of another era"[11]—we could go so far as to call "aura."

In the 1987 painting discussed earlier, this sense of internal animation, which separates artworks from everyday objects, is achieved through the tension between real and suggested shape. In the series of 2019 paintings composed of nested rectangles, the same tension is played out on the level of composition, as the implied forms are so simple that we cannot help but look at the paintings as if their coloured areas were executed in a uniform and complete manner, while the frayed edges of the shapes and the exposed patches of raw linen simultaneously undo this perceived gestalt. However simple and serenely immobile these paintings appear, they are enlivened by contradictory forces, tending in two directions at once. We might find a related sense of internal division in the 2020 monochromes on found canvases: painted over discarded works by unknown artists, the monochrome surface registers as an unresolved interaction between two subjects, the obscured image pressing forward as a shadowy modulation of the monochrome colour field.

Newman's recent gestural paintings often create this sense of internal conflict though the inclusion of crudely concealed pentimenti, traces of decisions made and then abandoned in the moment of painterly improvisation but retained on the finished surface. In a beautiful large painting predominantly in yellow from 2020, a similar effect is created simply by leaving a substantial area of primed canvas visible along the bottom edge, generating a tension between the suggested all-over composition of hovering forms and the reality in which this scheme has been prematurely abandoned. This patch of exposed canvas pushes the different layers visible on the surface into a tussle in which the abstract forms that occupy much of the canvas are forced into the position of illusionistic image in contrast to the cruder materiality of the exposed ground.

8 Hal Foster, "Signs Taken for Wonders," in *Abstract Art in the Late Twentieth Century*, ed. Frances Colpitt (Cambridge: Cambridge University Press, 2002), 111.

9 See Eve Sullivan, "Elizabeth Newman: Interesting Times, the 1980s and 1990s" in *Elizabeth Newman: More Than What There Is* (Melbourne: 3-ply, 2013), 27.

10 See David Joselit, "Painting Beside Itself," *October* 130 (Fall, 2009): 124–134.

11 Newman, "2008," 25

Do these large lyrical abstract paintings, which have occupied much of Newman's attention in the last few years, also possess that "second-order" quality present in so much of her work? In writing about some of these works in 2018, struck by their relative formal complexity and the lushness of their surfaces, I suggested that they did not, and should rather be seen as the "real thing."[12] I'm now inclined to question my judgment that these works represent something of a transformation or departure in Newman's practice. Though these paintings, mainly made up of large amorphous patches of colour either loosely abutting or hovering separately over luminous grounds of feathery brushstrokes or areas of blank canvas, and sometimes including collage elements, are bigger and bolder than anything else Newman has produced, the distance that separates them from what appear to be their models (the 1948–49 "multiform" works of Mark Rothko, for instance) strikes me as a key to understanding the impression they make.

In his essay "In Defence of Abstract Expressionism," T.J. Clark fixes on the quality of "vulgarity" as the defining quality of New York Abstract Expressionist painting, naming with this term the "empty intensity" of the painters' enacted belief that their surfaces could embody both the infinity of the sublime and "individualism in pure form."[13] Modernism, Clark reminds us, often derived its power from a "range of characteristics that had previously come under the worst kind of pejorative description": ugliness, base materiality, the formless. The specifically Abstract Expressionist form of this "lowness" is vulgarity.[14]

The strident, swaggering vulgarity is precisely what is missing from Newman's paintings in related forms, and what, when compared to Abstract Expressionist models, gives them their sense of second-order remove. But what, then, is the particular form of Newman's "lowness"? Perhaps we might best call it the unresolved. Not the "unfinished," as this too strongly calls up the energetic sketchiness that appalled critics of the nineteenth-century avant-garde, but the look of something hesitant, undecided. Just as the vulgarity of Abstract Expressionism dangerously courts what Clark calls "ludicrousness,"[15] so Newman's embrace of the unresolved courts the inconsequential. To call these paintings gestural or lyrical, as I have, is in a sense quite wrong. They make no bold, bodily gestures nor do they sing of private emotions. Their forms and their scale might derive from mid-century abstraction, but looking at them one sometimes has the feeling that Newman has reconnected with what Carter Ratcliff calls the "acausal blanks" that dot the late works of Manet and Degas: moments of painterliness that do no representational work yet also "make no strong argument for abstraction," refusing any didactic "recognition of the painting's independence" or forceful demonstration of the expressive qualities of the medium.[16] Rather, they simply open "a blank space in the texture of institutionally recognised meaning."[17]

While some might perceive here a similarity between Newman and an artist like Michael Krebber, the differences between the two strike me as more profound. Krebber's elegantly flaccid, pointedly lazy paintings can be interpreted as part of a dandyish institutional critique: the near-disappearing quality of Krebber's work is a strategy, John Kelsey has argued, designed "to go to work on the wider system that makes painting what it is today."[18] Newman is also concerned with what "makes art what it is and not something else" but her answer is fundamentally different.[19] Rather than being institutional, it is a quality of the individual object, of the painting that somehow managed to live, the found object that possesses "soul."[20] If her work insists on remaining unresolved, on presenting us with almost nothing, it is precisely to propose a heightened experience of what divides artworks from other objects, of what allows a material thing to be no longer simply an object among other objects. Unlike many works of contemporary art, Newman's are meant to be looked at, puzzled over, lived with. They reward this engagement through the subtlety of their effects, the nearly imperceptible movements with which they cross the line separating lifeless object from auratic presence.

***

When they first emerged in the late 1980s, Newman's text paintings appeared to disrupt the modernist dimension of her work, opposing discourse to the mute image. In the early text painting, statements ("I believe in other possible worlds," "The AUTHORITY of Art rests upon an invisible platform of KNOWLEDGE and POWER") seem to introduce a transparent, confessional relationship between artist and reader opposed to the opaque connection between Newman's paintings and the viewer. However, as this body of work has developed over the years, it has become clear that there is no basic contrast between this aspect of the artist's

12 See my essay for the exhibition *So many lights and so much darkness*, Darren Knight Gallery, Sydney, 2018.
13 See T.J. Clark, "In Defence of Abstract Expressionism" in *Farwell to an Idea: Episodes from a History of Modernism* (New Haven: Yale University Press, 1999), 371–403.
14 Ibid., 375
15 Ibid., 401.
16 Carter Ratcliff, "Dandyism and Abstraction in a Universe Defined by Newton," *Artforum* 27, no. 4 (December 1988): 85.
17 Ibid., 87.
18 John Kelsey, "Stop Painting Painting," *Artforum* 44, no. 2 (October 2005): 224
19 Newman "2008," 27.
20 See Newman, "Introduction" in *Texts*, 35.

production and the other forms to which she continually returns (such as the monochrome, abstract painting, and the use of found objects). The texts show an increasing tendency toward brevity and ambiguity (as well as, we might note, an increased use of other languages—French, Spanish, Latin), that makes the experience of looking at them as immediate and confounding as her other works. The mode of engagement the text paintings now propose is, like the rest of Newman's work, ultimately contemplative. When discussing these works with me, the artist reached for a phrase from Lacan, explaining the ideal text painting as "oracular and enigmatic."[21]

The 2020 work on which is painted "Las Pinturas Negras," the Spanish title for Goya's black paintings, exemplified this tendency of the recent text paintings. At first, the phrase, merely naming a major moment from European art history, appears almost aggressively banal, as blank as a monochrome surface or the mischievous gouaches depicting the Coca-Cola logo the artist produced in 2019. But, presented in isolation on its raw linen surface, the possible meanings of the phrase multiply—referring back to the dark paintings the artist has produced over the years and in this naming constituting them as a distinctive subset of her oeuvre, or giving a general title to a series of related works produced around the same time that contain equally dark phrases ("radix malorum," "all against all"). Or perhaps it simply names itself: it is, after all, painted in black.

The early text paintings are painted in a sans-serif print that "approximates a studious neatness," giving the paintings a faint whiff of childish cuteness.[22] The words of "Las Pinturas Negras" look as if they are the product of a drunken sign-painter who has neglected proper planning, resulting in unevenly sized letters squeezed into the closely packed lines that fill almost the entire surface. In both the early and current text paintings, the presentation of the text is insistently handmade without being notably expressive. While the texts themselves can have an enigmatic, even solemn quality, their presentation introduces a comic levity.

A 1990 text painting and a large wooden sculpture designed in 2007 both spell out the two letters of "No," alerting us to the role of negation in Newman's work: the negation of representation, of finish, of resolution, of spectacle, of clarity, of the saturation of contemporary life in superficial and overly literal discourse.[23] However, described in these terms, her works sounds serious, even academic, and this misses another fundamental aspect of Newman's work: the negation of seriousness. Newman's work refuses the solemnity that reigns in mainstream contemporary "biennale" art, the value of which is so often understood as inseparable from its critical commentary on a host of pressing contemporary issues.

Newman has described the sumptuous colour palette used in her paintings—an extensive range of lilacs and mauves, pale greens, apricots, pastel pinks, blacks and greys barely tinted with blues and purples, among many others—as a challenge to "various prejudices about what is allowed in serious painting."[24] While certainly conscious, this negation of "serious" or rationalised approaches to colour is primarily intuitive and felt. As she wrote to me once about Barnett Newman: "primary colours, yuk!"[25] Newman's approach to colour affirms and embraces taste in the most everyday sense of likes and dislikes almost impossible to analyse. In a long series of works stretching back to 2009 inspired by the German late-modernist Imi Knoebel, a large monochrome rectangle (a wonderful buttery yellow in the example included here) is bordered on all four sides by stripes of different colour. The schemes used in these studies in colour combination are not derived from any pre-existing program. Rather, they are discovered in the visual materials that impress Newman in everyday life: in posters, clothes, Picasso paintings, pictures in magazines. Here, as always in Newman's work, this "no" to an impersonal seriousness is also a "yes": an affirmation of the fleeting, ungraspable reality of taste, a dimension of subjectivity inaccessible to rationalisation.

21 Conversation with the author, August 17, 2021.

22 Naomi Evans, "Elizabeth Newman: Is that a 'No'?", 4.

23 The latter negation is the subject of one Newman's best essays, "The Distance Between Representation and Domination" in *Texts*, 59–74.

24 Newman, "Two Works," 116.

25 Email to the author, March 8, 2014.

P.101 *Untitled*, 2019, oil on linen, 45 × 35 cm. Private collection.
P.102 *Untitled*, 2018, oil on board, 40 × 35 cm. Private collection.
P.103 *E3. Untitled*, 2019, oil on linen, 45 × 35 cm. Collection of Erik Jensen.
P.104 *Untitled*, 2020, oil on timber 50 × 40 cm.
P.105 *Untitled*, 2019, oil on linen 40 × 30 cm. Private collection.
P.106 *Untitled*, 2019, oil on linen. 40 × 30 cm. Private collection.
P.107 *Untitled*, 2019, oil on timber 40 × 30 cm.
P.108 *Black flag Red flag*, 2022, oil on linen 60 × 50 cm.
P.109 *Untitled*, 2018, oil on linen 35 × 28 cm. Collection of Francis Plagne.
P.110 *One All Alone*, Installation view, Disneyland Paris, 2020.
P.111 *One All Alone*, 2020, found object, 185 × 10 × 5.5 cm.
P.112 *Untitled*, 2022, oil on linen, 140 × 96 cm.
P.113 *Untitled*, 2022, oil on linen, 141 × 100 cm.
P.114 *Untitled*, 2017, oil on linen, 77.5 × 52.5 cm.
P.115 *Untitled*, 2017–18, oil on linen, 137 × 104 cm.
P.116 *Untitled*, 2022, oil on linen, 50 × 40 cm.
Untitled, 2022, oil on linen, 100 × 70 cm. Private Collection.
P.117 *Untitled*, 2017–18, oil on linen, 46 × 36 cm.
P.118 *Untitled*, 2017, oil on linen, 100.5 × 69.5 cm.
P.119 *Untitled*, 2017–18, oil on linen, 40.5 × 30.5 cm. Collection of Susan Taylor and Peter Jones.
P.120 *Untitled*, 2020, oil on found painting, 35 × 28 cm.
P.121 *Untitled*, 2020, oil on found painting, 76 × 51 cm.
P.122 *Untitled 1*, 2019, oil on linen, 50 × 40 cm.
P.123 *Found object*, 2020, painted timber, 120 × 79 cm.
P.124 *To Bradley Manning*, 2013, found object, 140 × 27cm.
P.125 *Untitled*, 2012, acrylic on linen, 145 × 35 cm.
Untitled, 2013, oil on linen, 130 × 50 cm.
P.126 *Untitled*, 2021, paper on timber stretcher, 56 × 40 cm.
P.127 *Untitled*, 2019, acrylic on cardboard, 90 × 68 × 2 cm.
P.128 *From the movement 3*, 2008, found image, 41 × 35 cm.
From the movement 1, 2008, found image, 41 × 35 cm.
P.129 *From the movement 4*, 2008, found image, 41 × 35cm.
From the movement 5, 2008, found image, 41 × 35cm.
From the movement 6, 2008, found image, 41 × 35cm.
From the movement 2, 2008, found image, 41 × 35cm.
P.130 *Untitled*, 2022, acrylic on cardboard, 25 × 19 × 9 cm.
P.131 *Untitled*, 2022, acrylic on cardboard, 17 × 13 × 5 cm.
P.132 *Two boxes*, 2010, acrylic paint on cardboard, 55 × 20 × 7.5 cm.
P.133 *Two boxes*, 2010, acrylic paint on cardboard.
P.134 *Small Sculpture*, 2009, mixed media, 40 × 20 × 22 cm.
P.135 *One*, 2021, timber and stone, various dimensions.
P.136 *The origin of life*, 2012, found object, various dimensions.
P.138 *Documenta*, 2012, framed photographs, 61 × 46 cm each.
P.139 *Documenta*, 2012, framed photographs, 61 × 46 cm each.
P.140 *Untitled*, 2013, pigment print and screenprint on paper, 110 × 79.5 cm, printed by Negative Press.
P.141 *Collateral Damage*, 2013, pigment print and screenprint on paper, 110 × 79.5 cm, printed by Negative Press.
P.142 *Bag*, 2014, fabric paint and fabric on cloth bag, 35 × 30 × 5 cm. Private collection.
P.143 *Black Sites Bag*, 2014, fabric paint and fabric on cloth bag, 35 × 30 × 5 cm. Private collection.
P.144 *Untitled*, 2010, acrylic paint on cardboard, 78 × 26 × 26 cm.
P.145 *Untitled*, 2010, painted cardboard, 78 × 26 × 26 cm.
P.146 *Untitled*, 2021, oil on linen, 80 × 70 cm.
P.147 *Untitled*, 2013, oil on linen, 100 × 75 cm. Private collection.
P.148 *Radix Malorum*, 2021, oil on linen, 50 × 40 cm.
P.149 *Untitled*, 2020, oil on linen, 50 × 40 cm.
Untitled (Hobbes), 2021, oil on linen, 50 × 40 cm.
P.150 *Untitled (humanity)*, 2022, oil on linen, 50 × 40 cm.
P.151 *Untitled*, 2021, oil on linen, 50 × 40 cm.

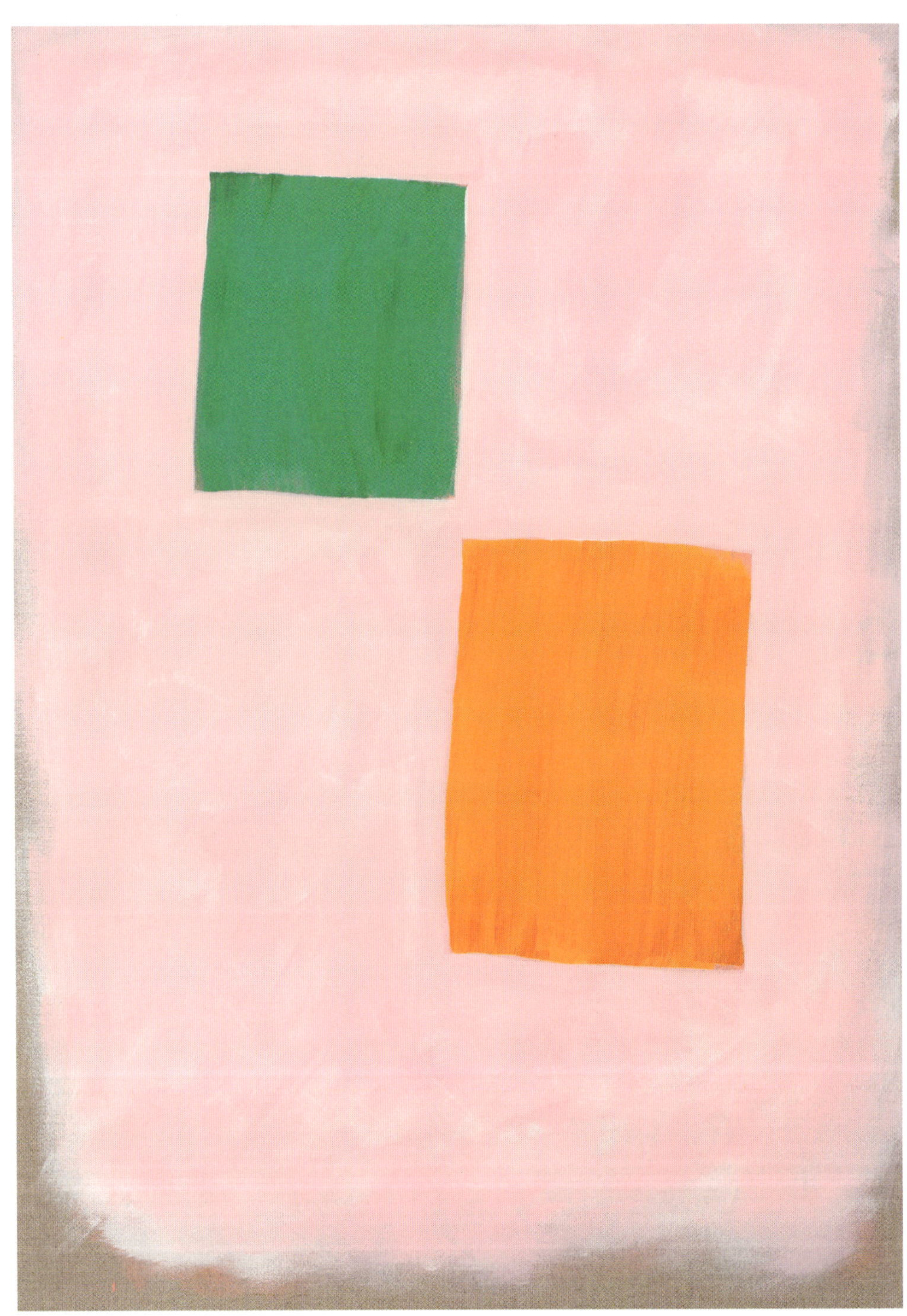

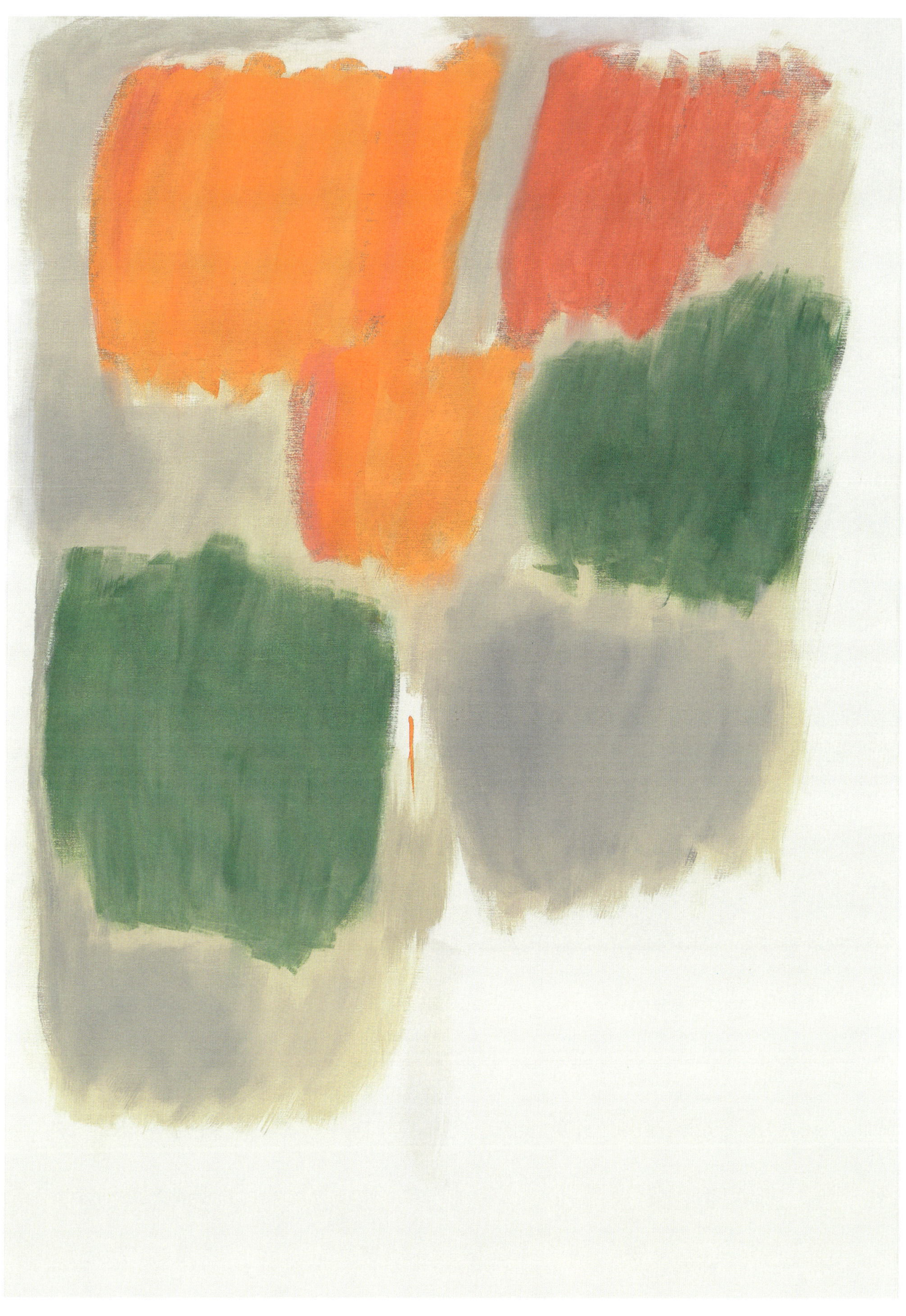

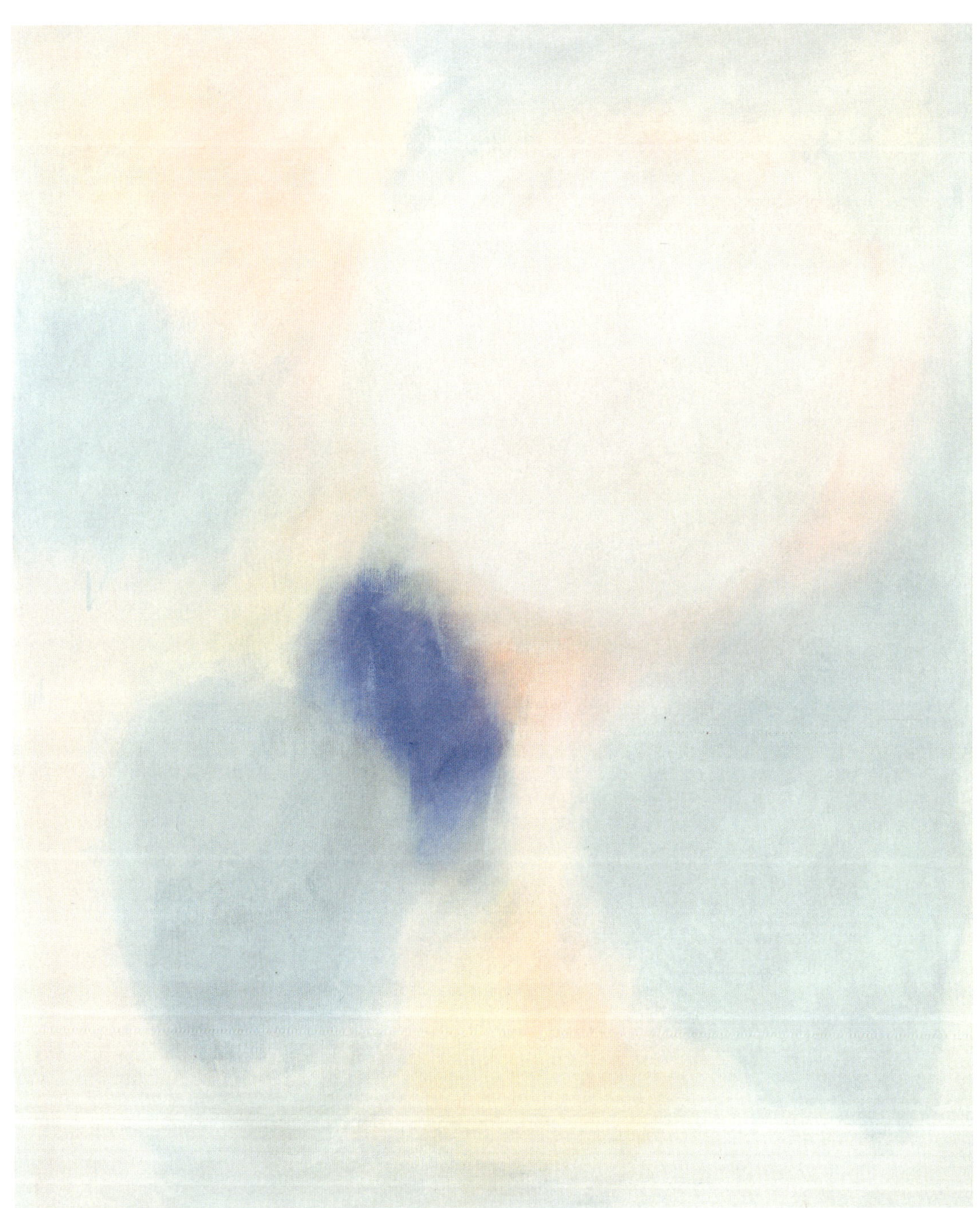

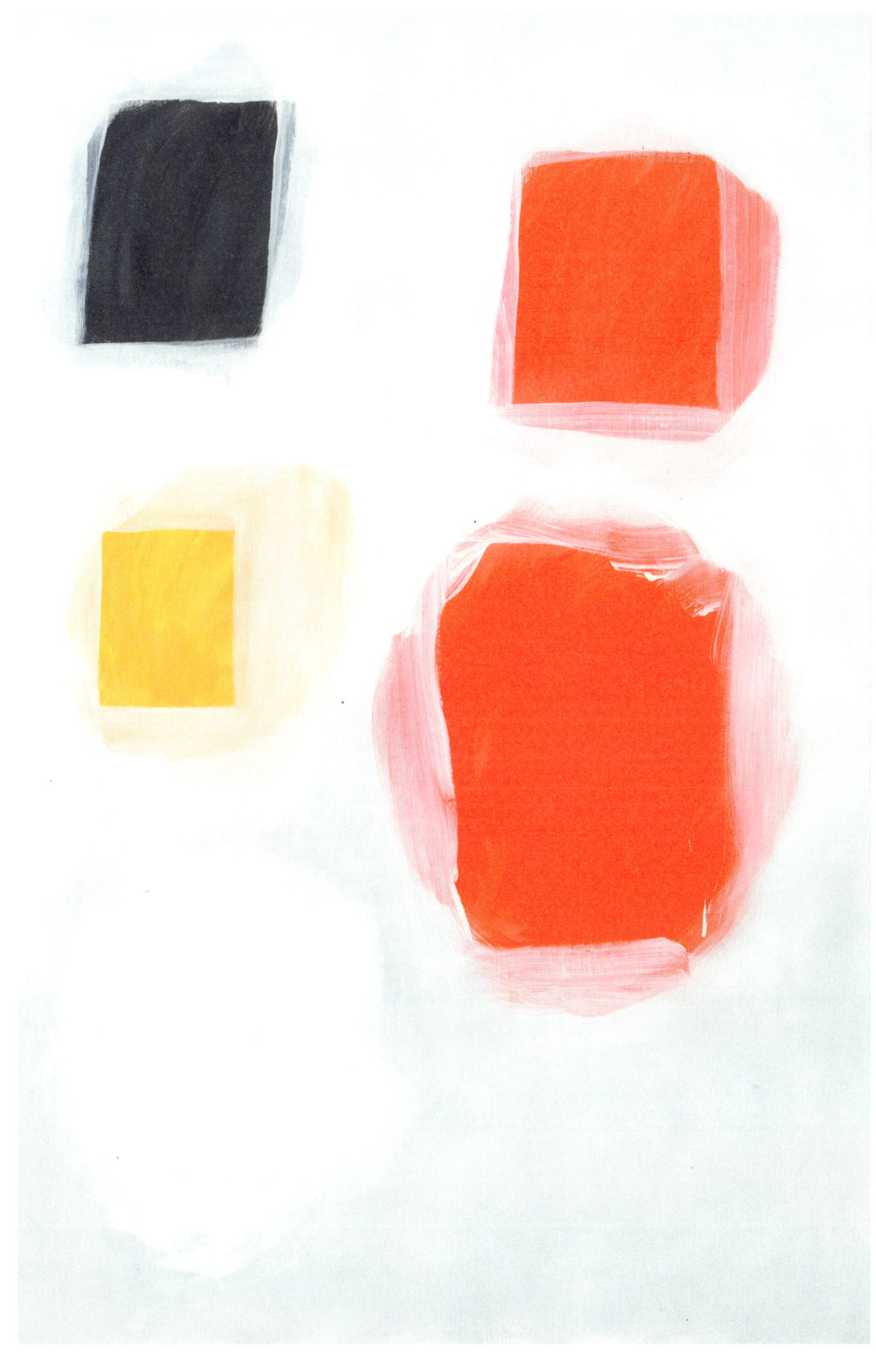

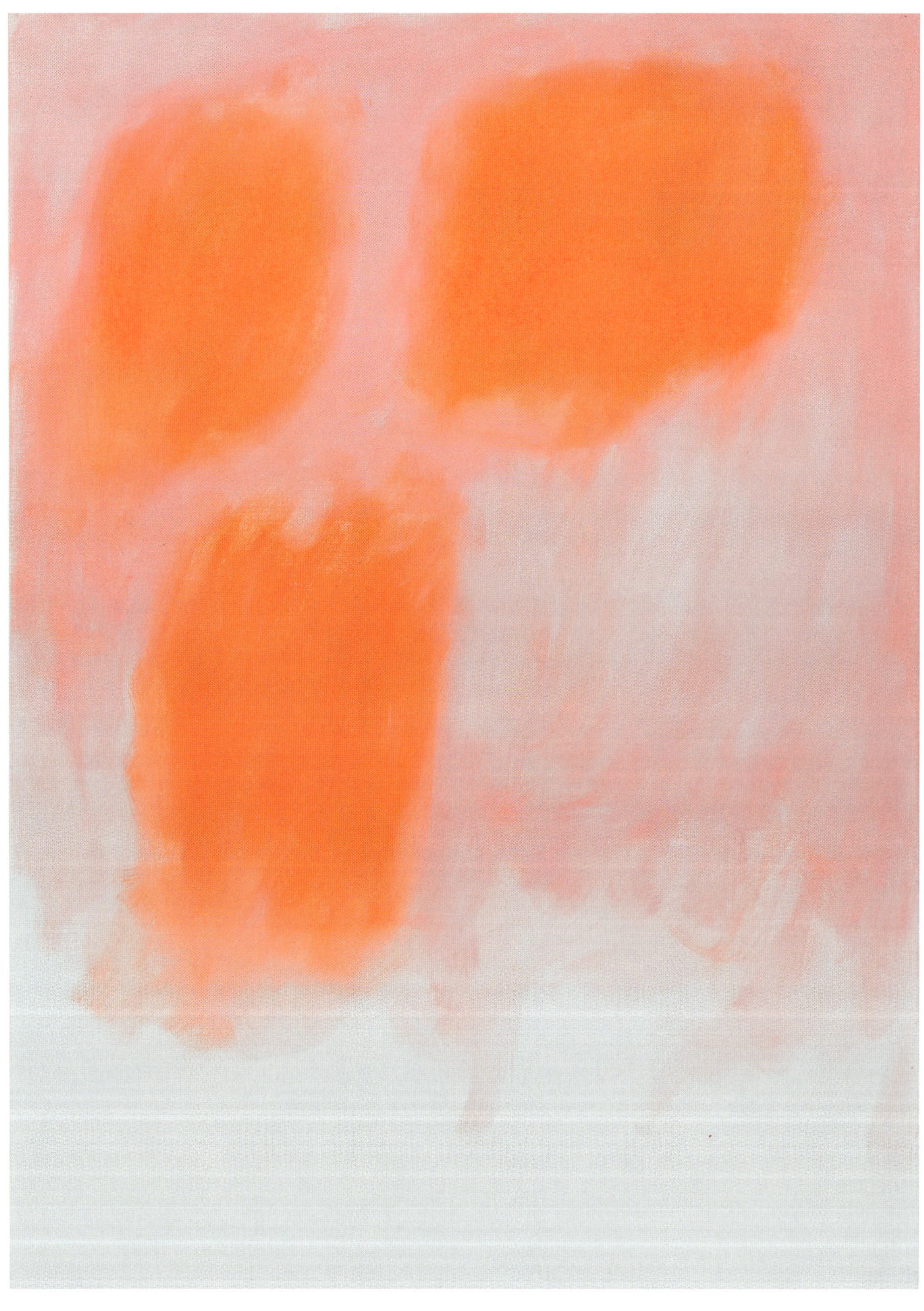

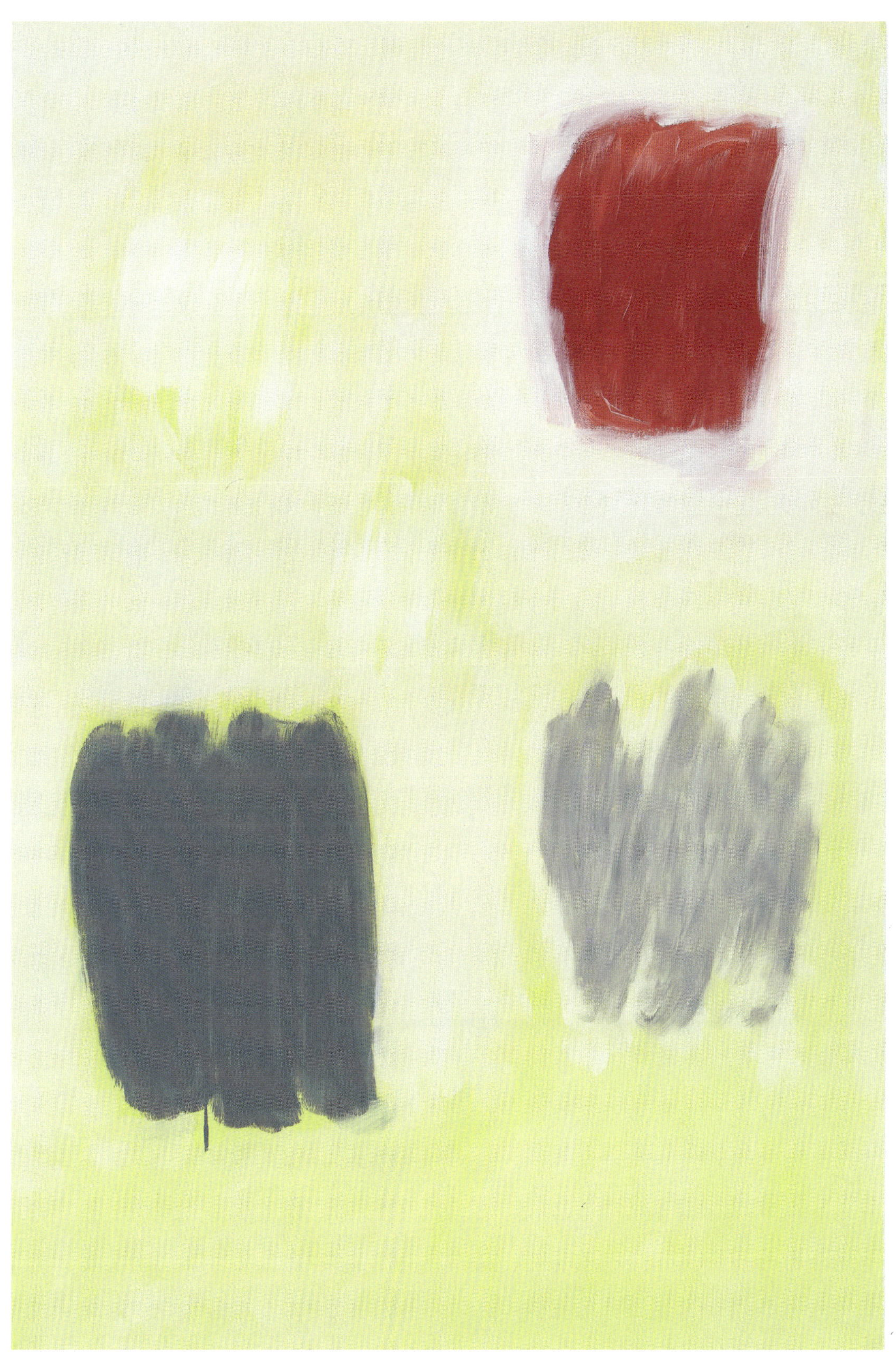

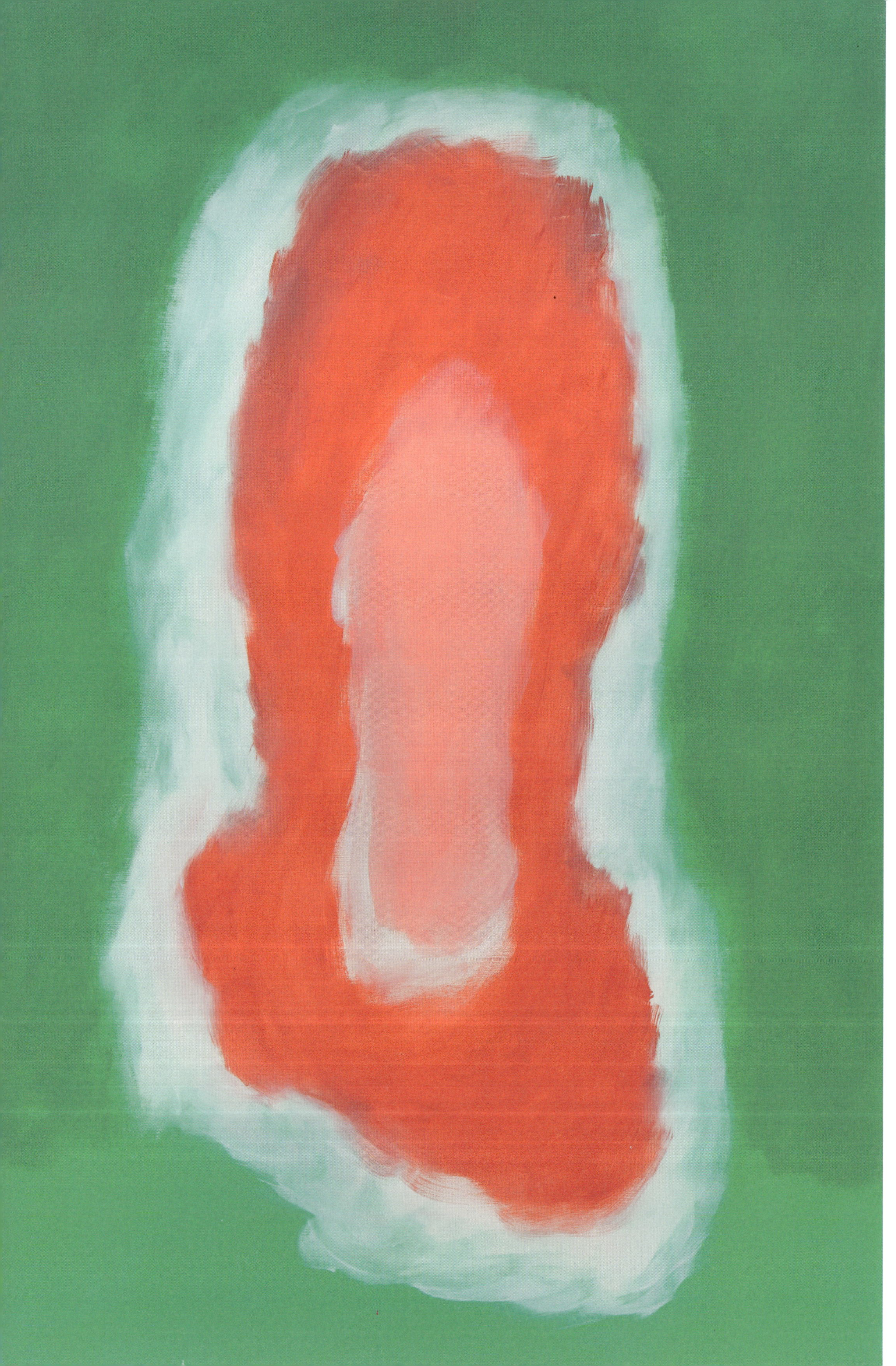

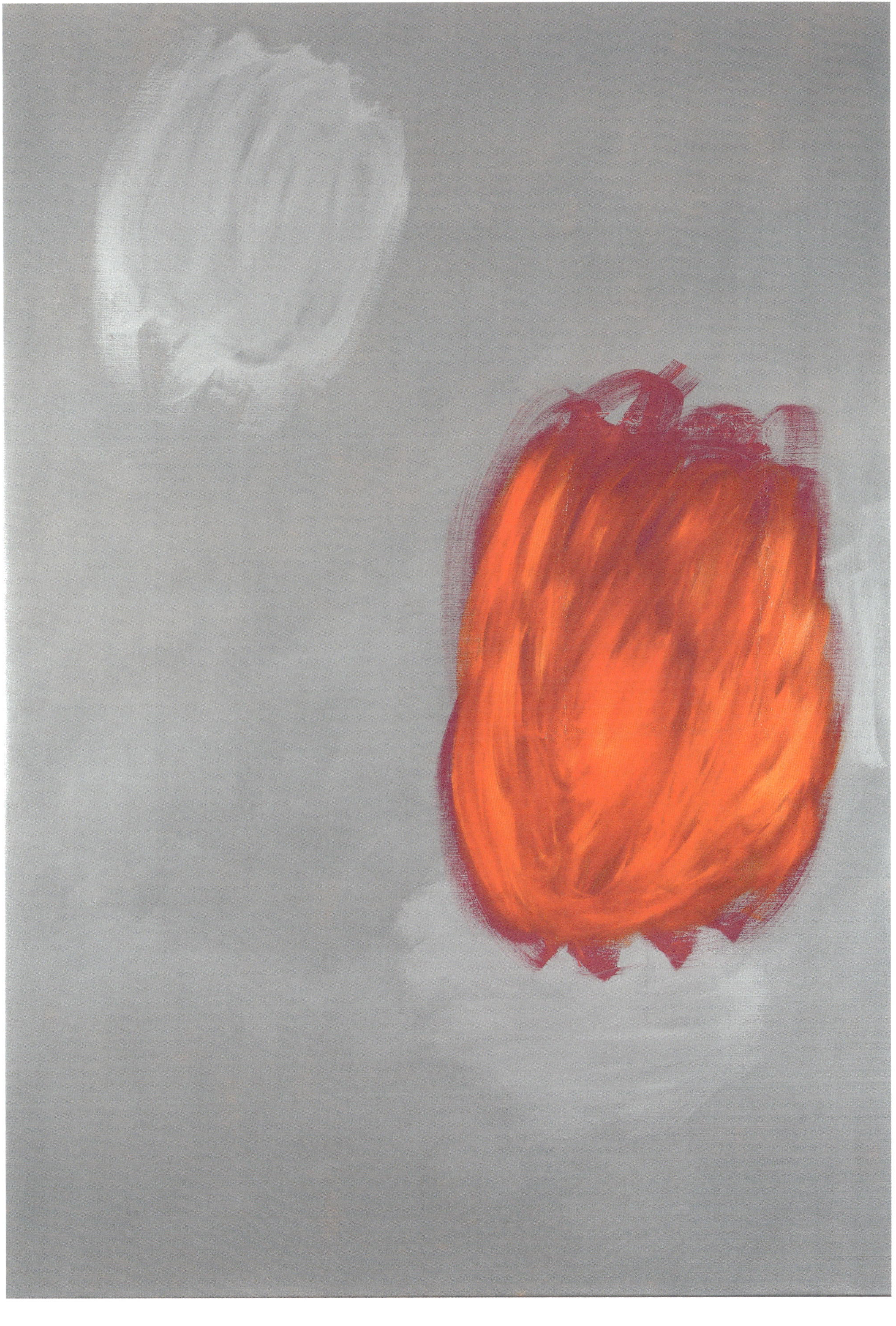

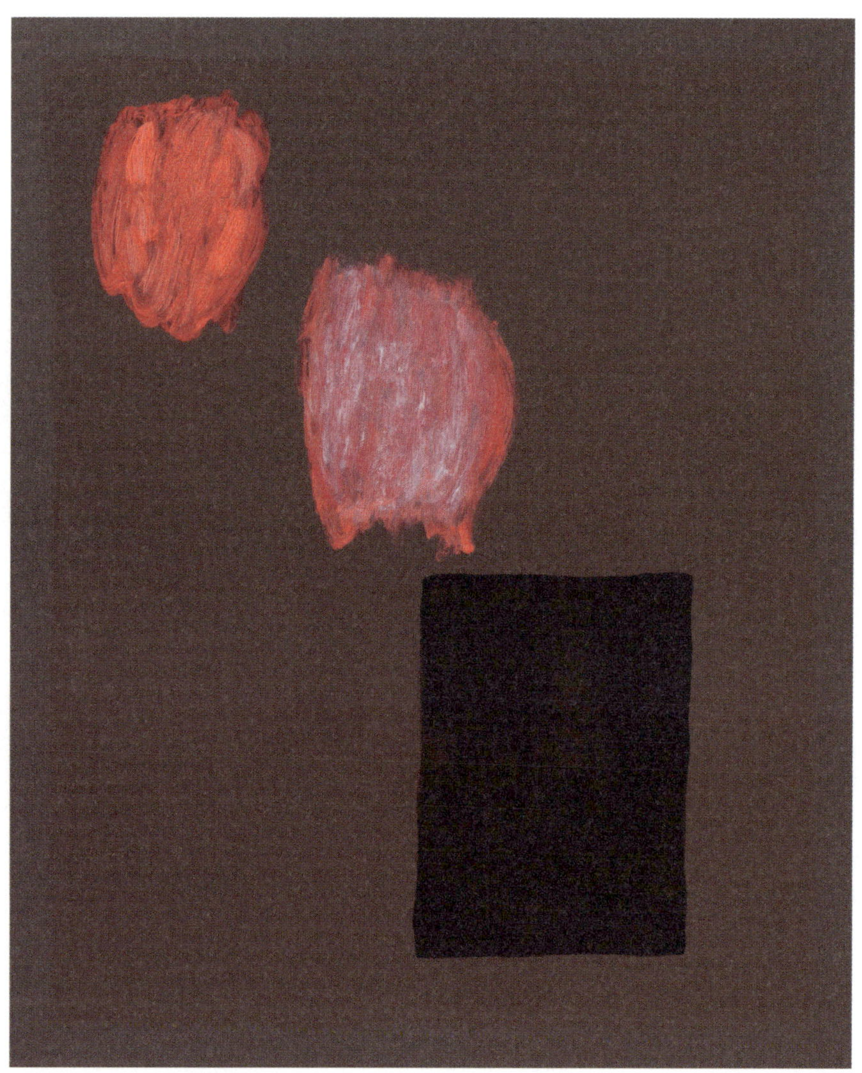

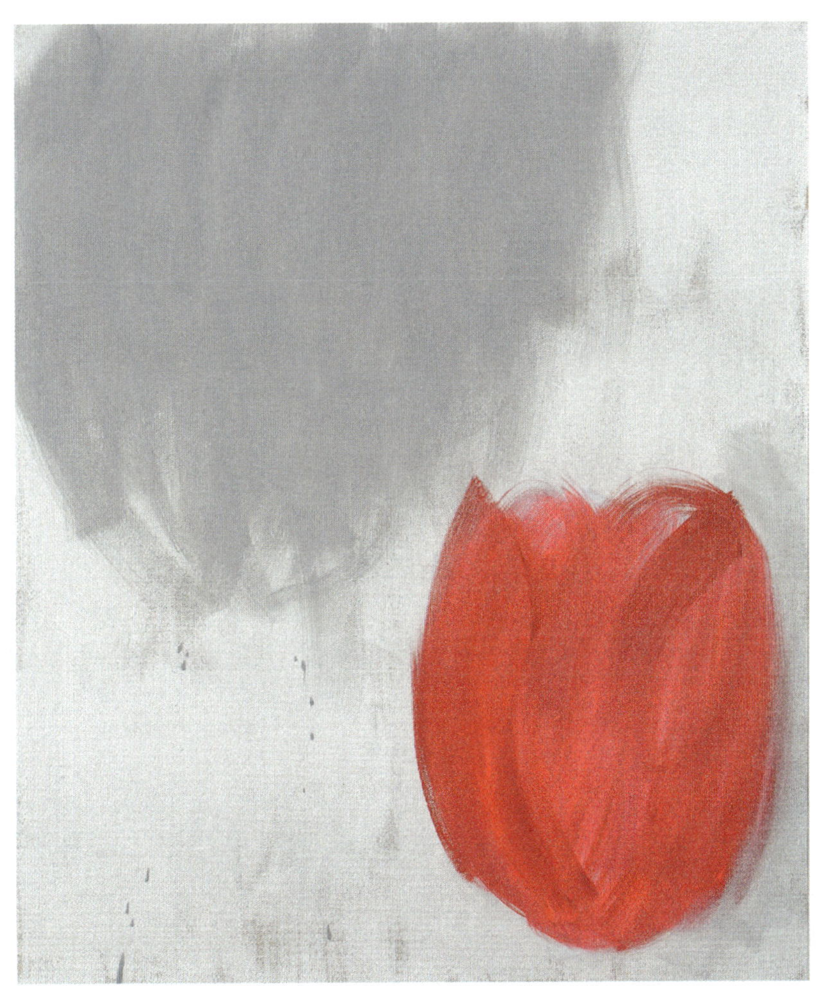

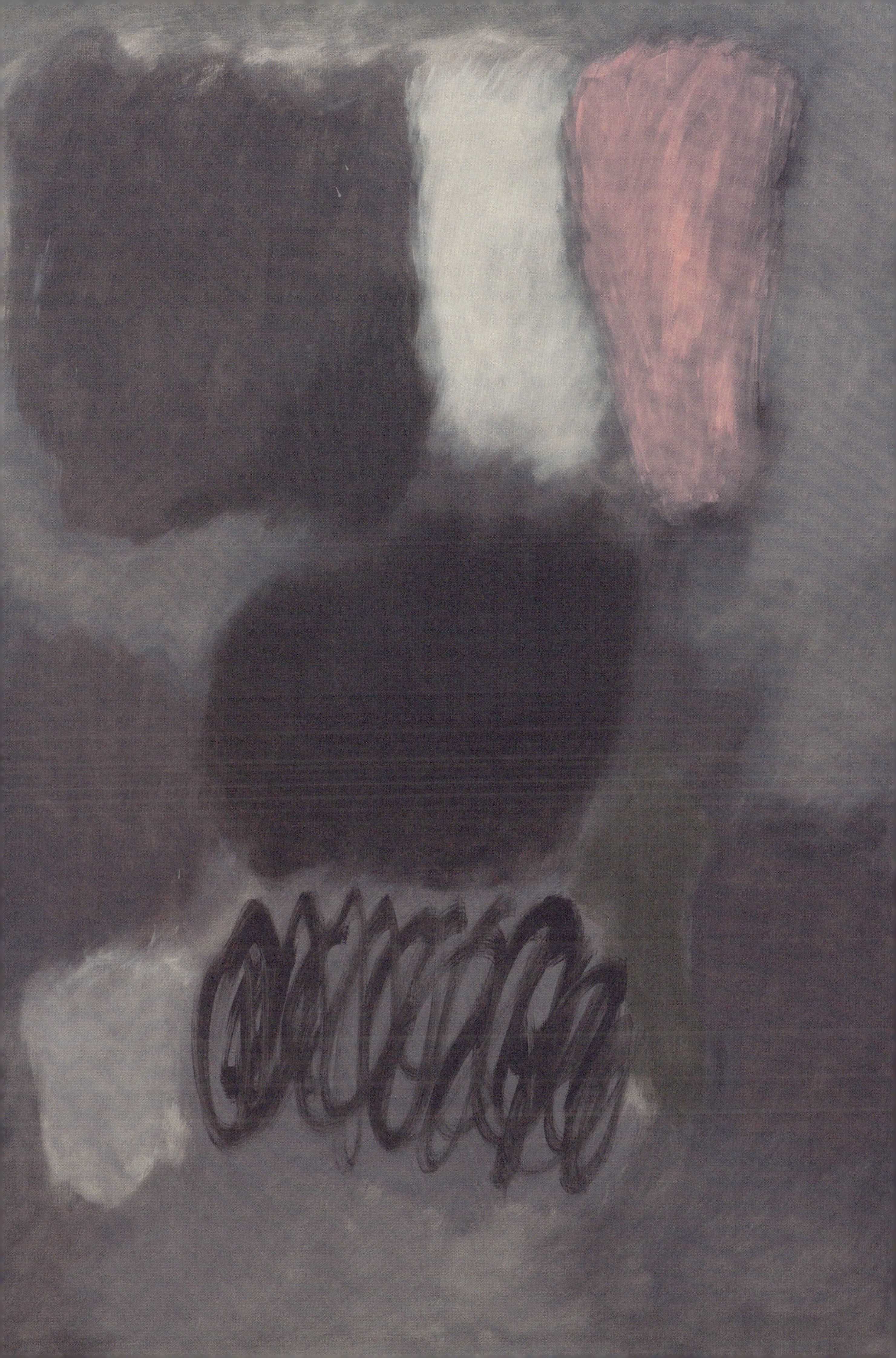

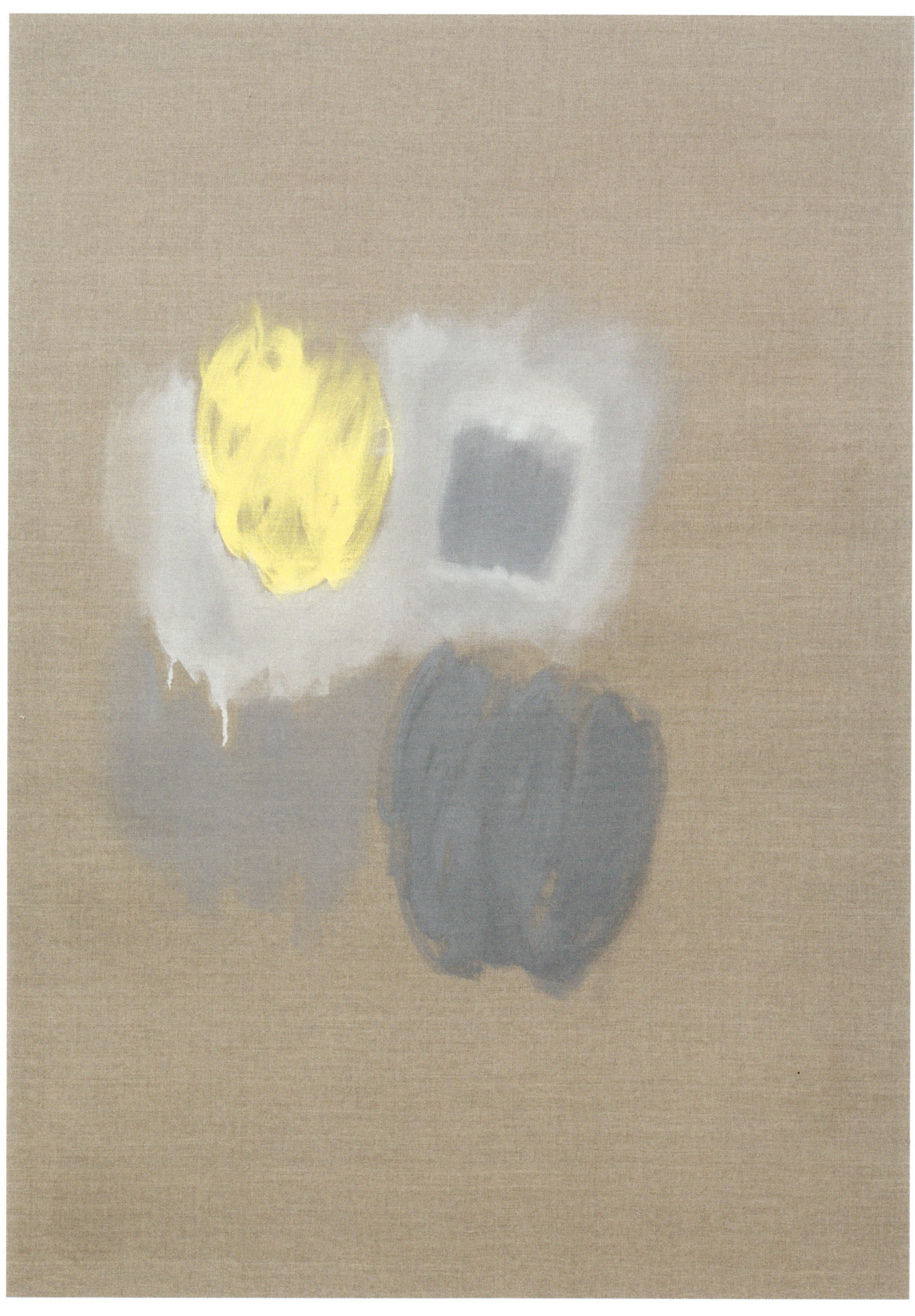

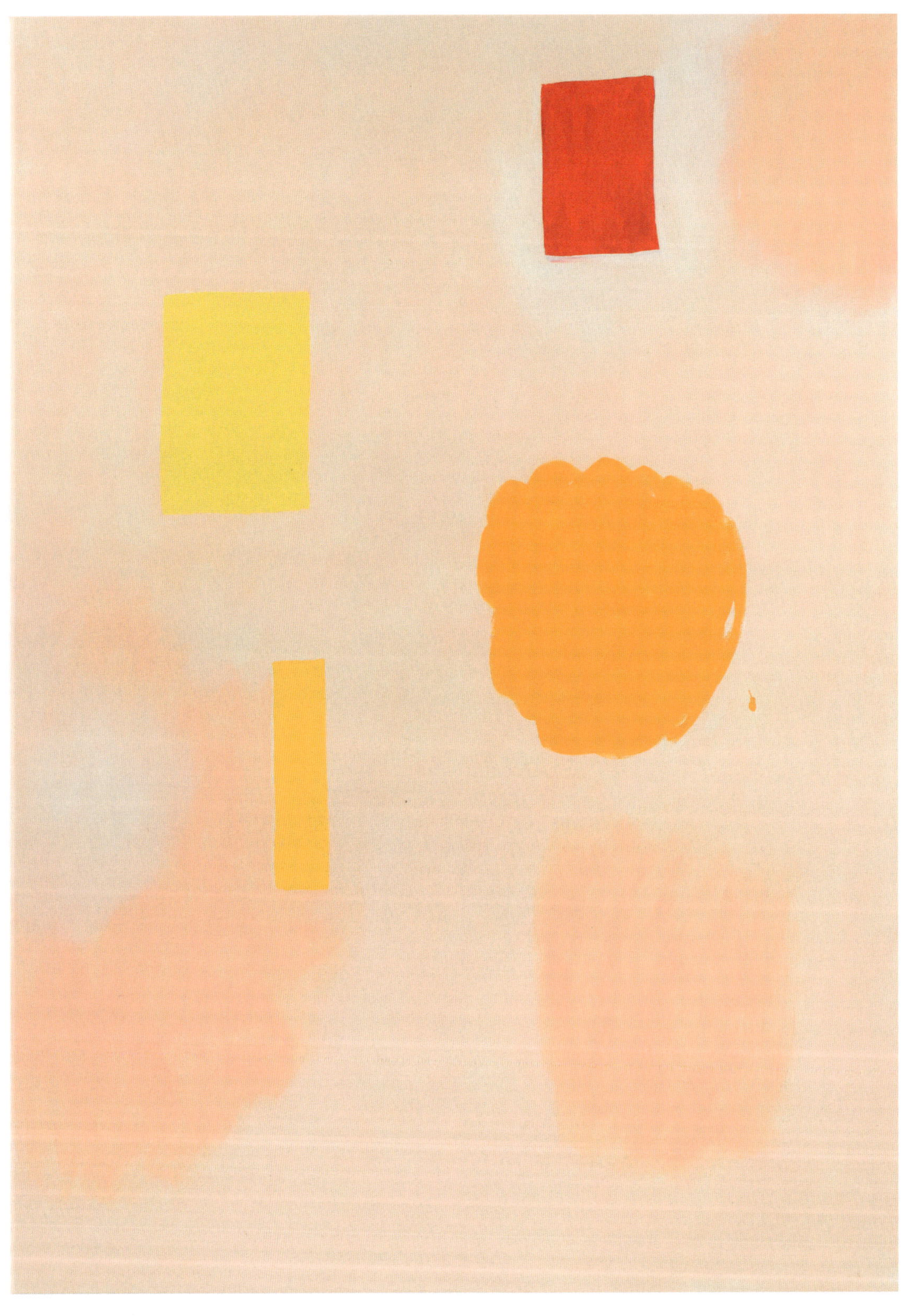

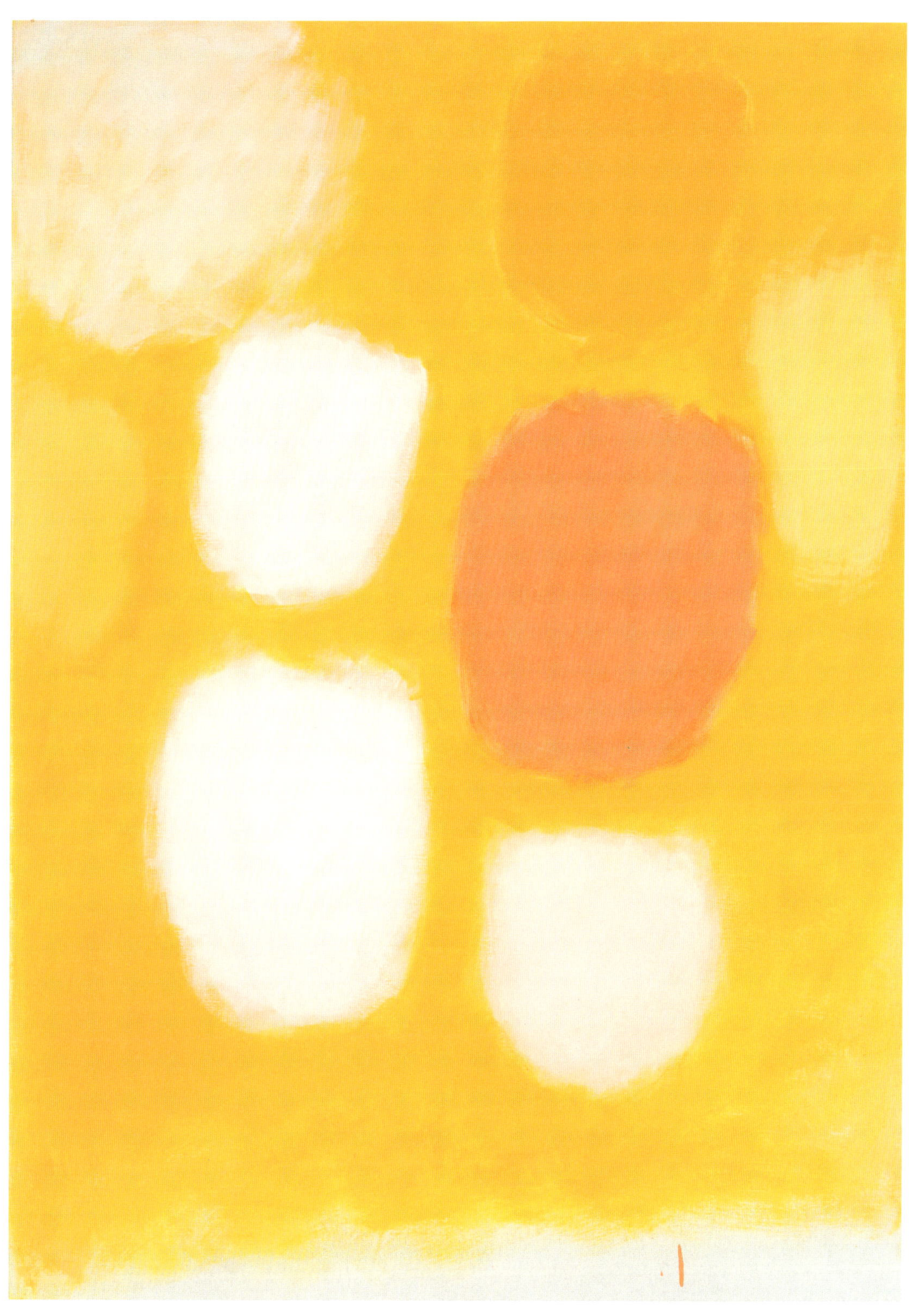

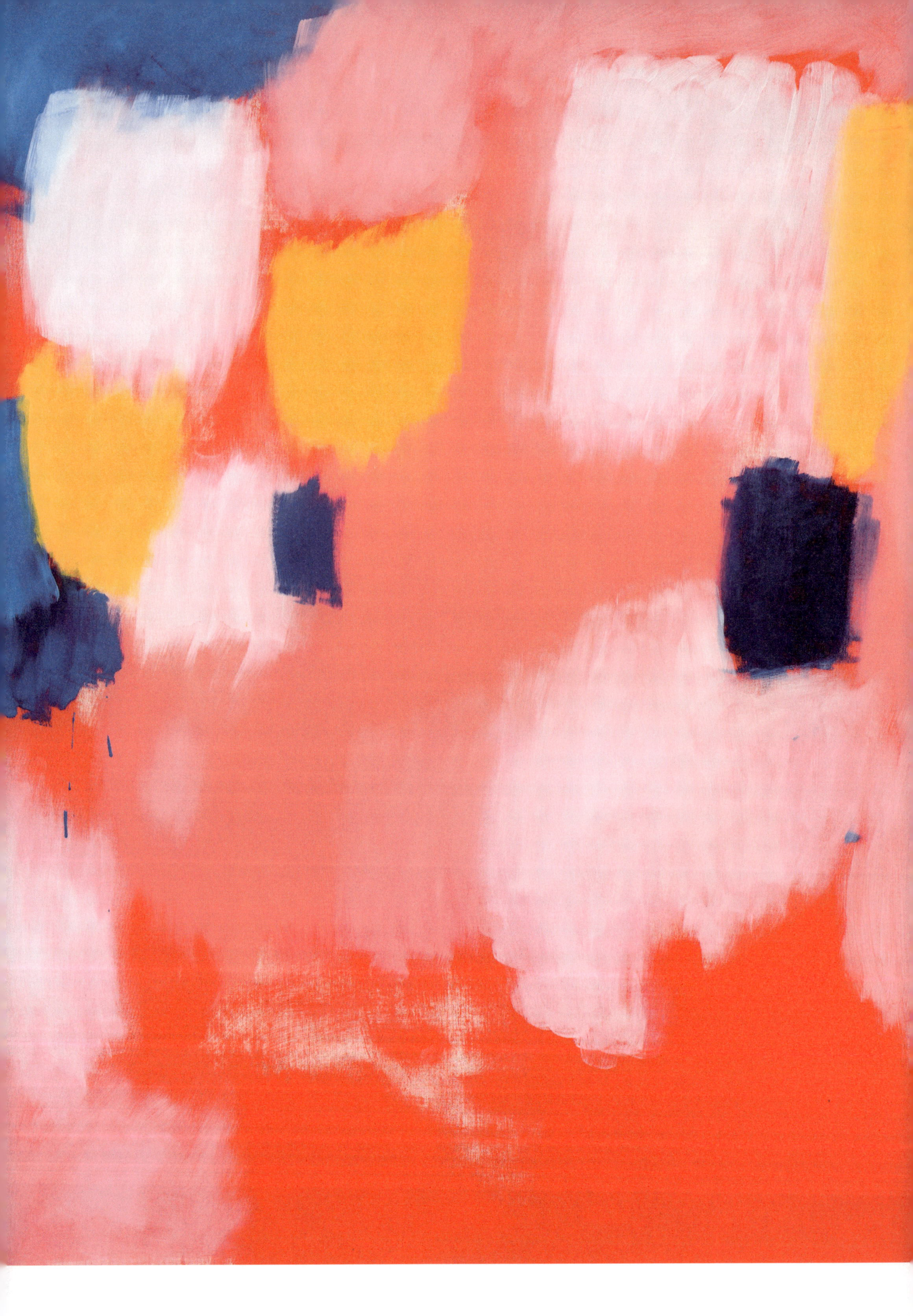

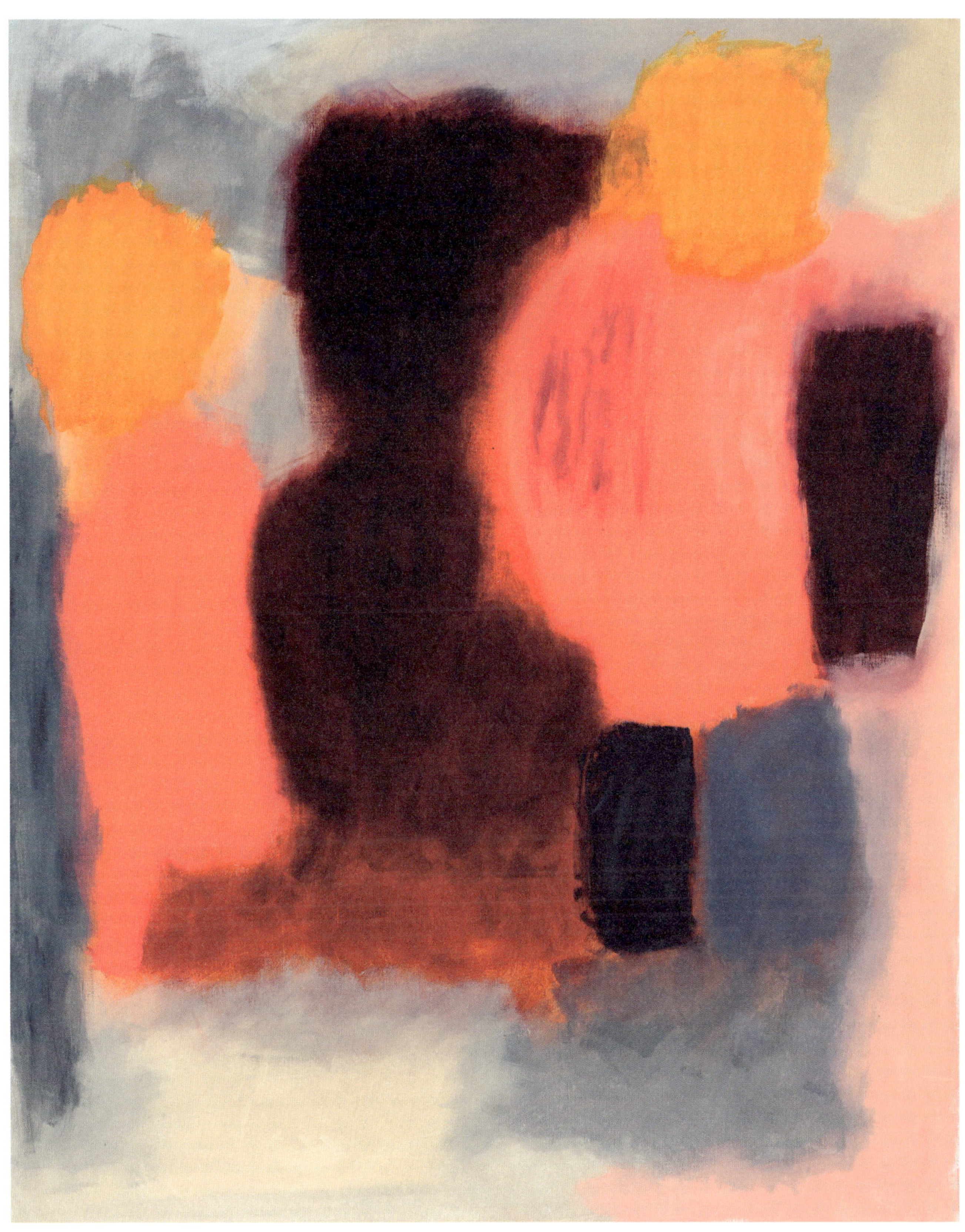

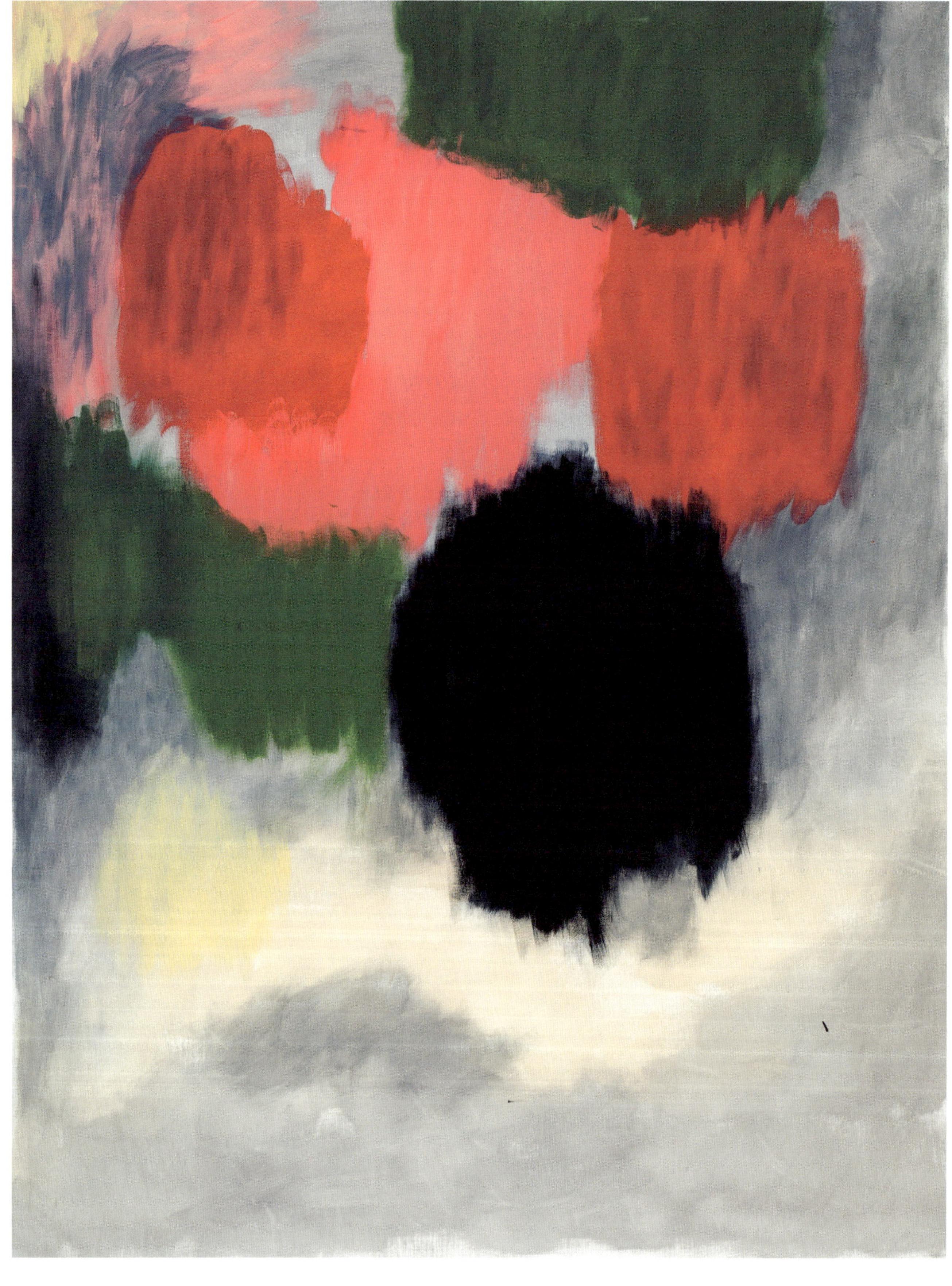

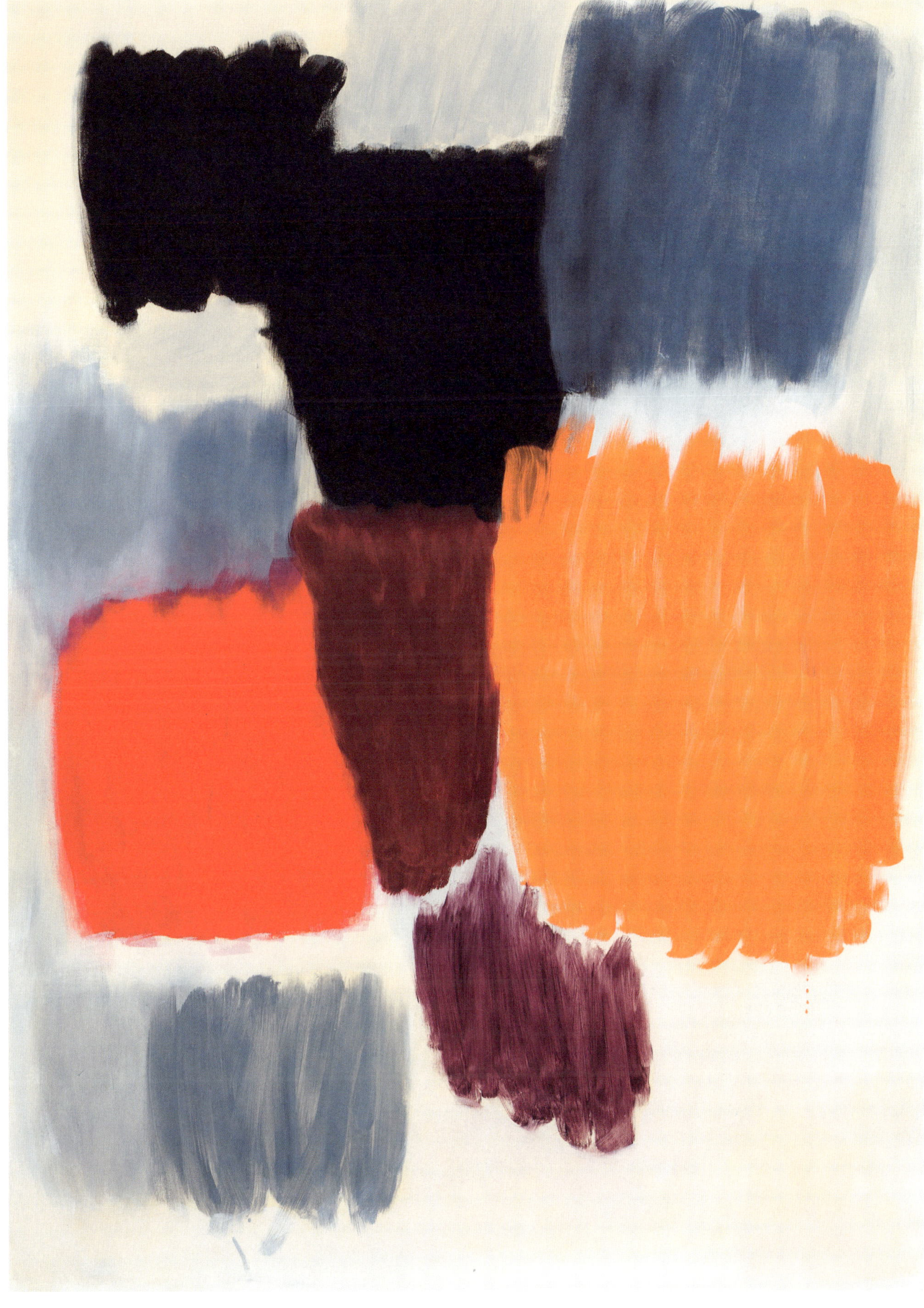

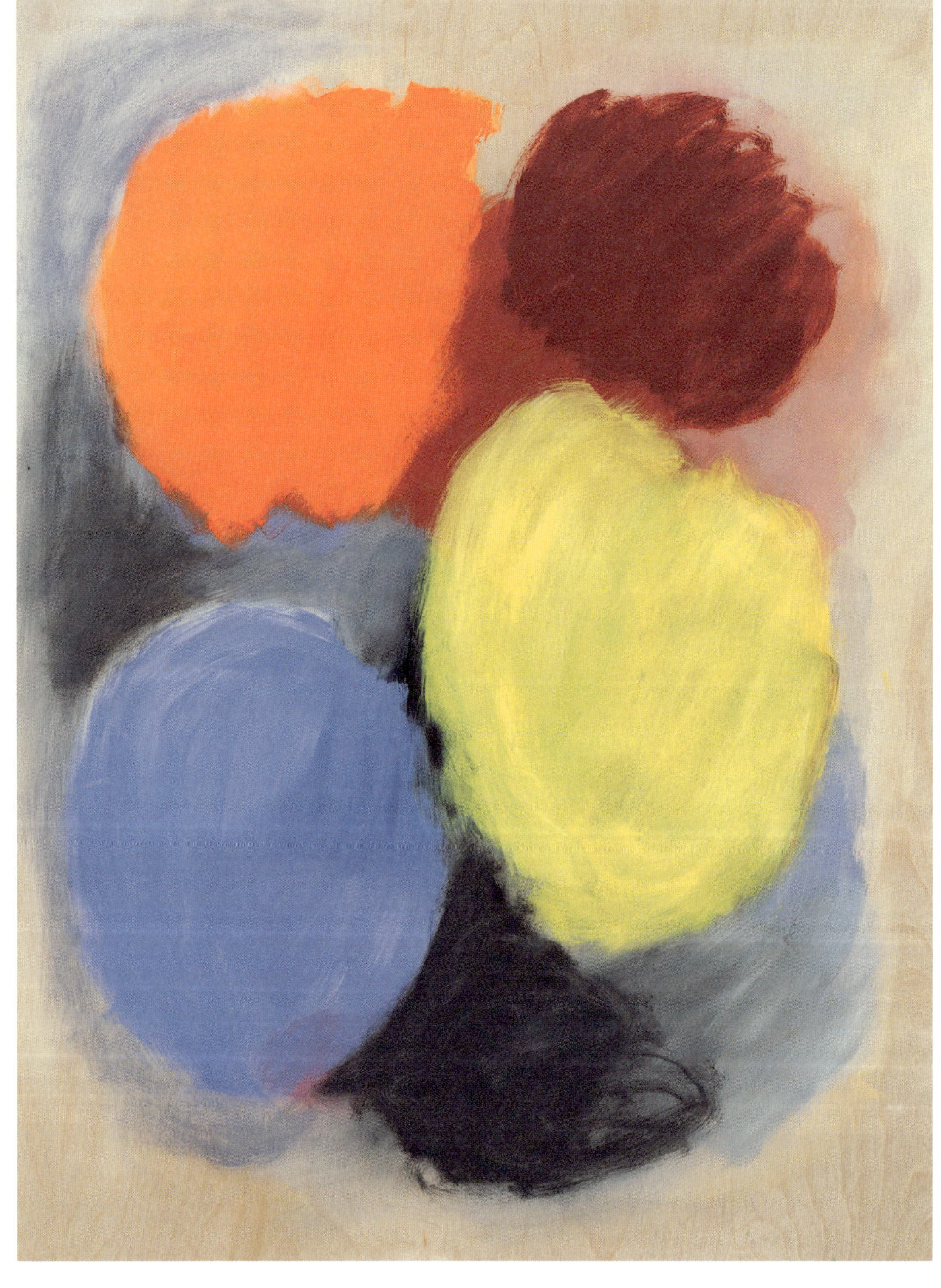

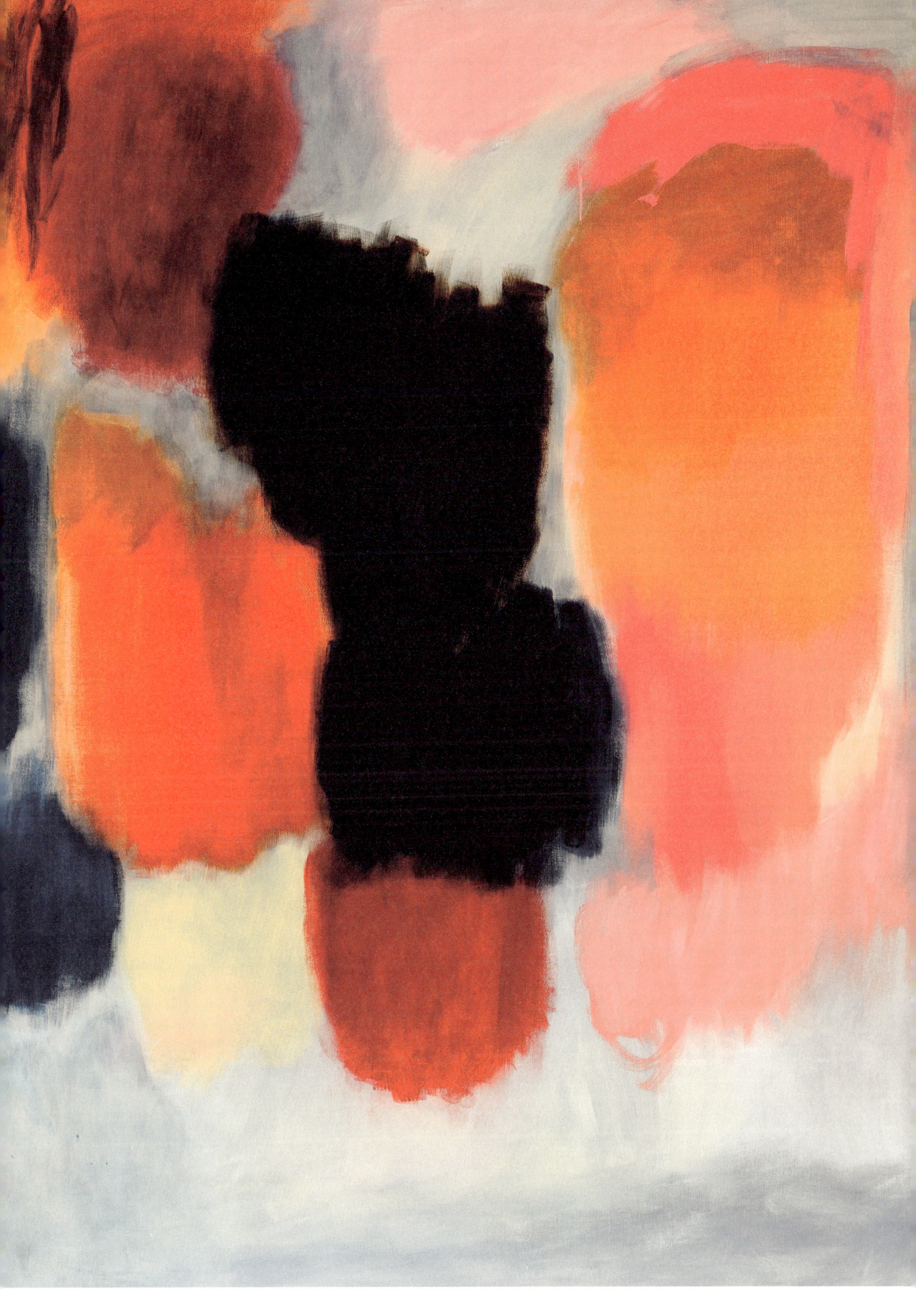

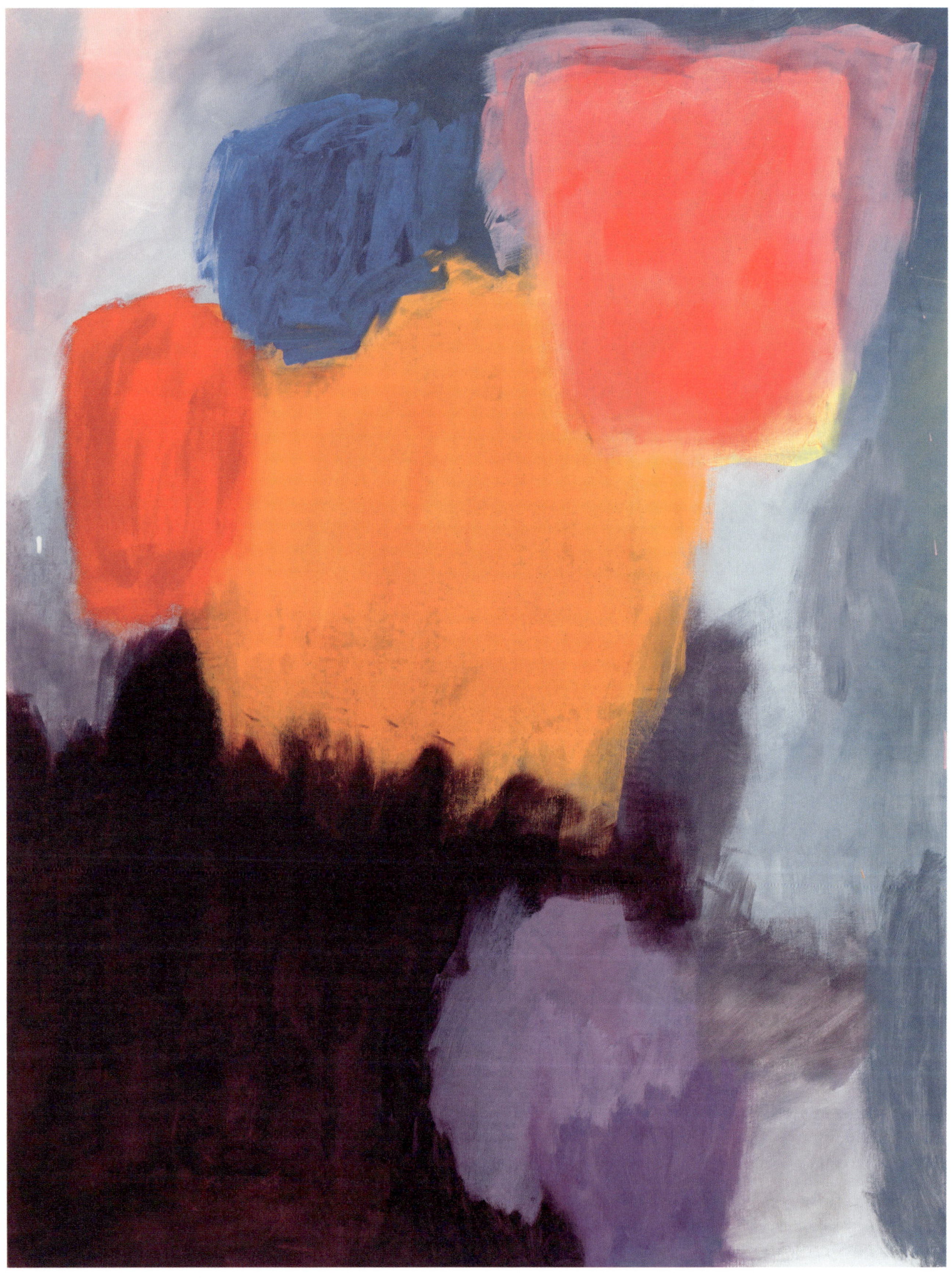

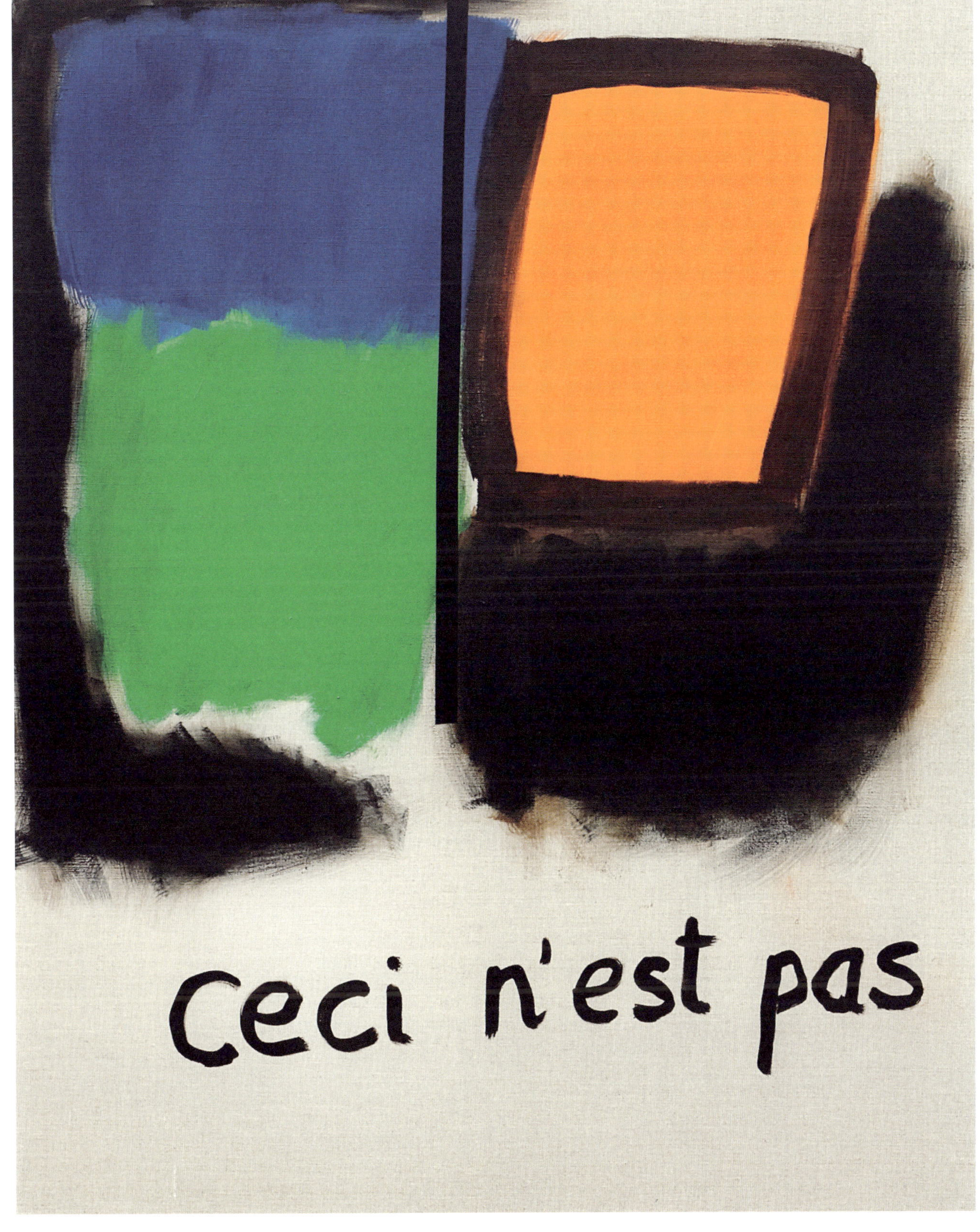
Ceci n'est pas

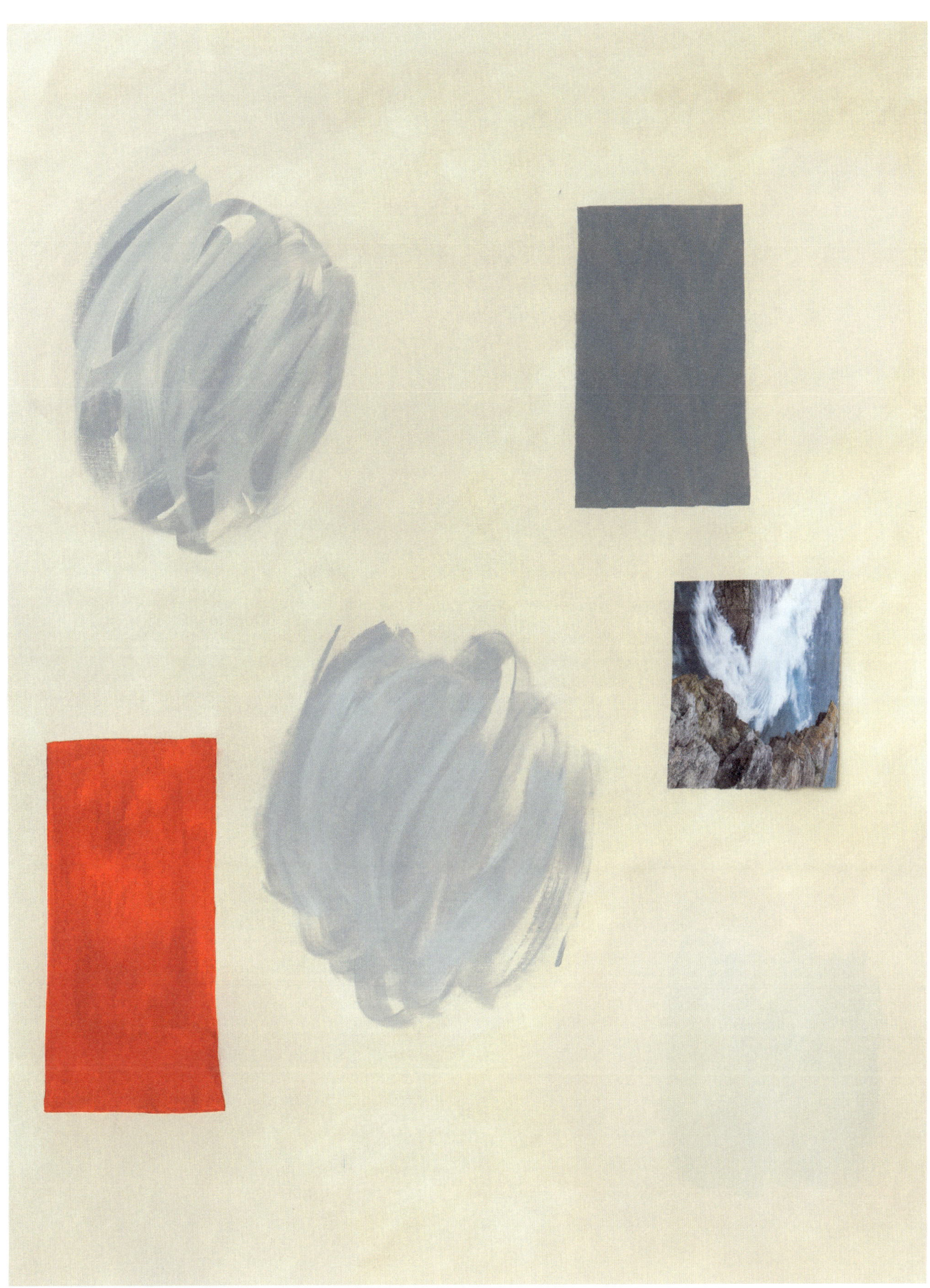

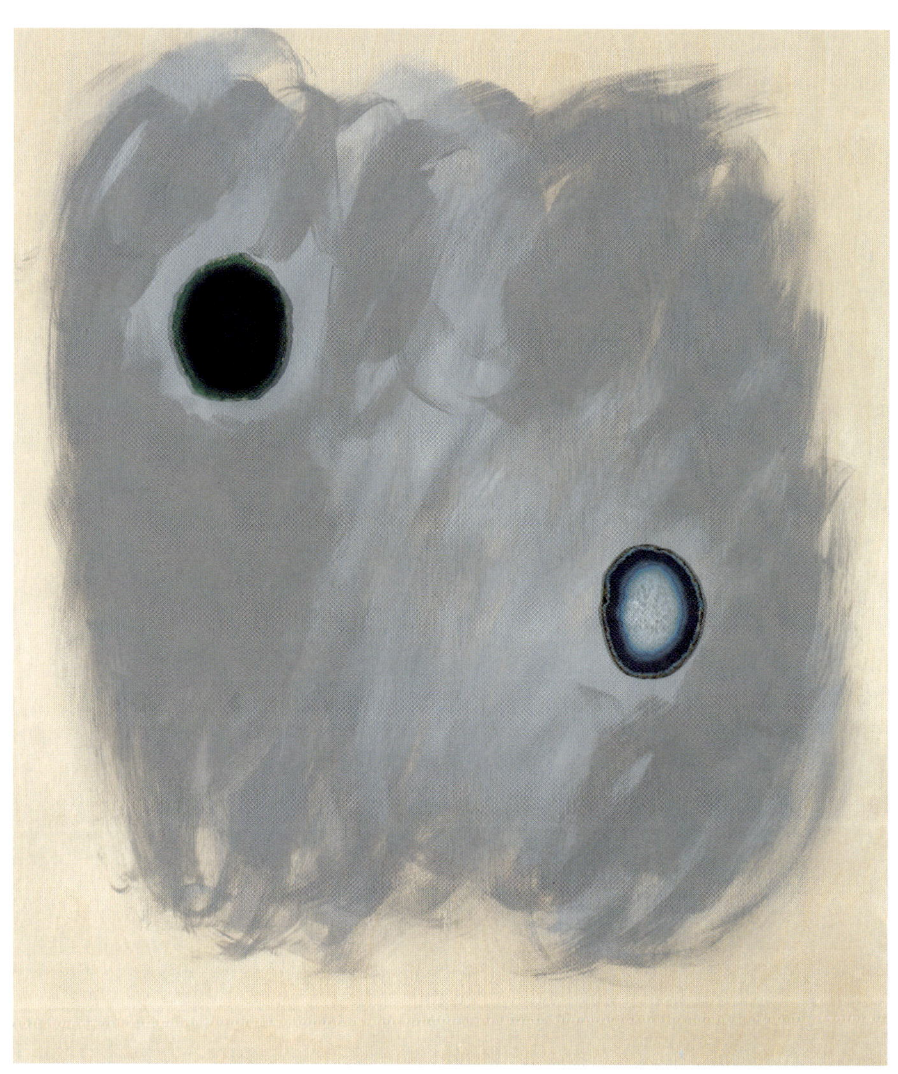

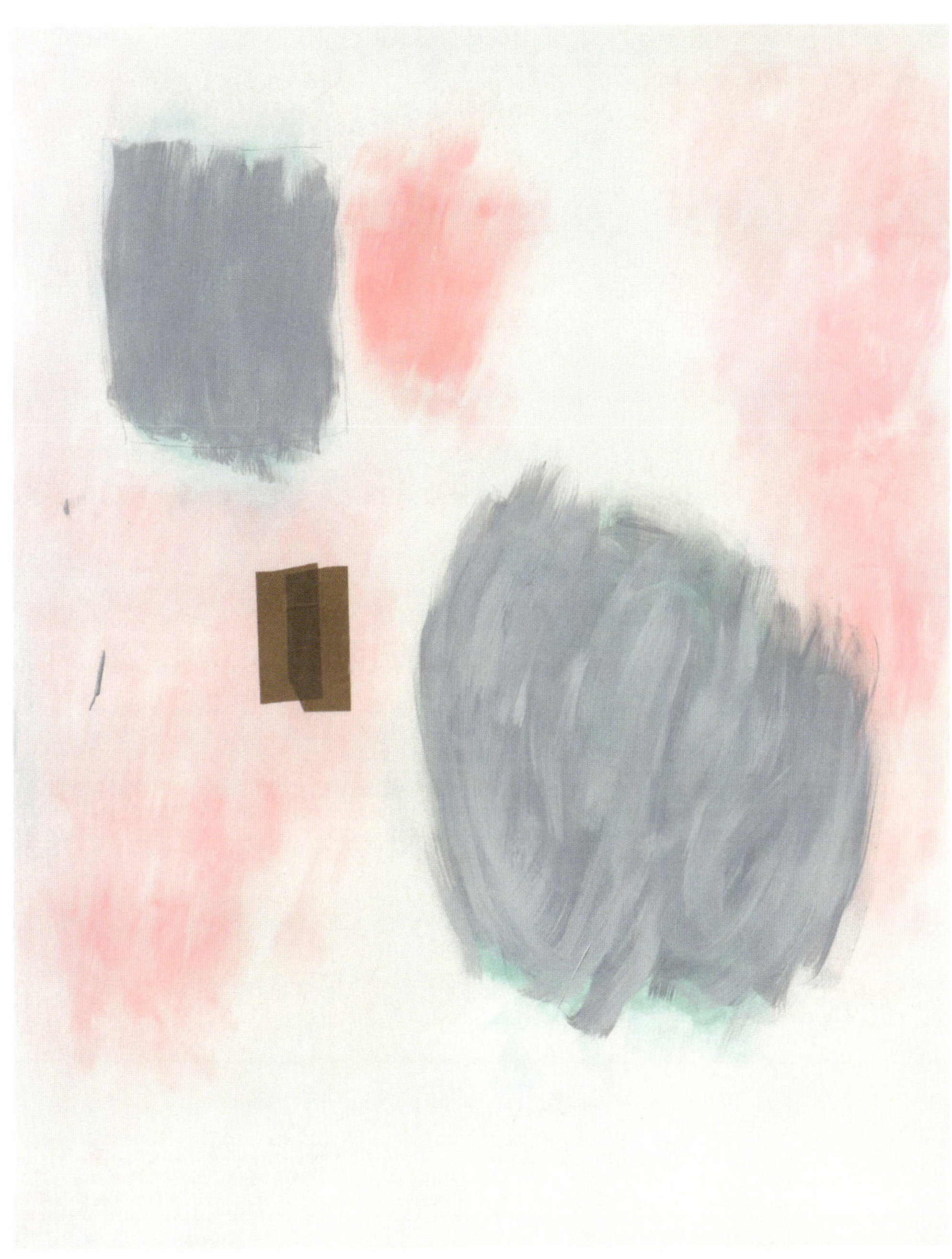

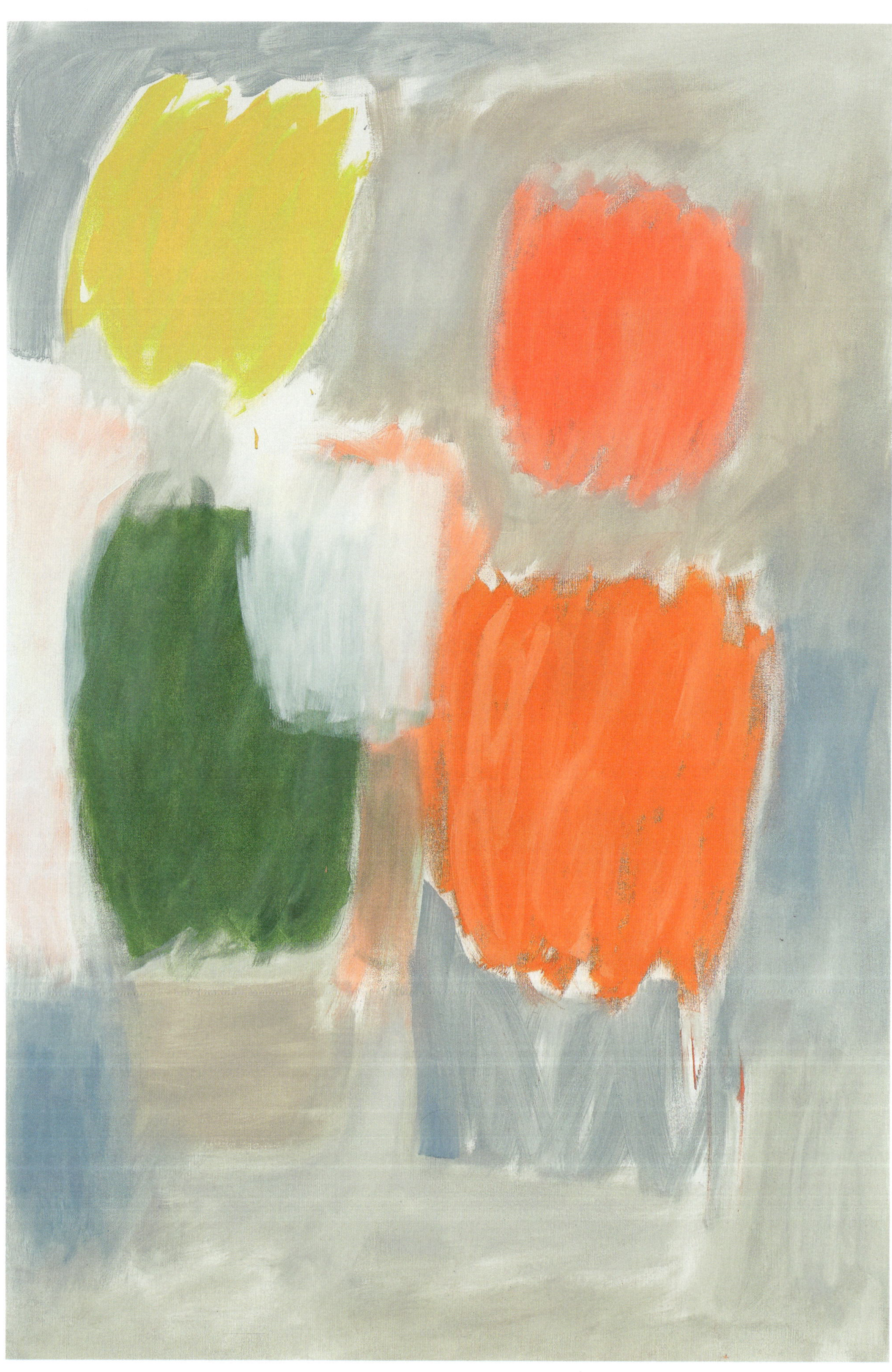

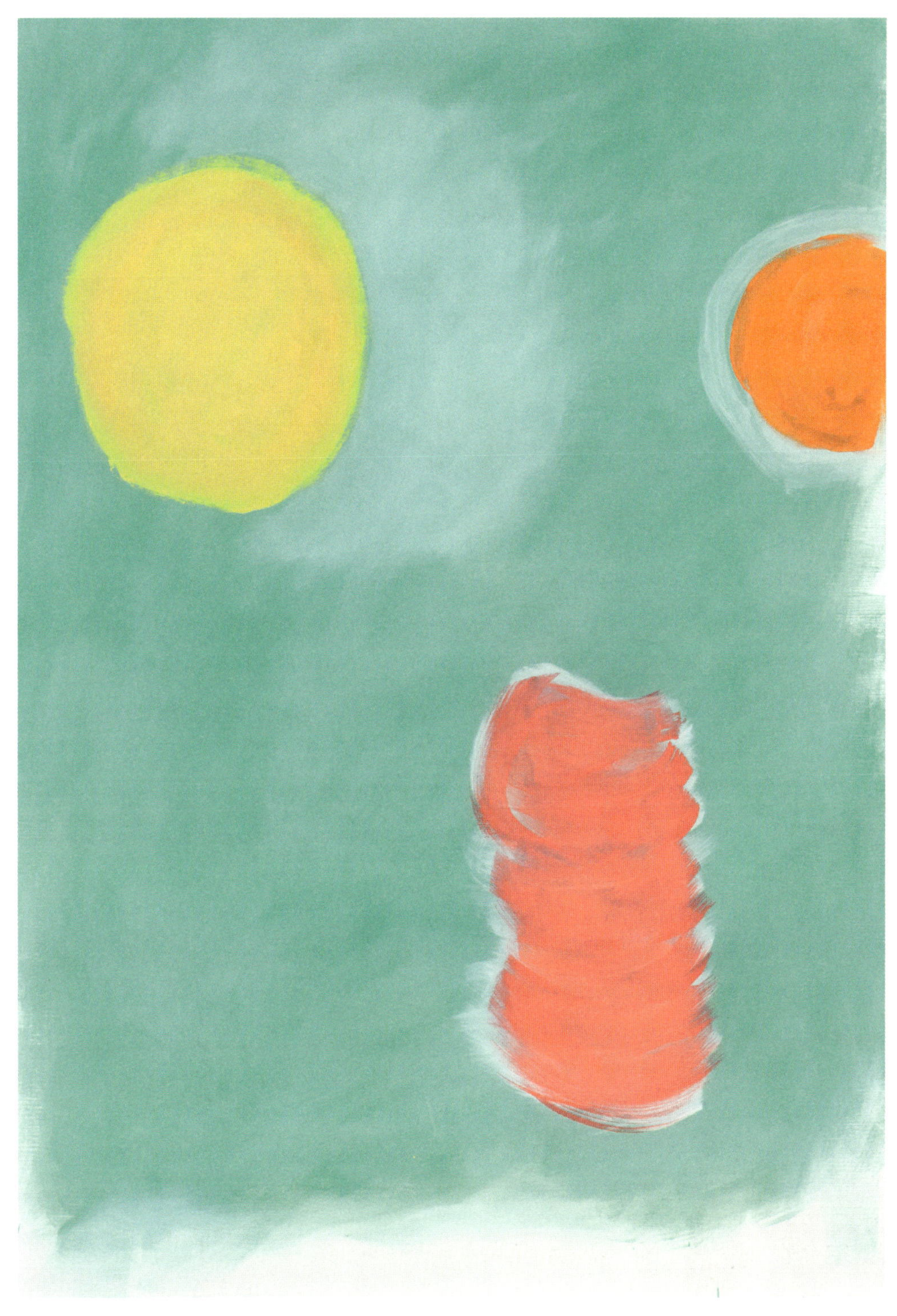

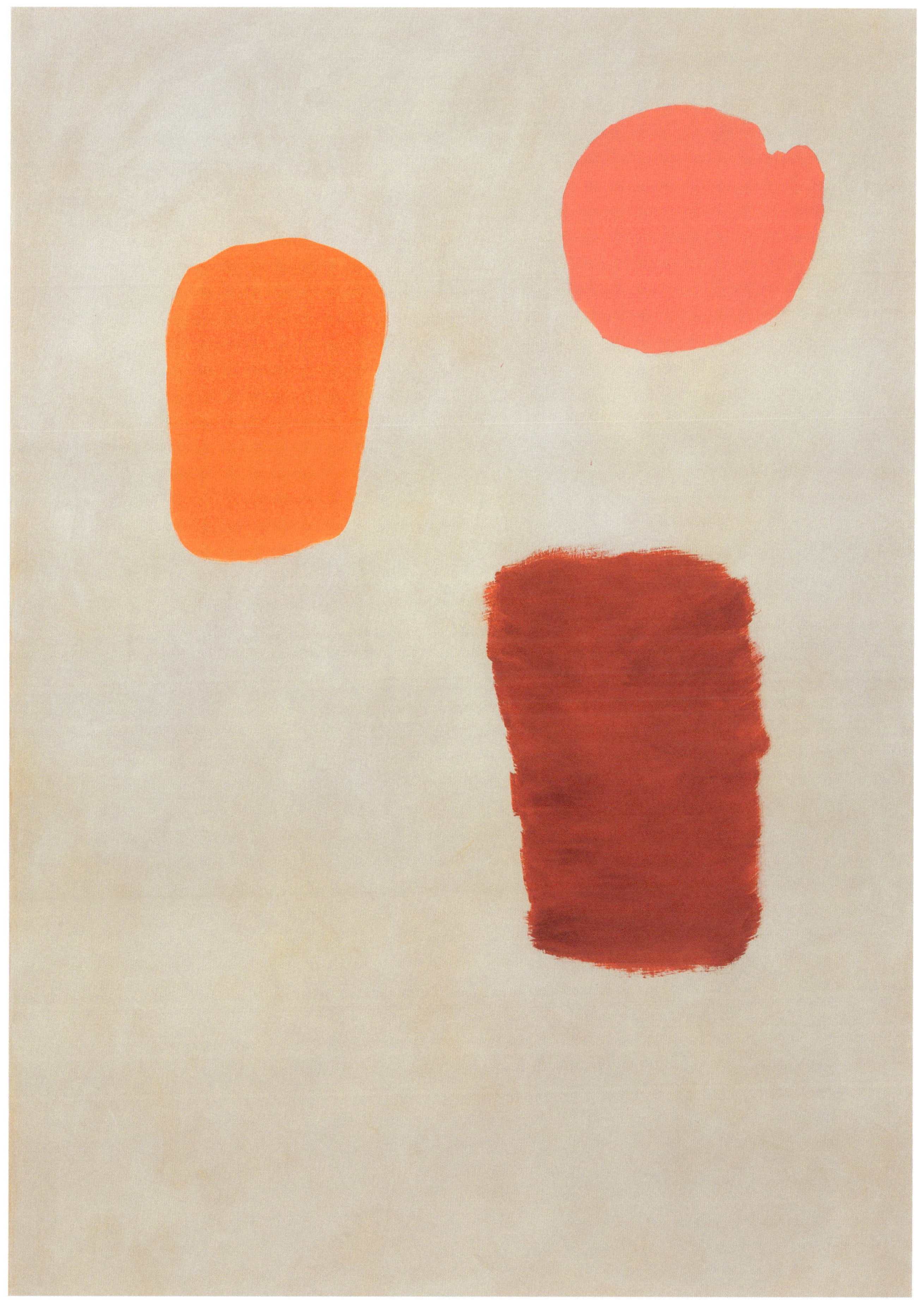

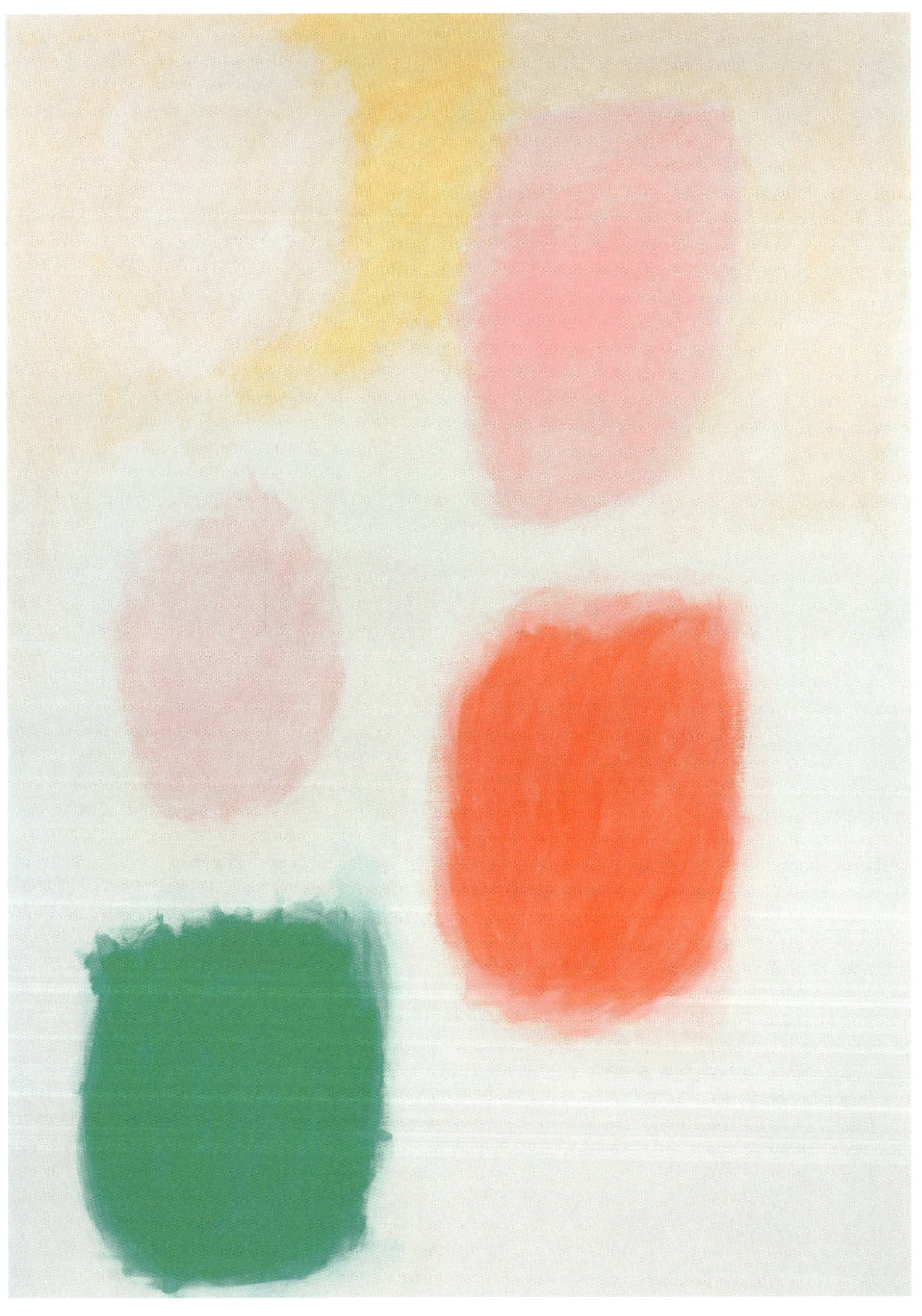

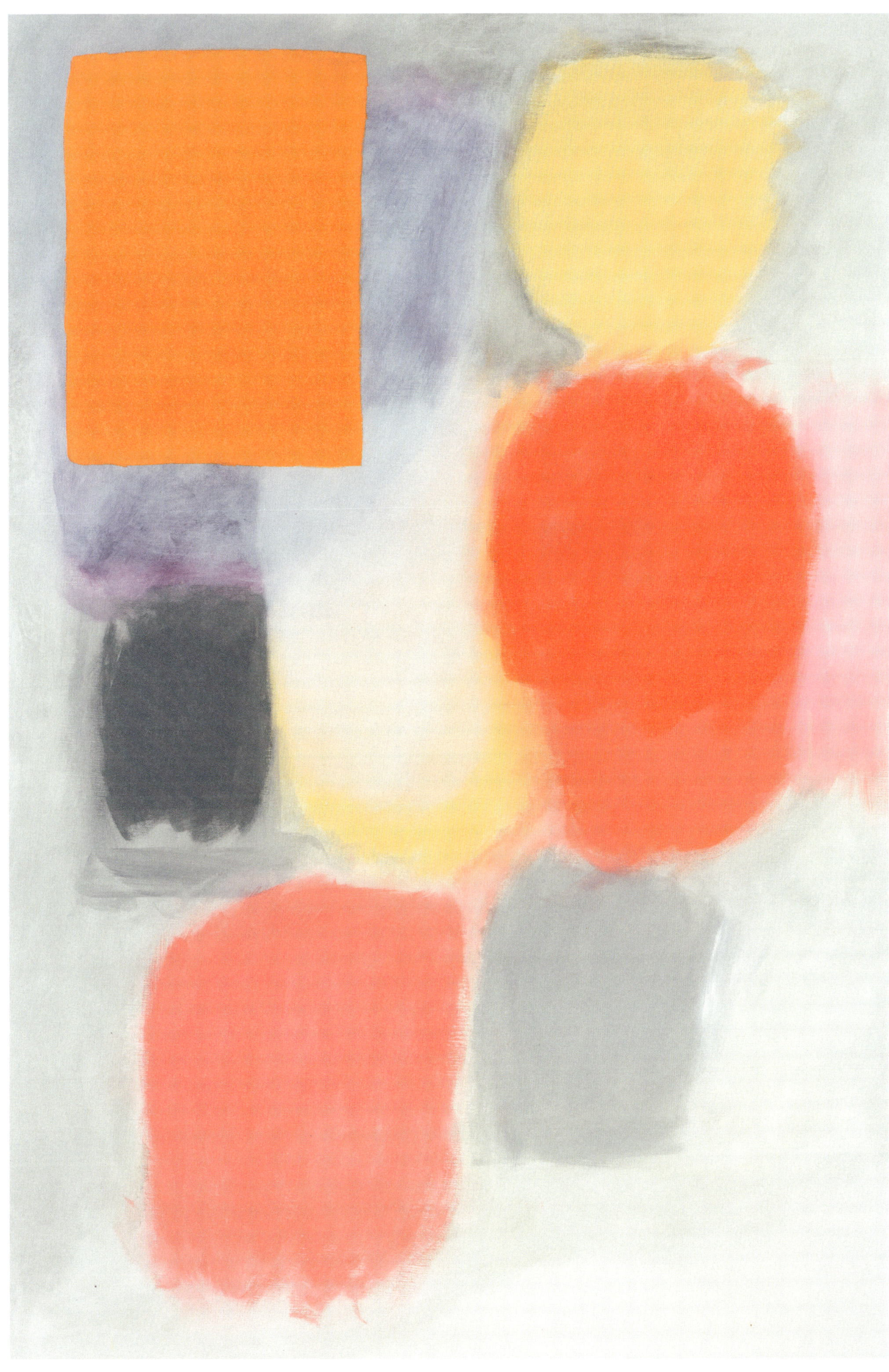

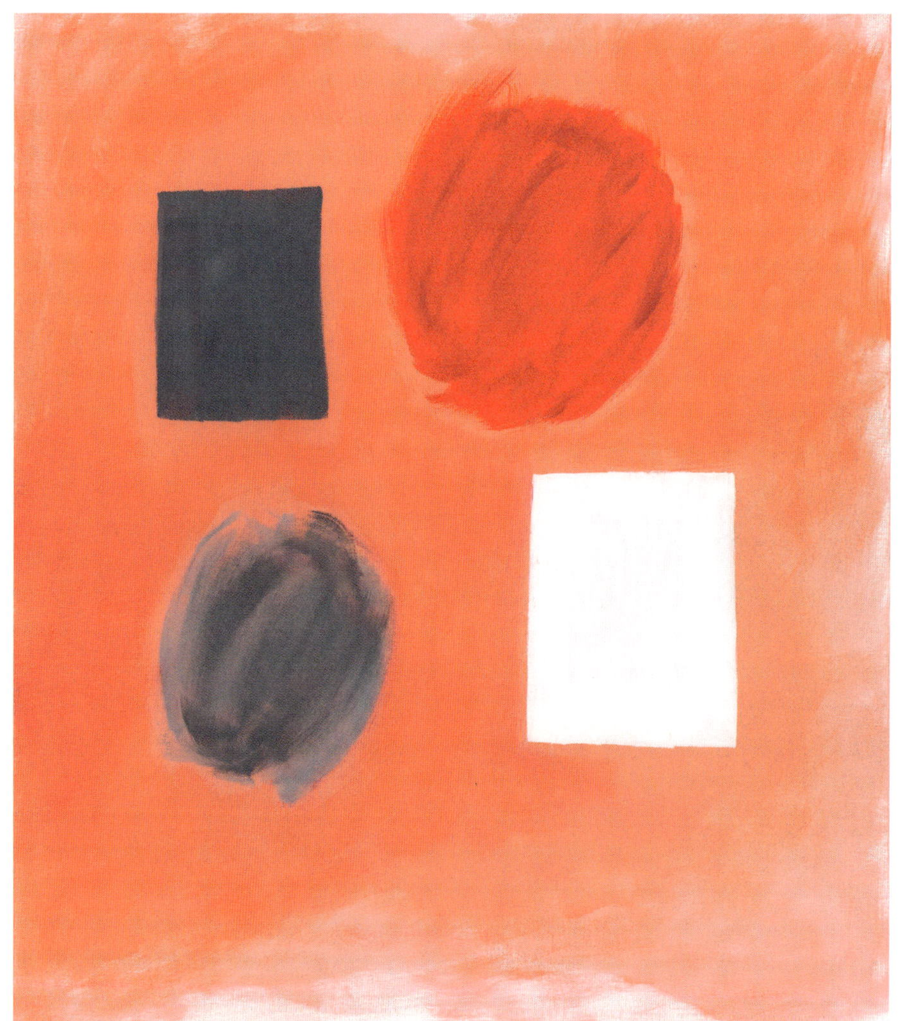

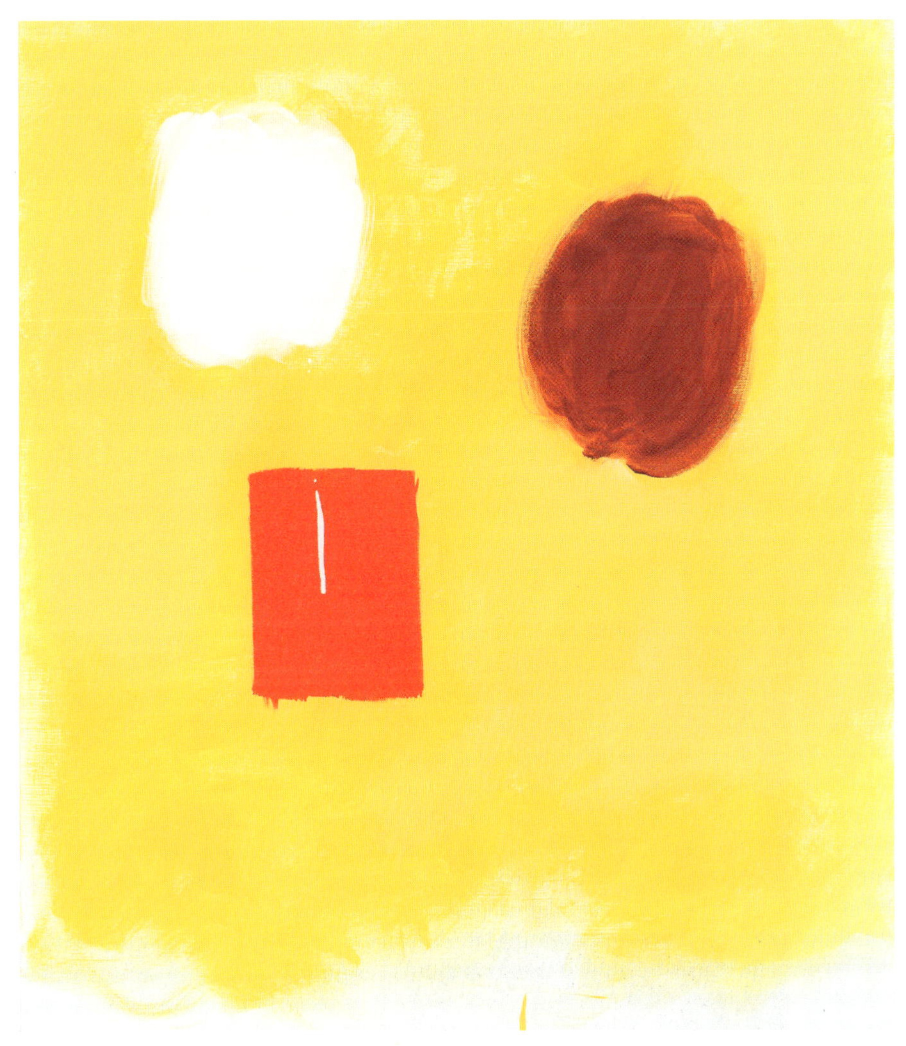

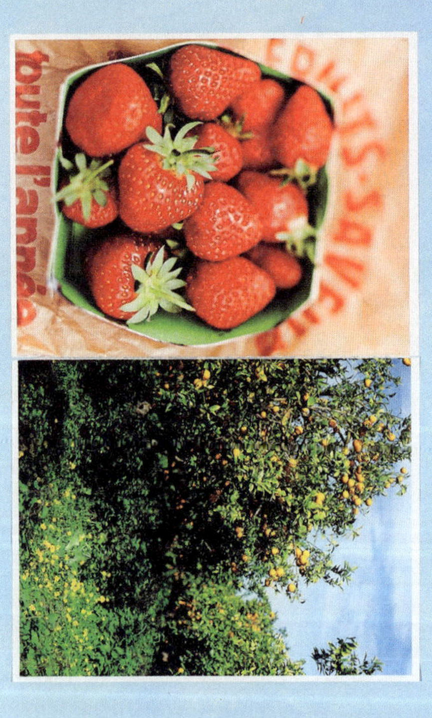

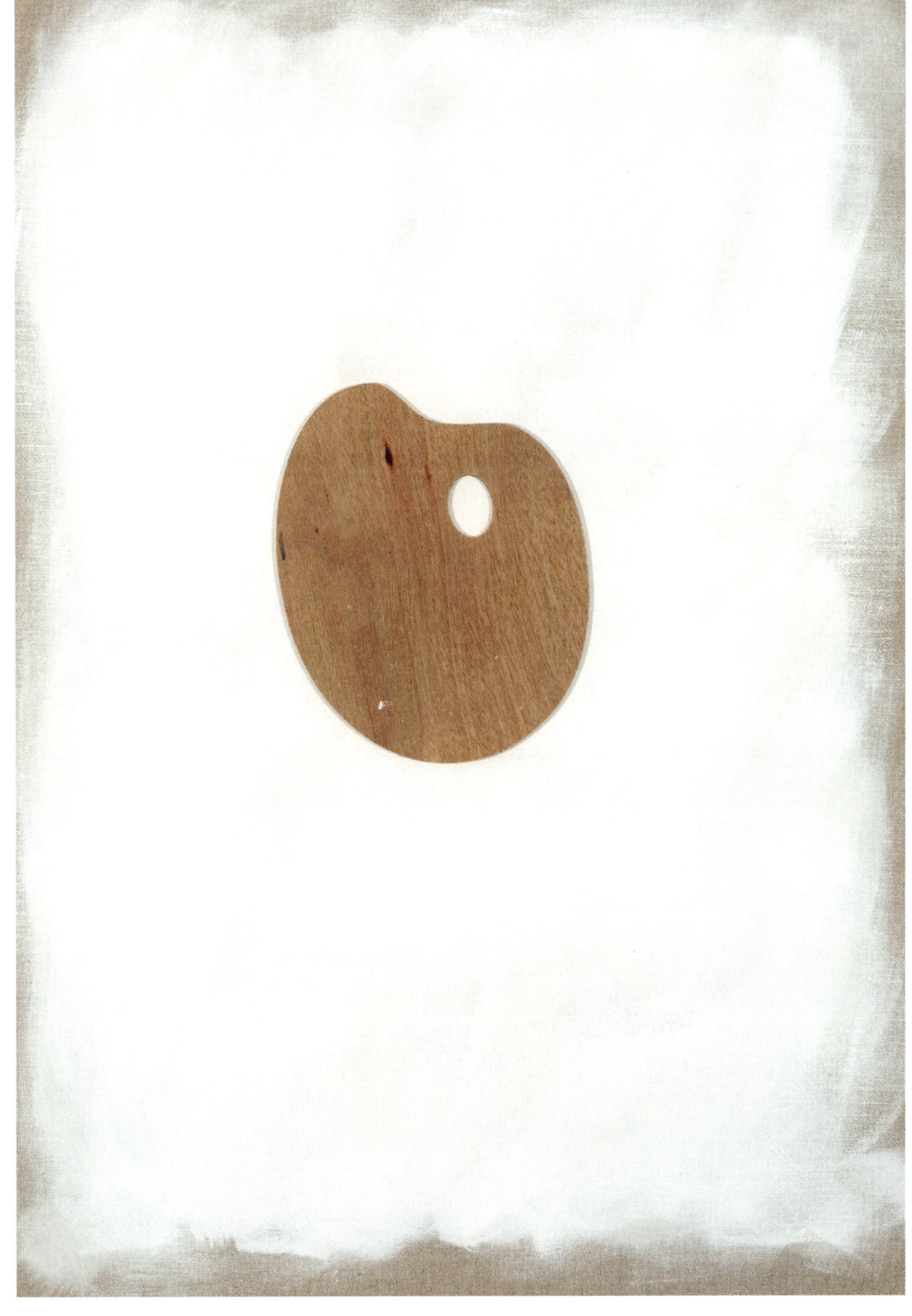

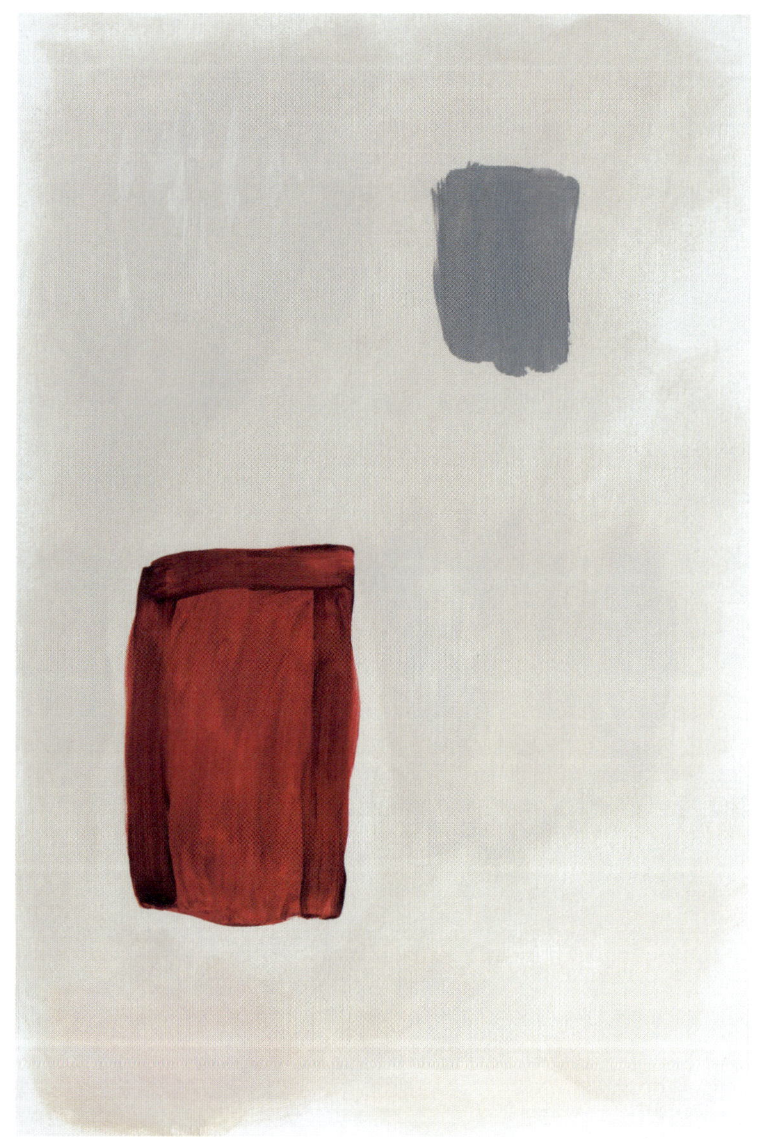

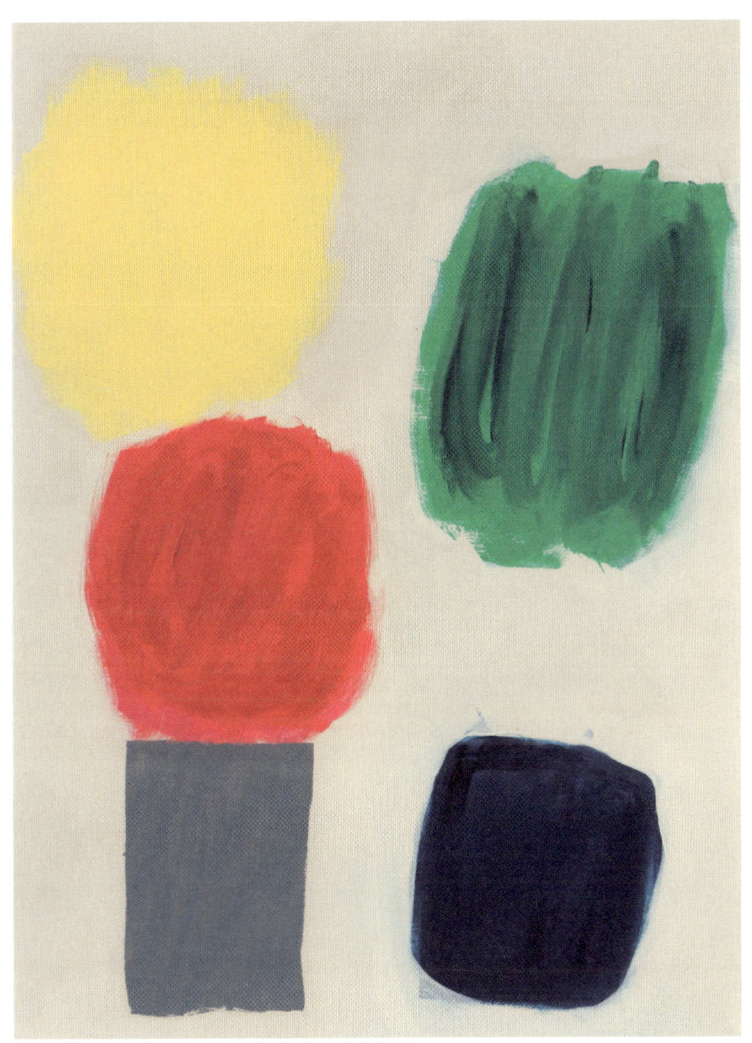

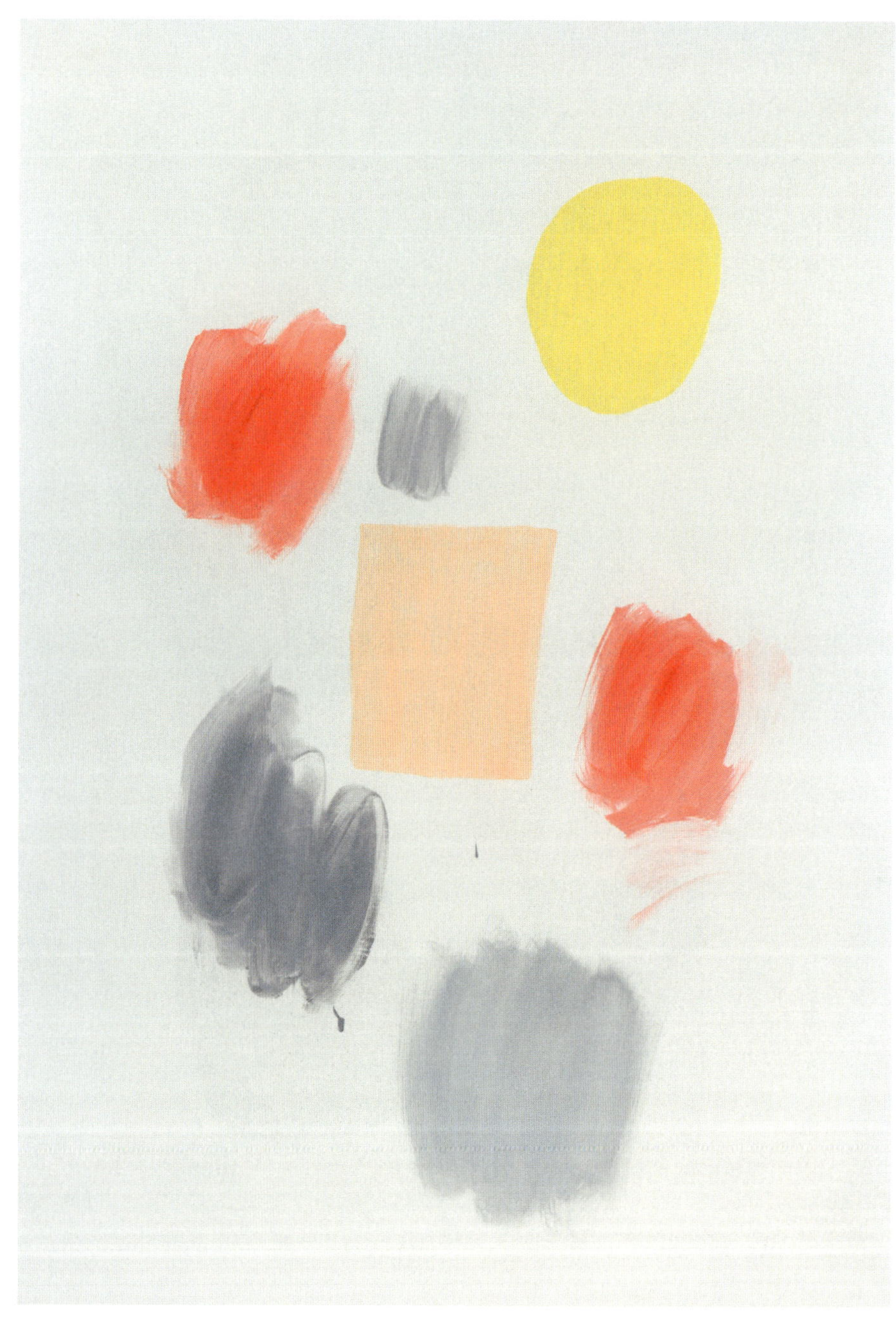

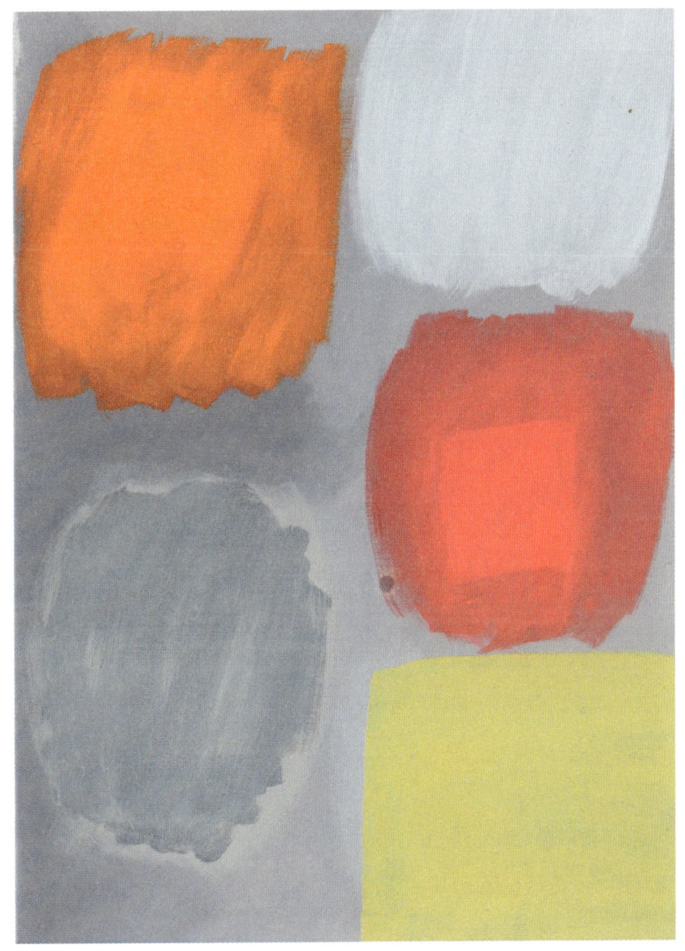

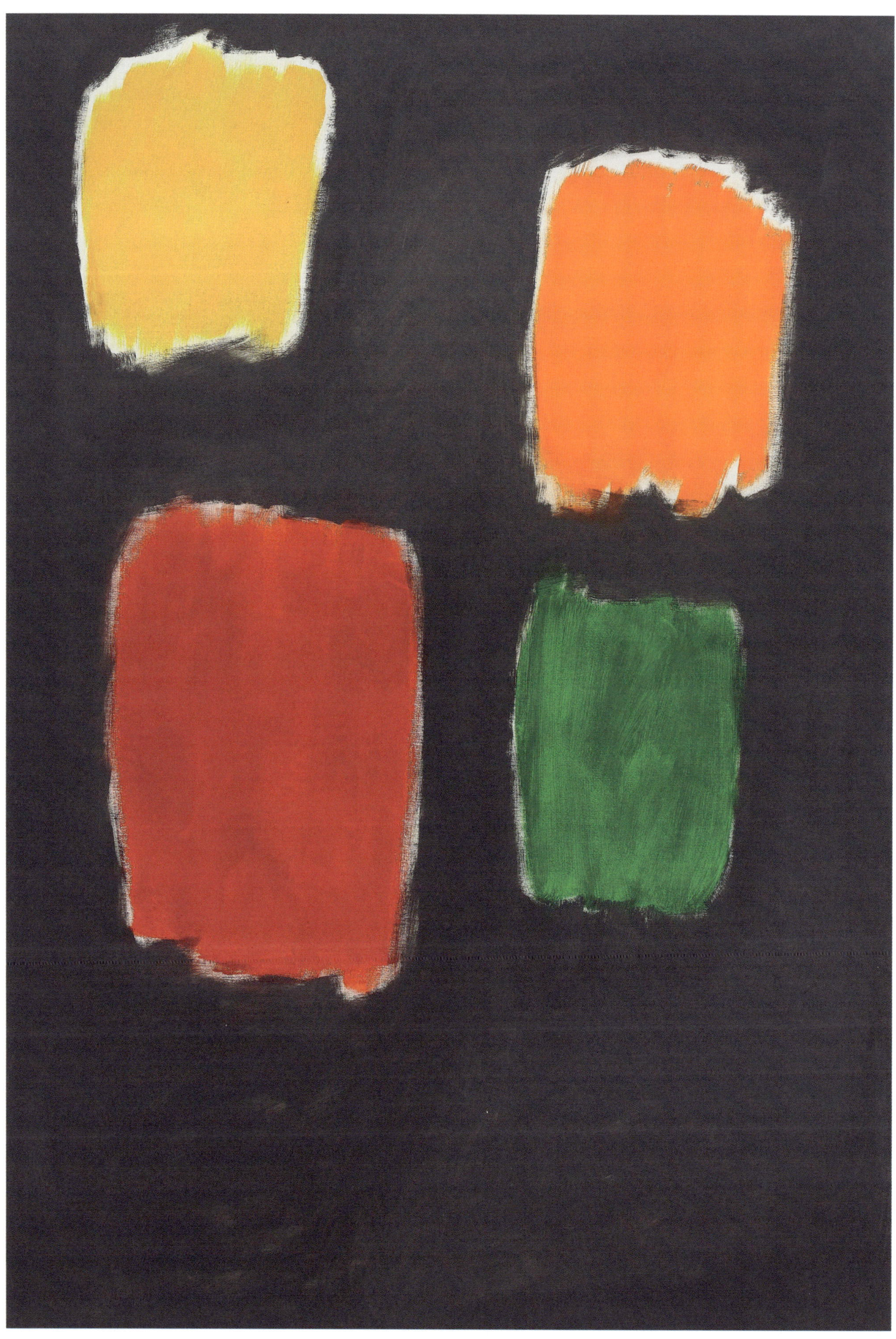

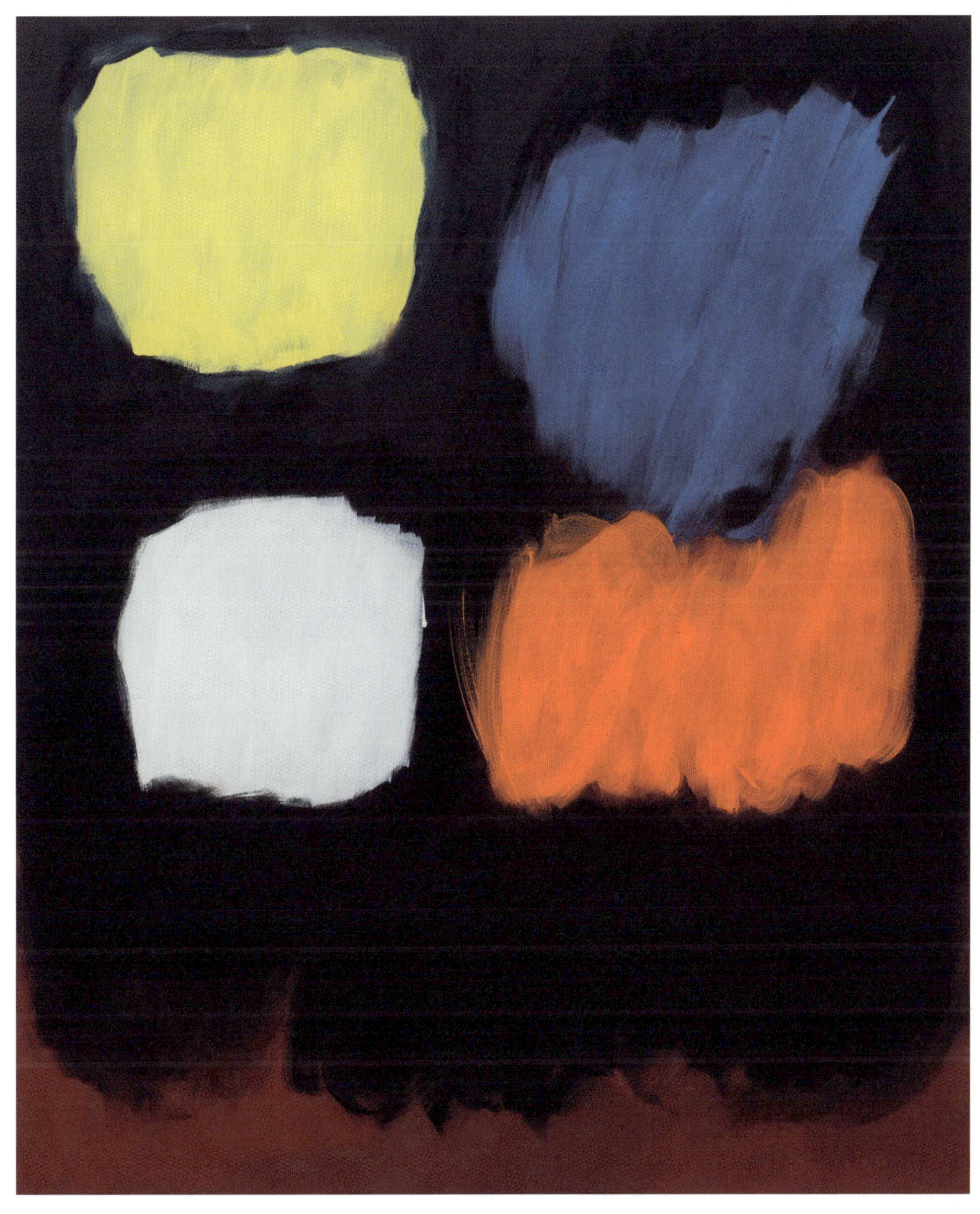

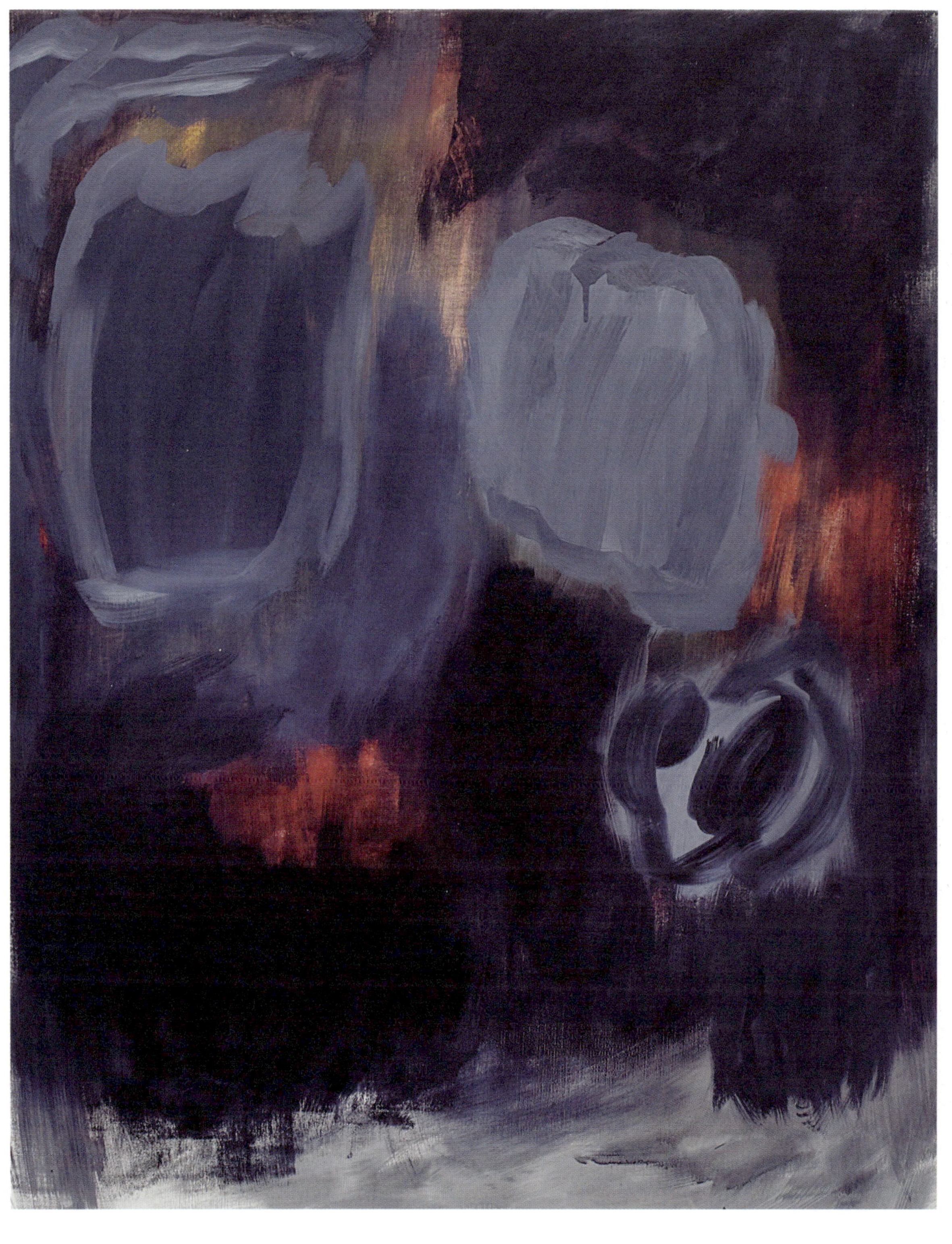

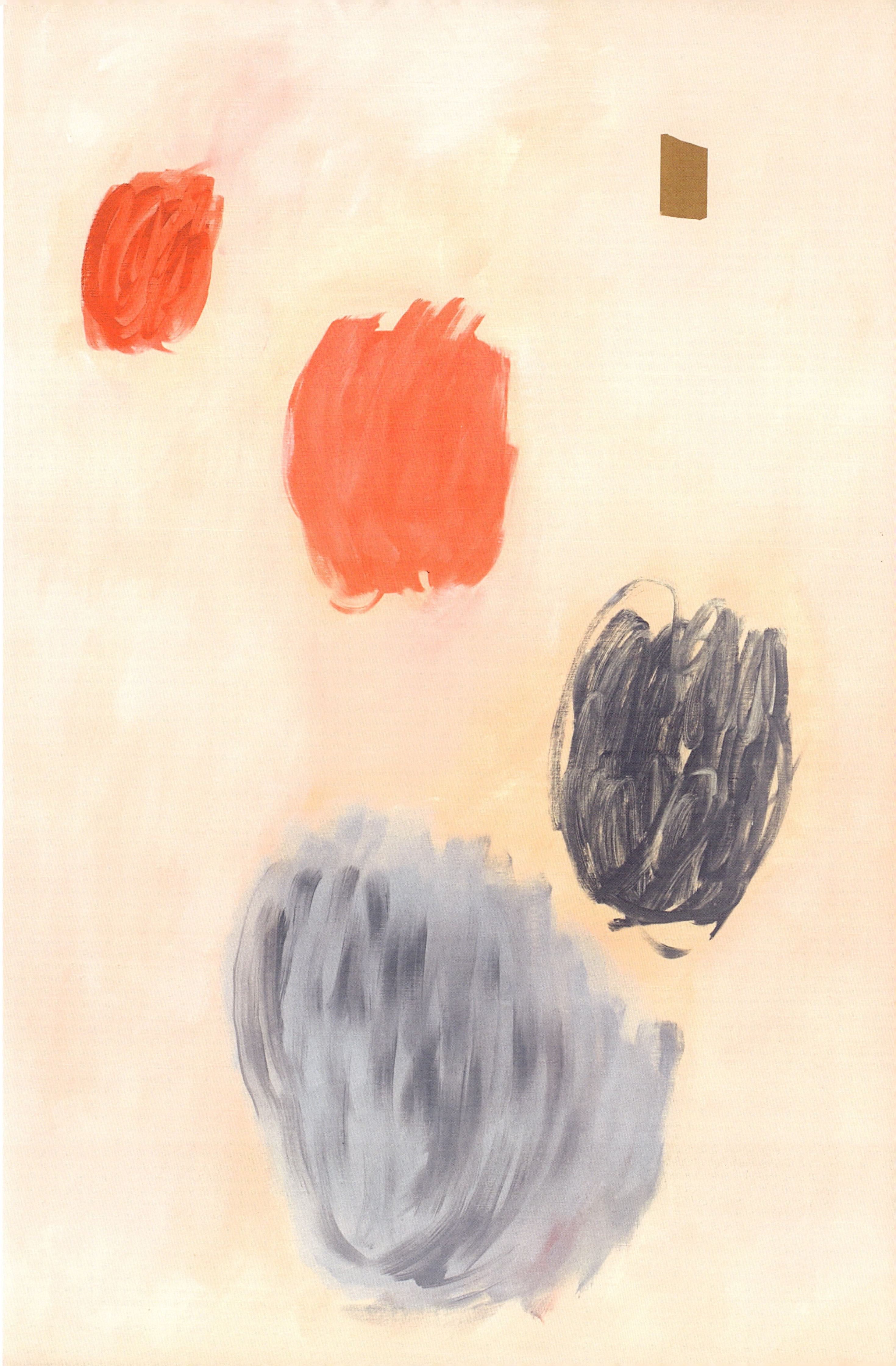

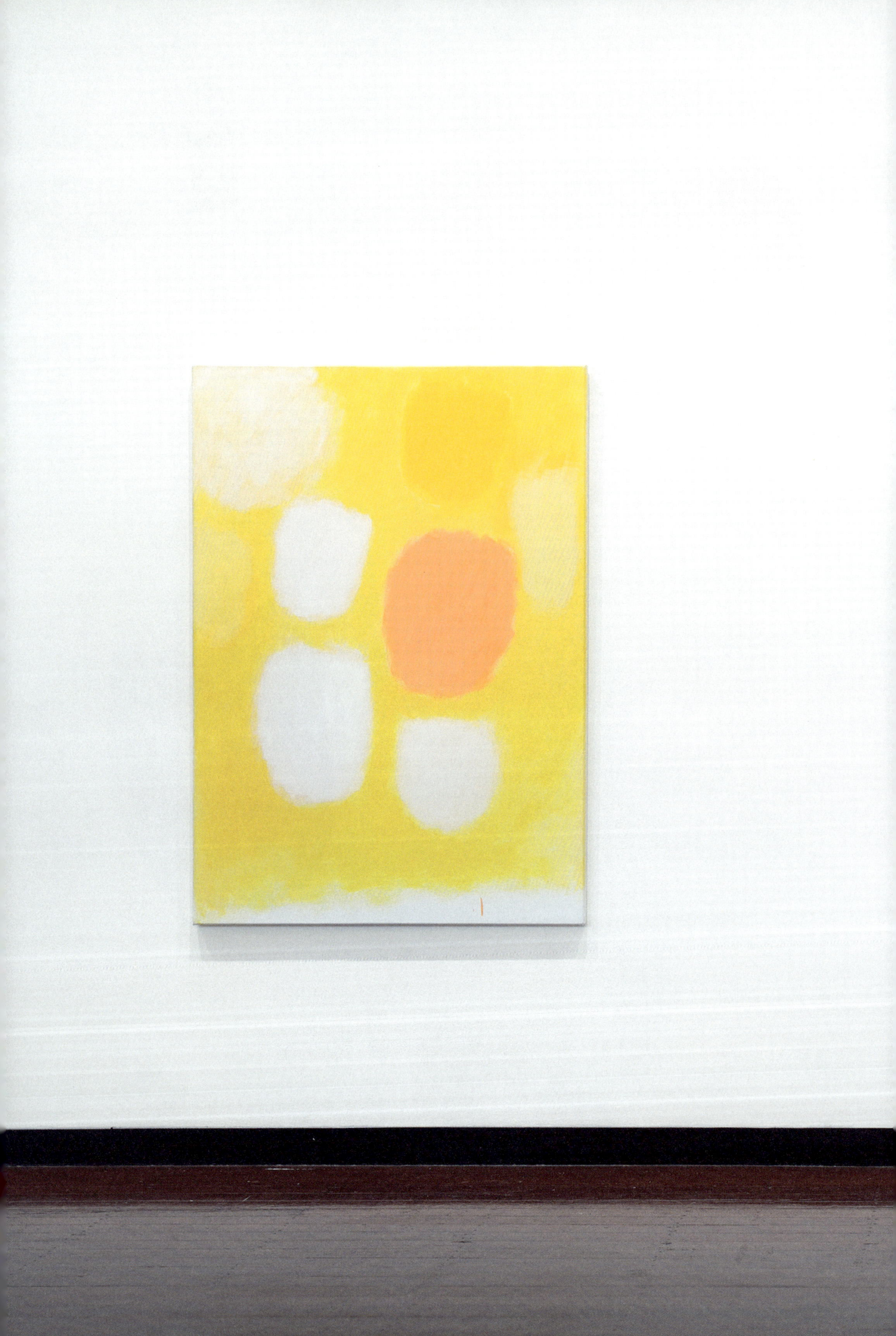

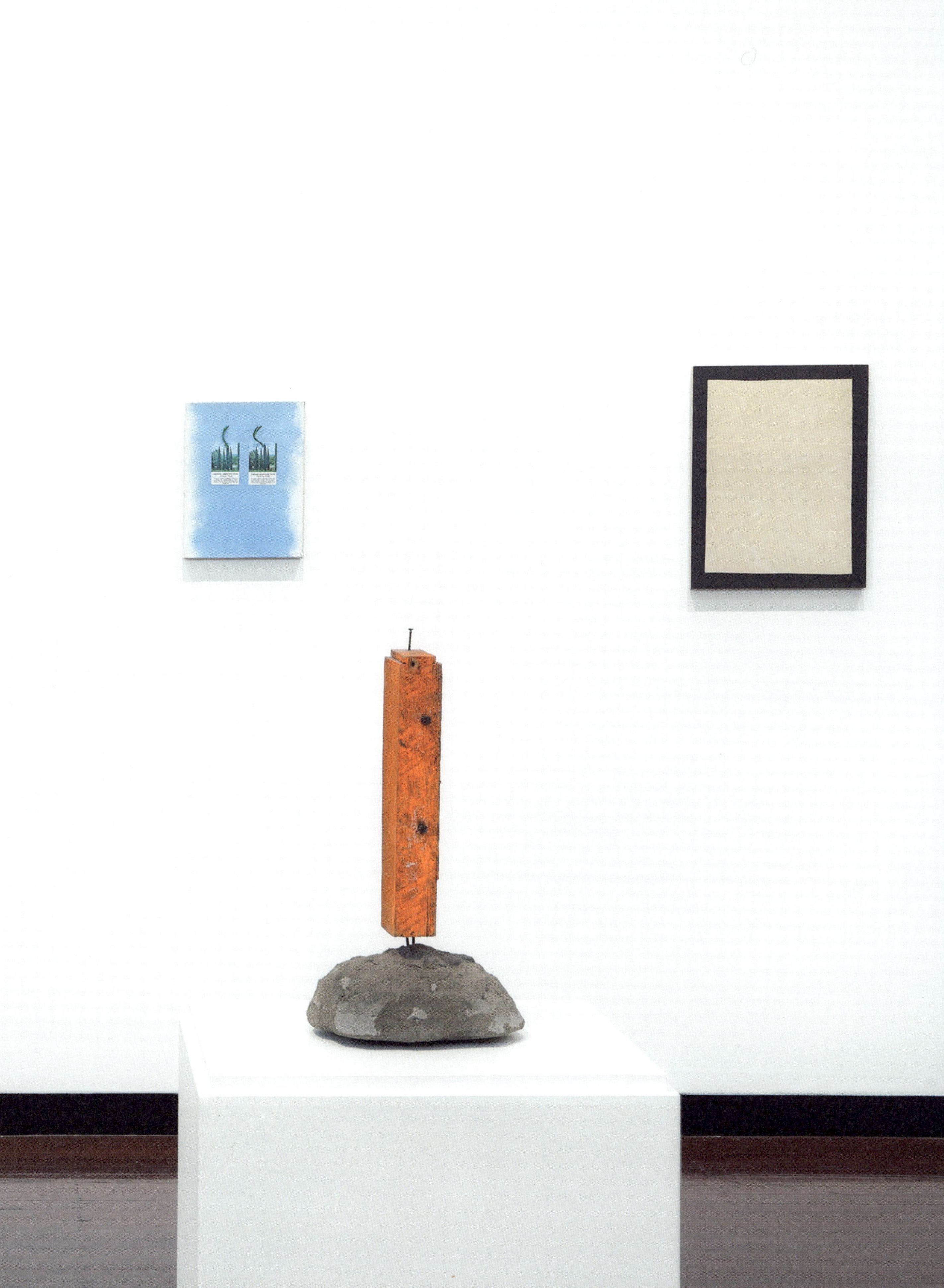

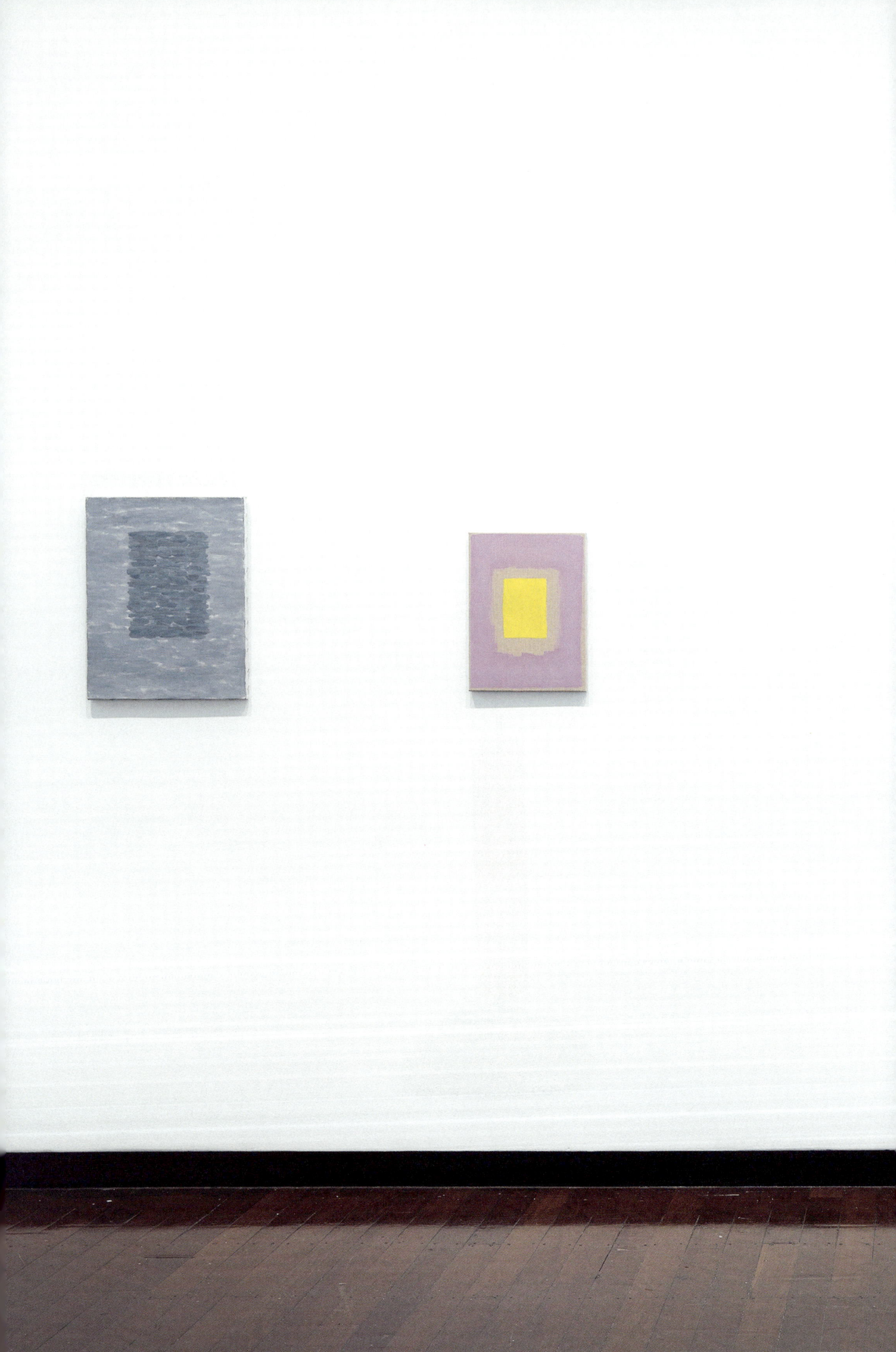

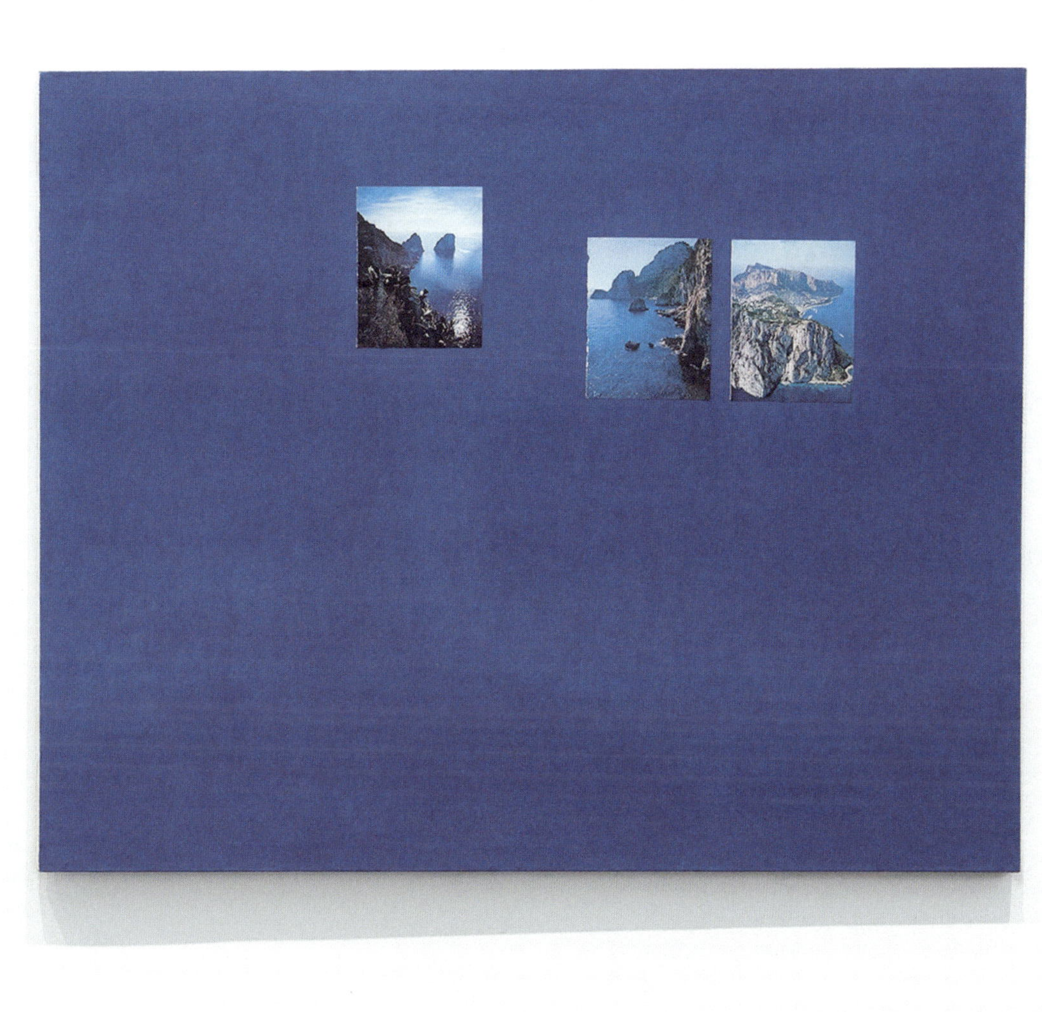

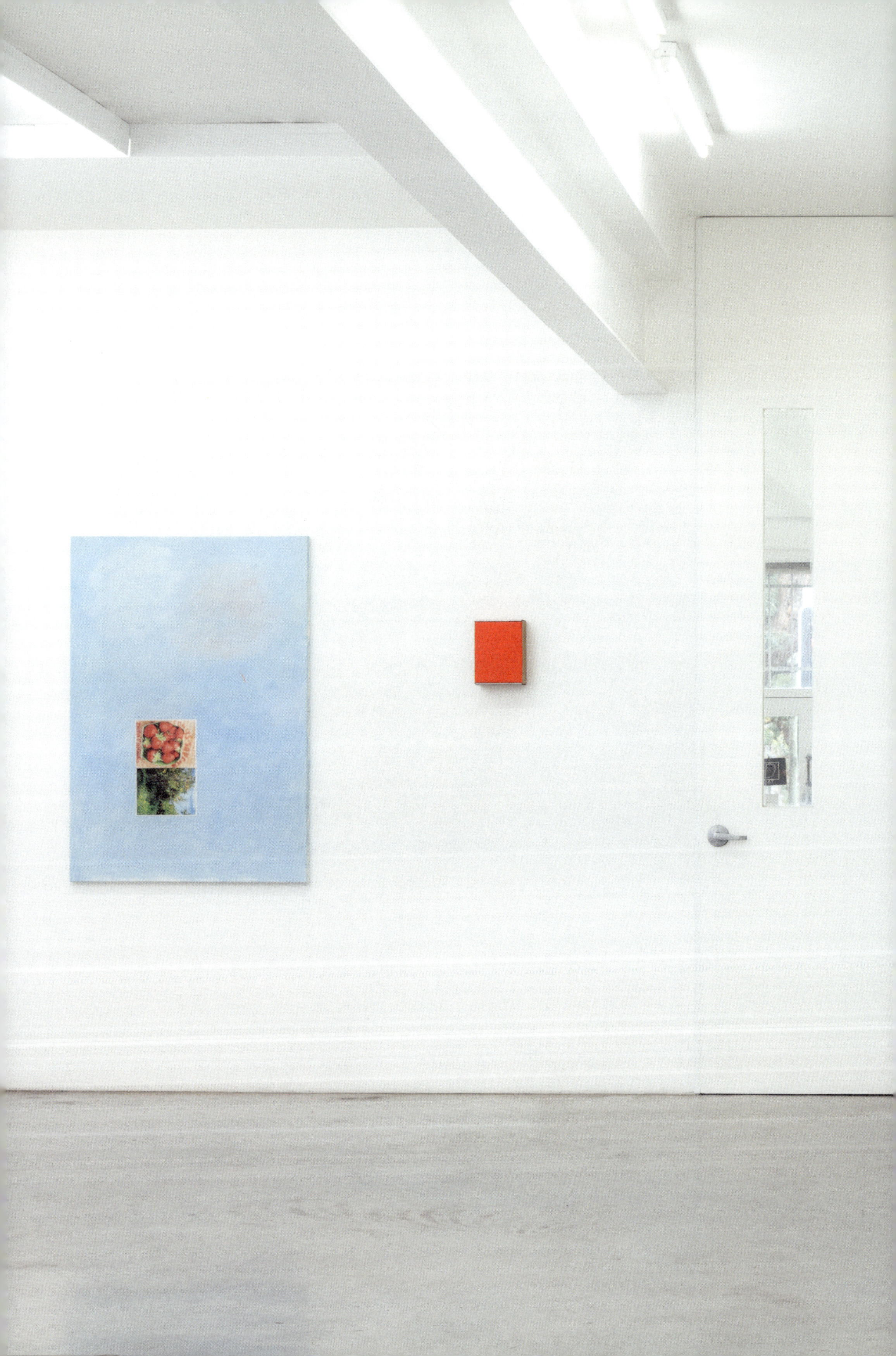

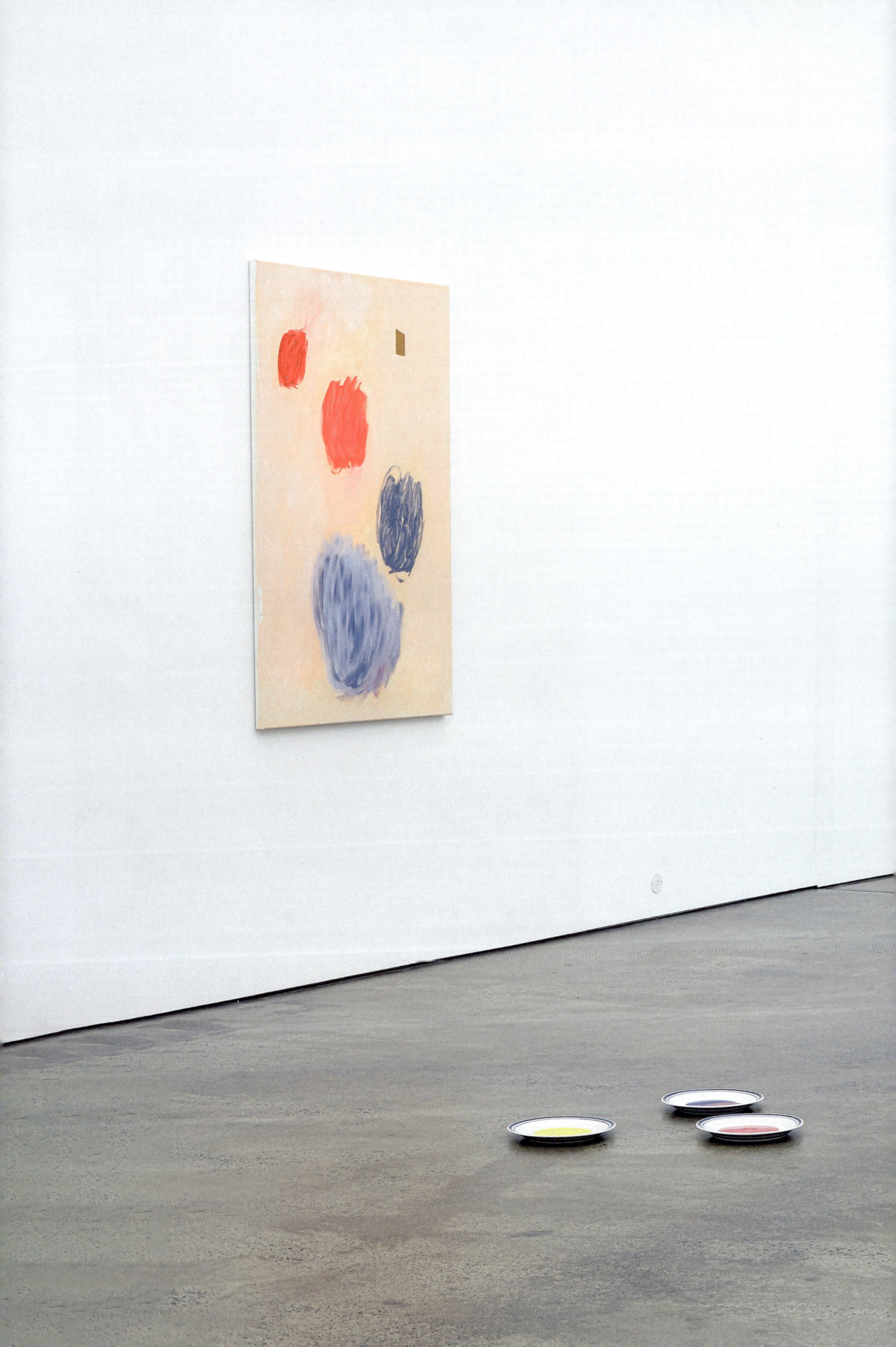

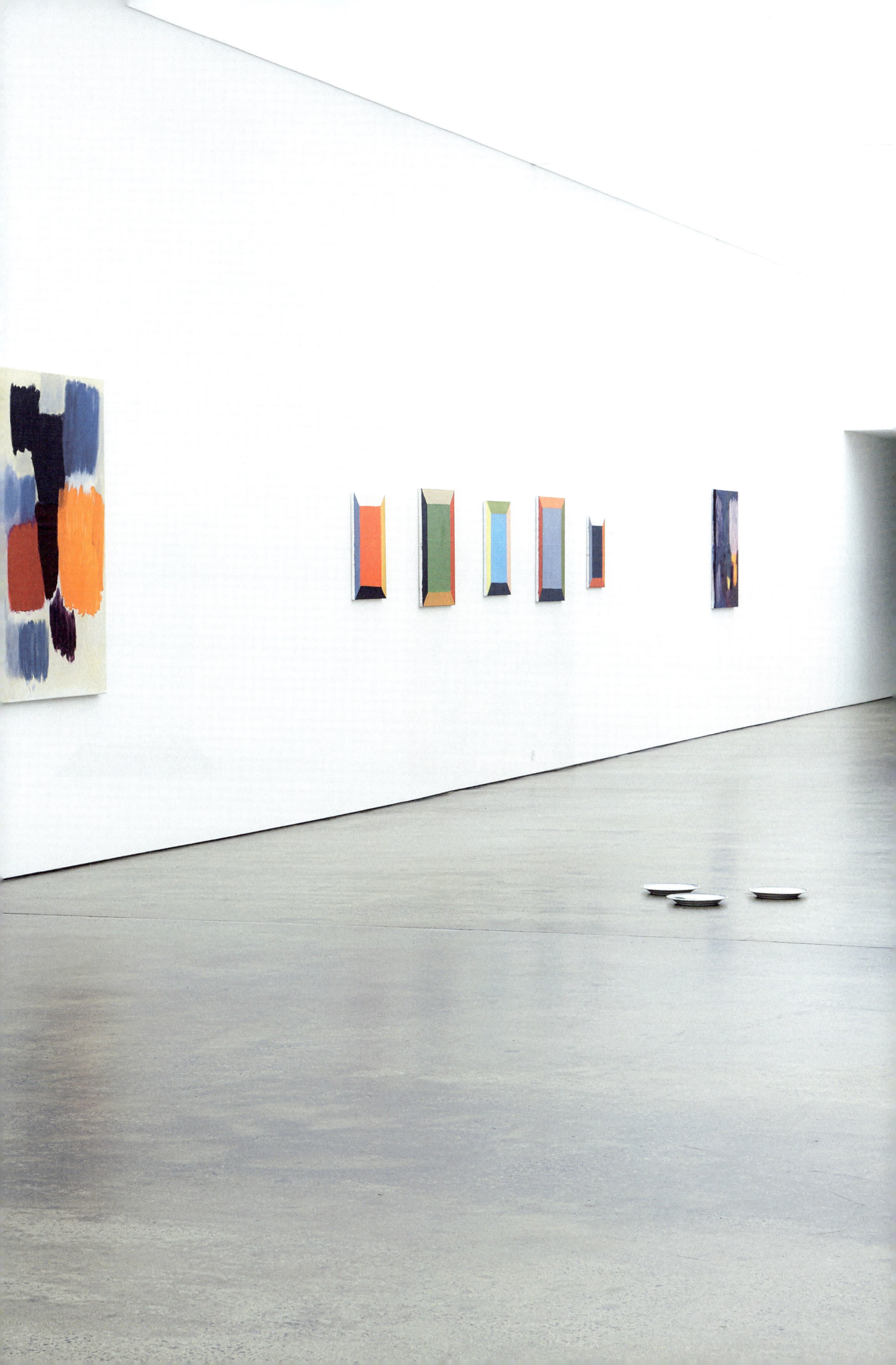

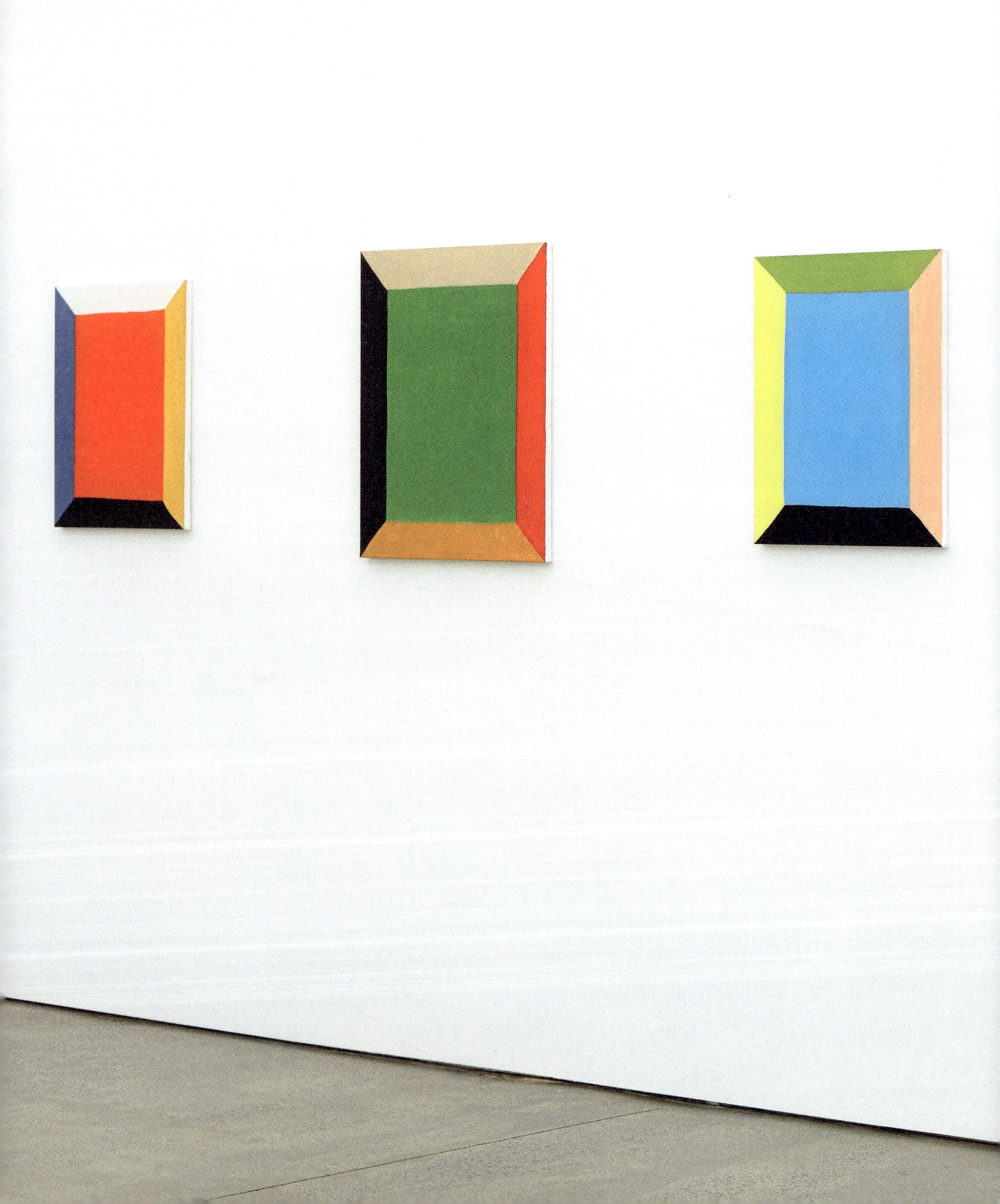

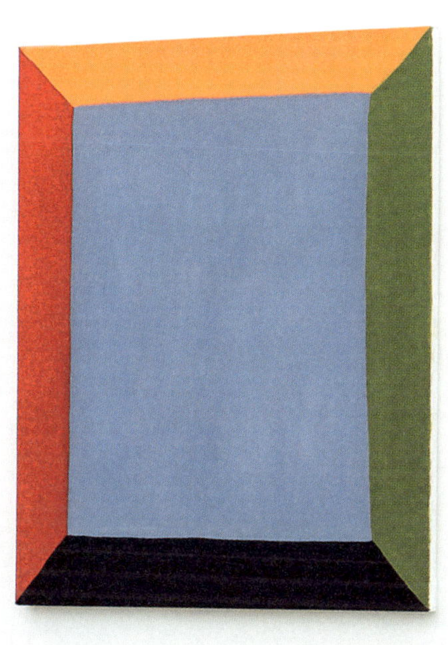

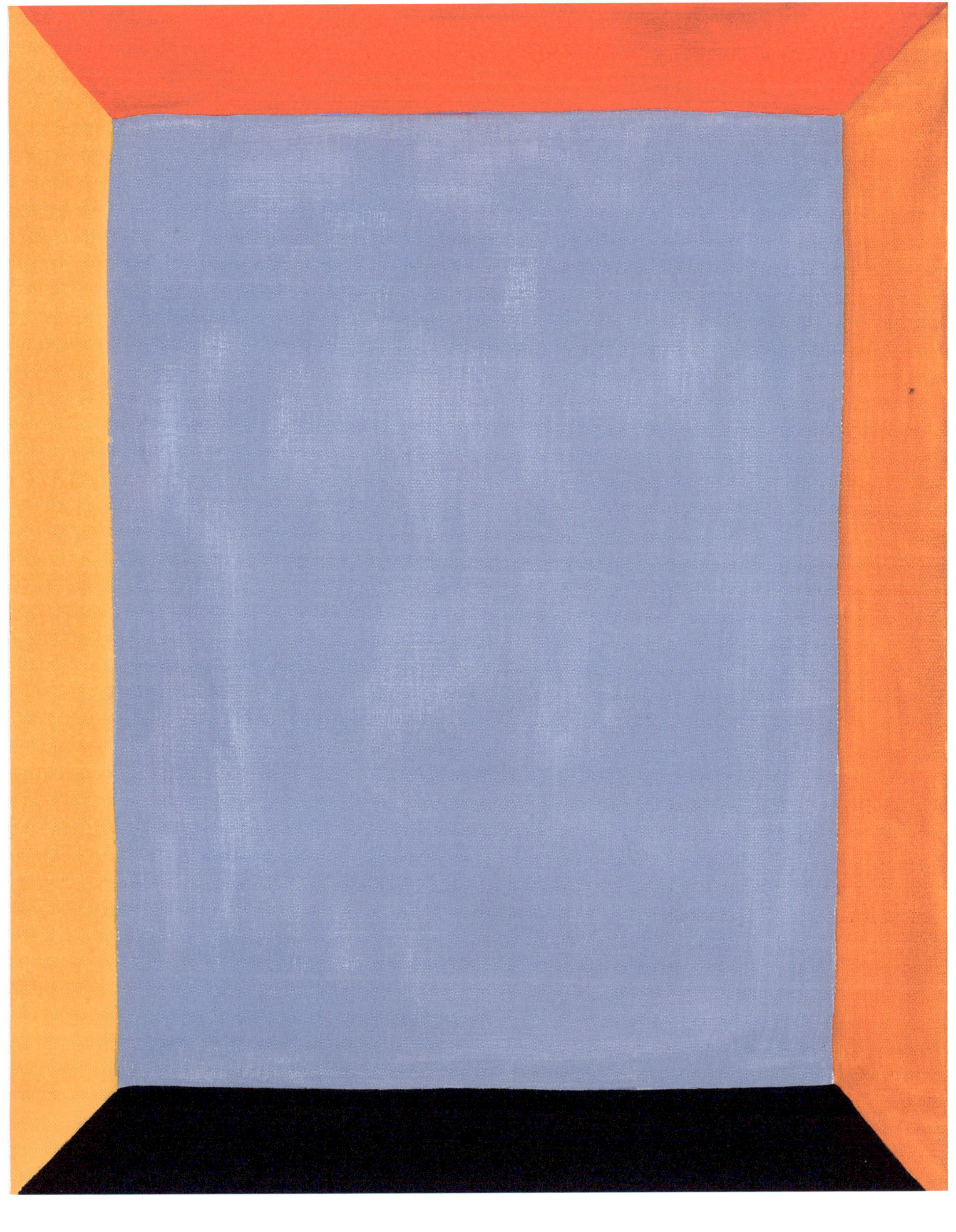

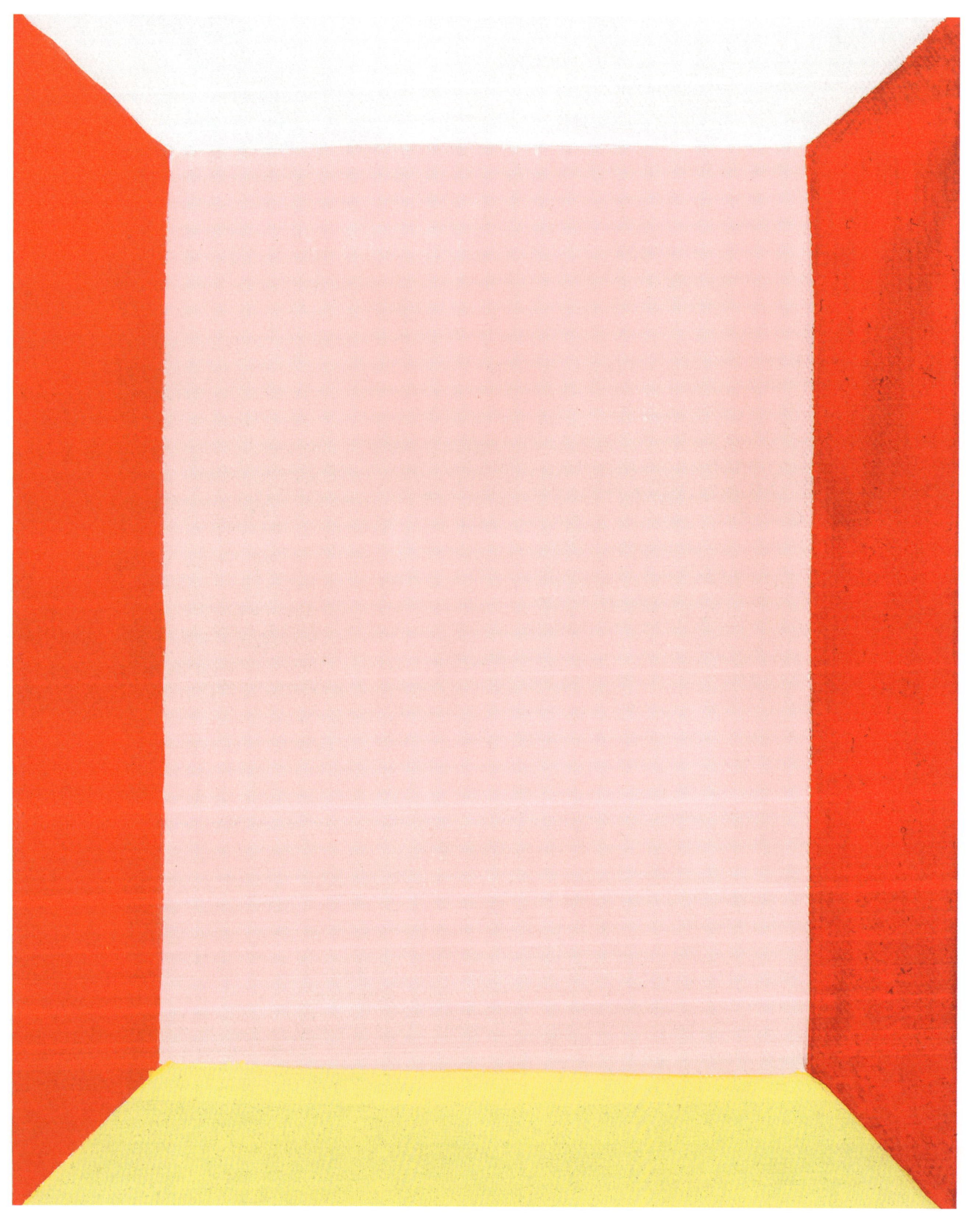

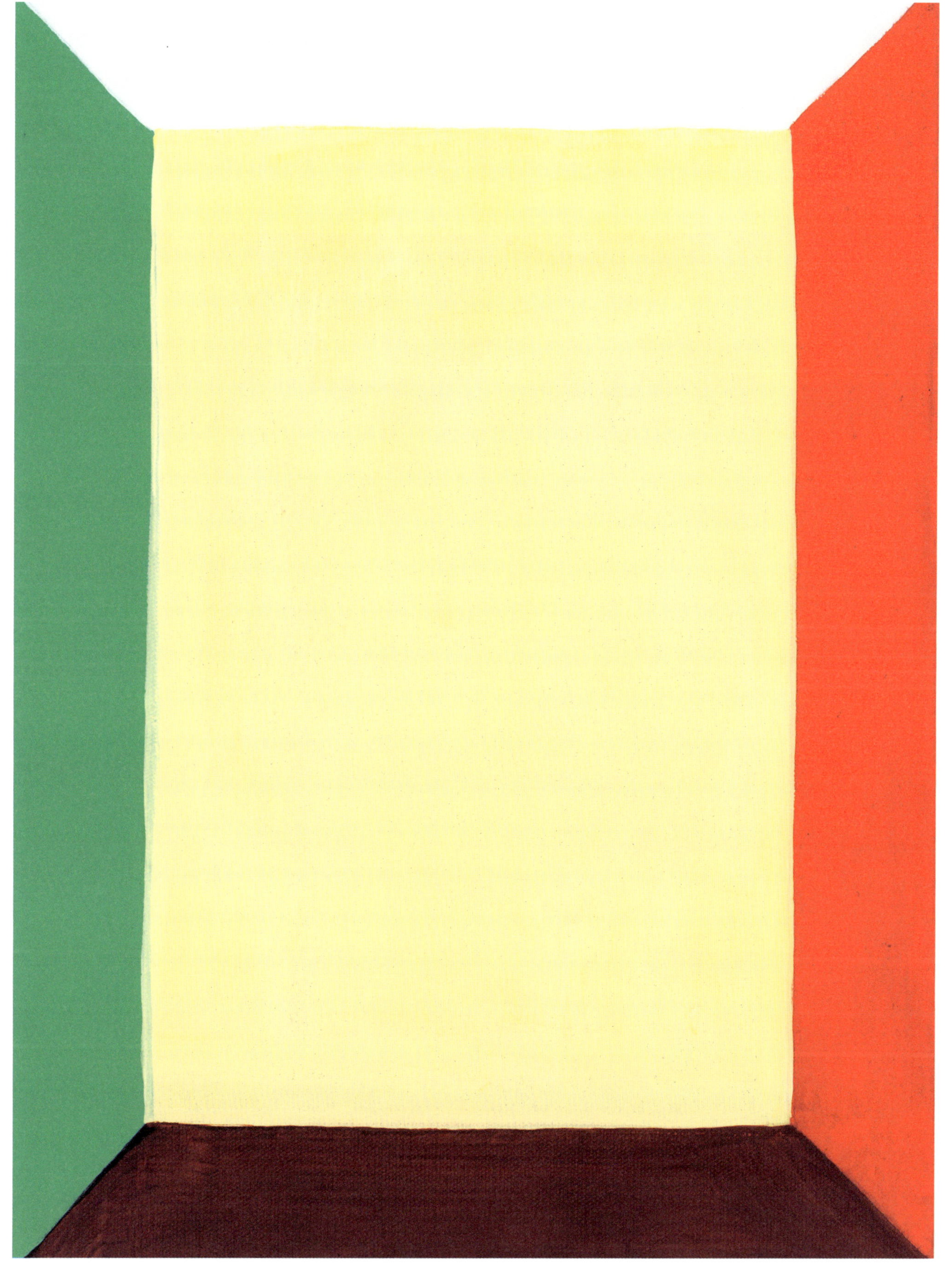

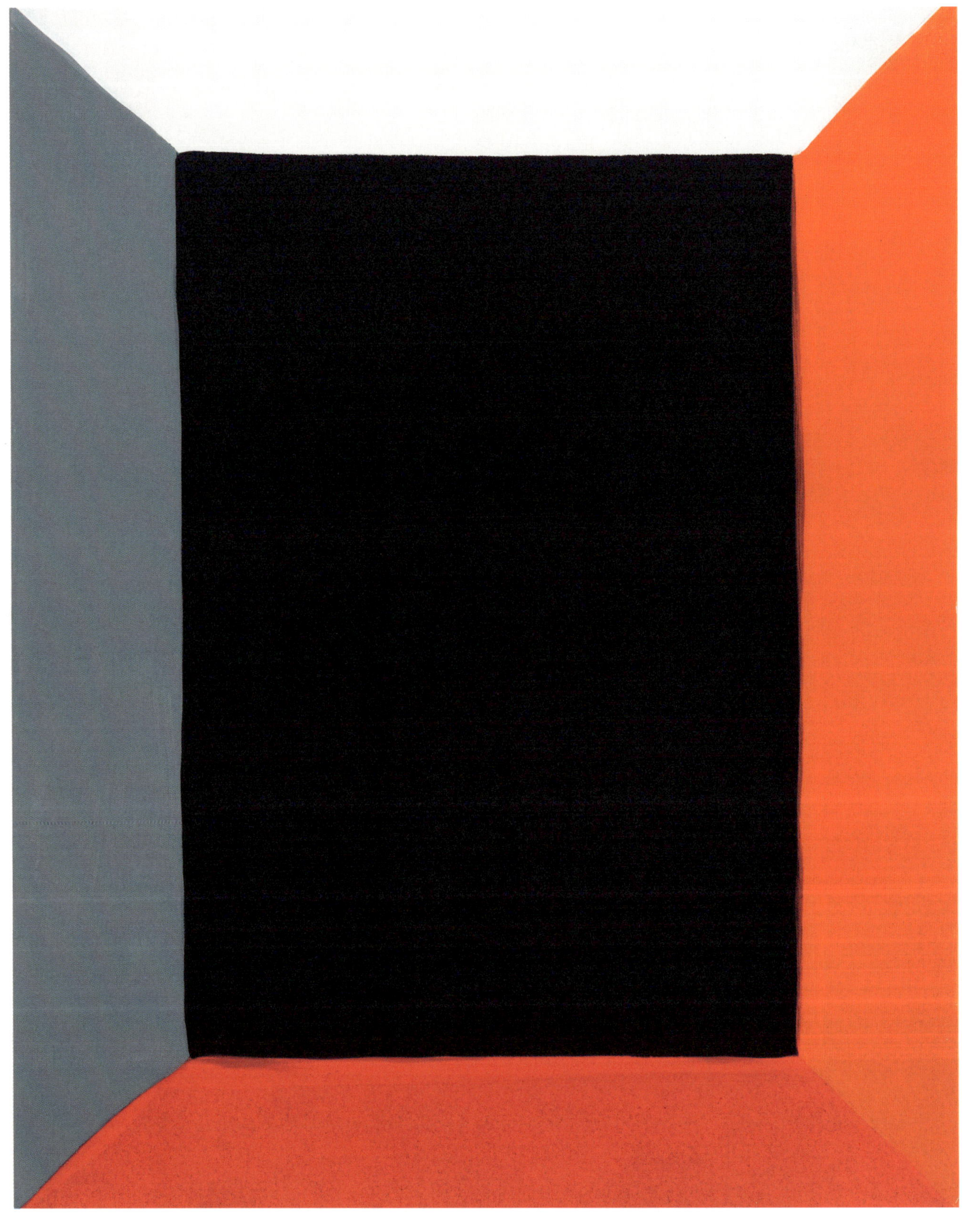

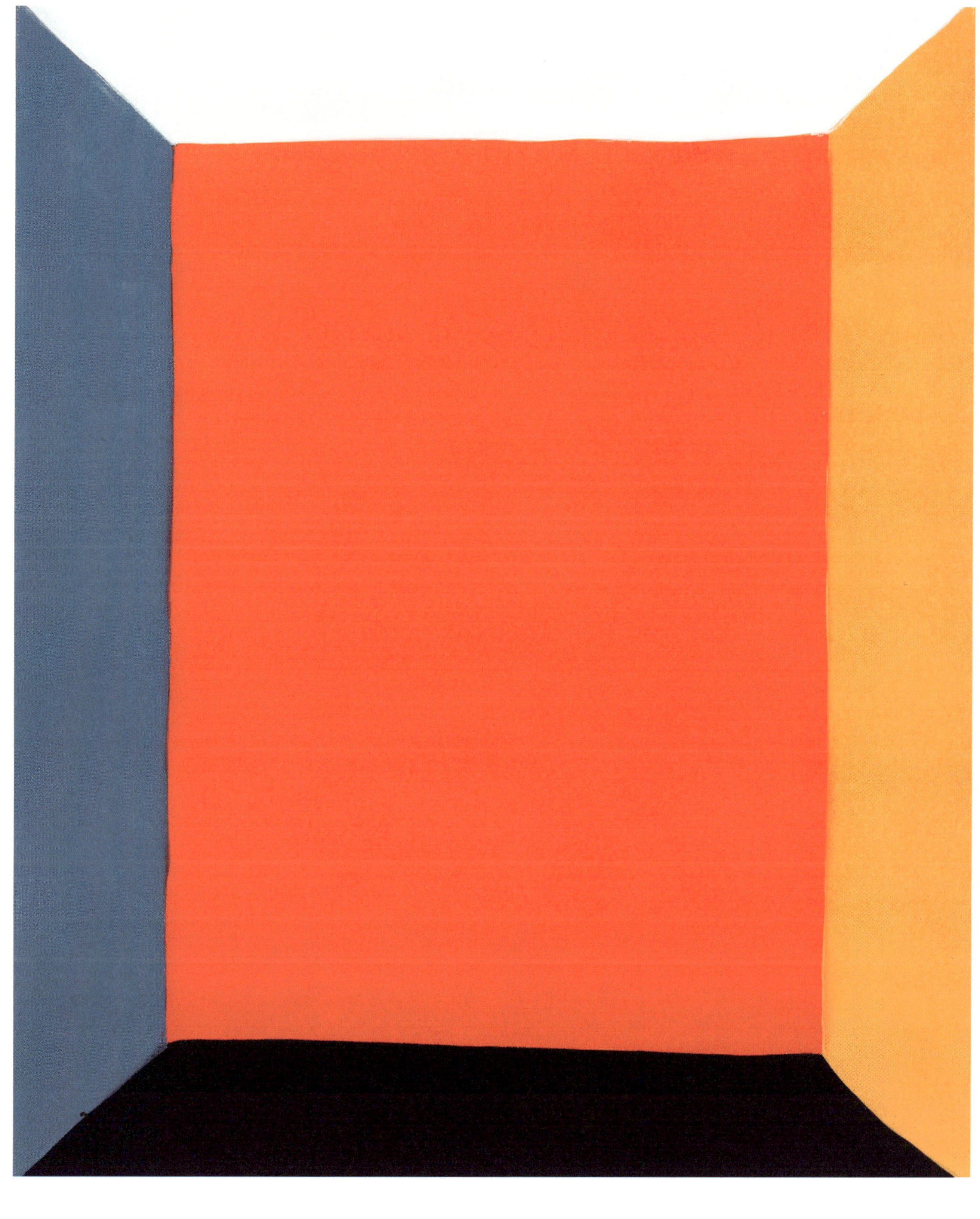

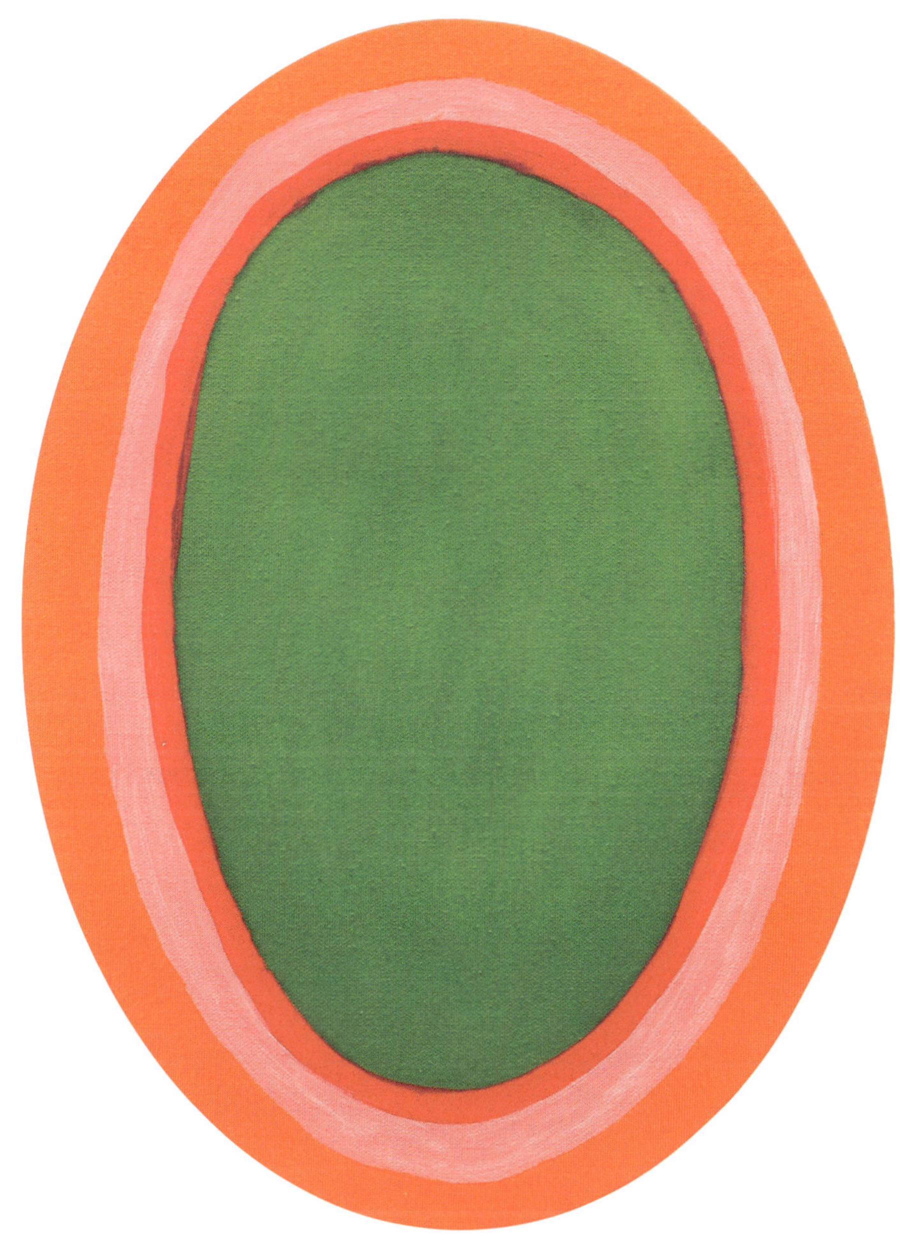

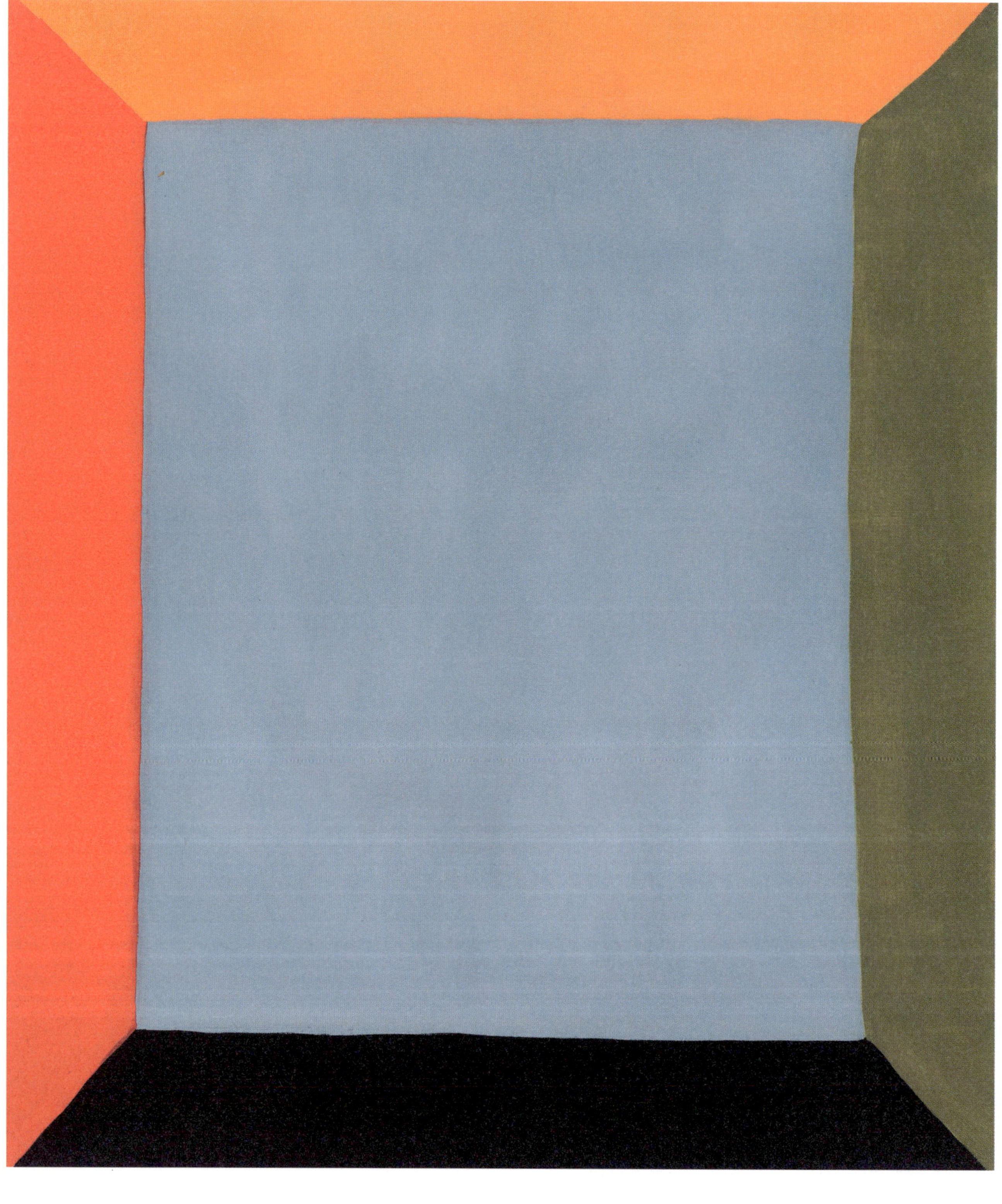

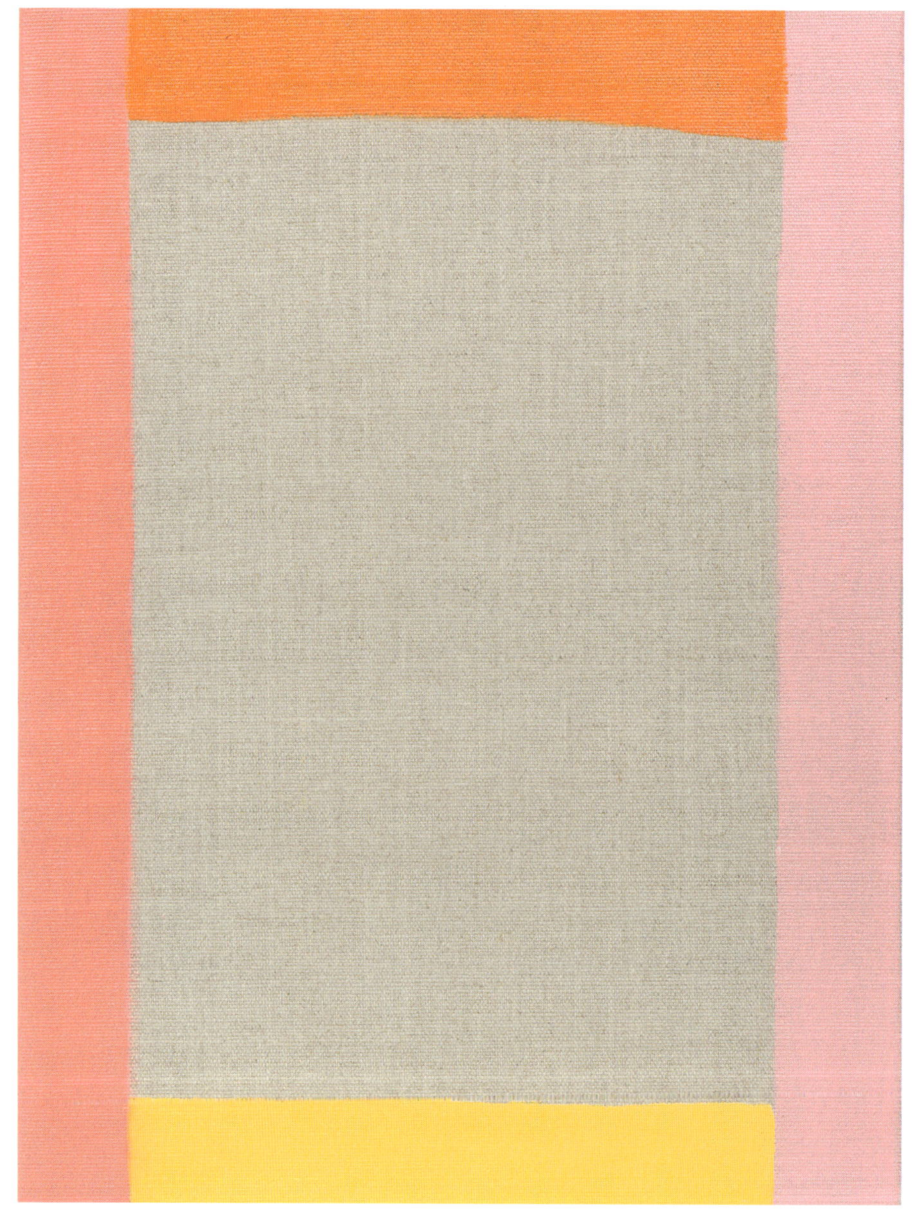

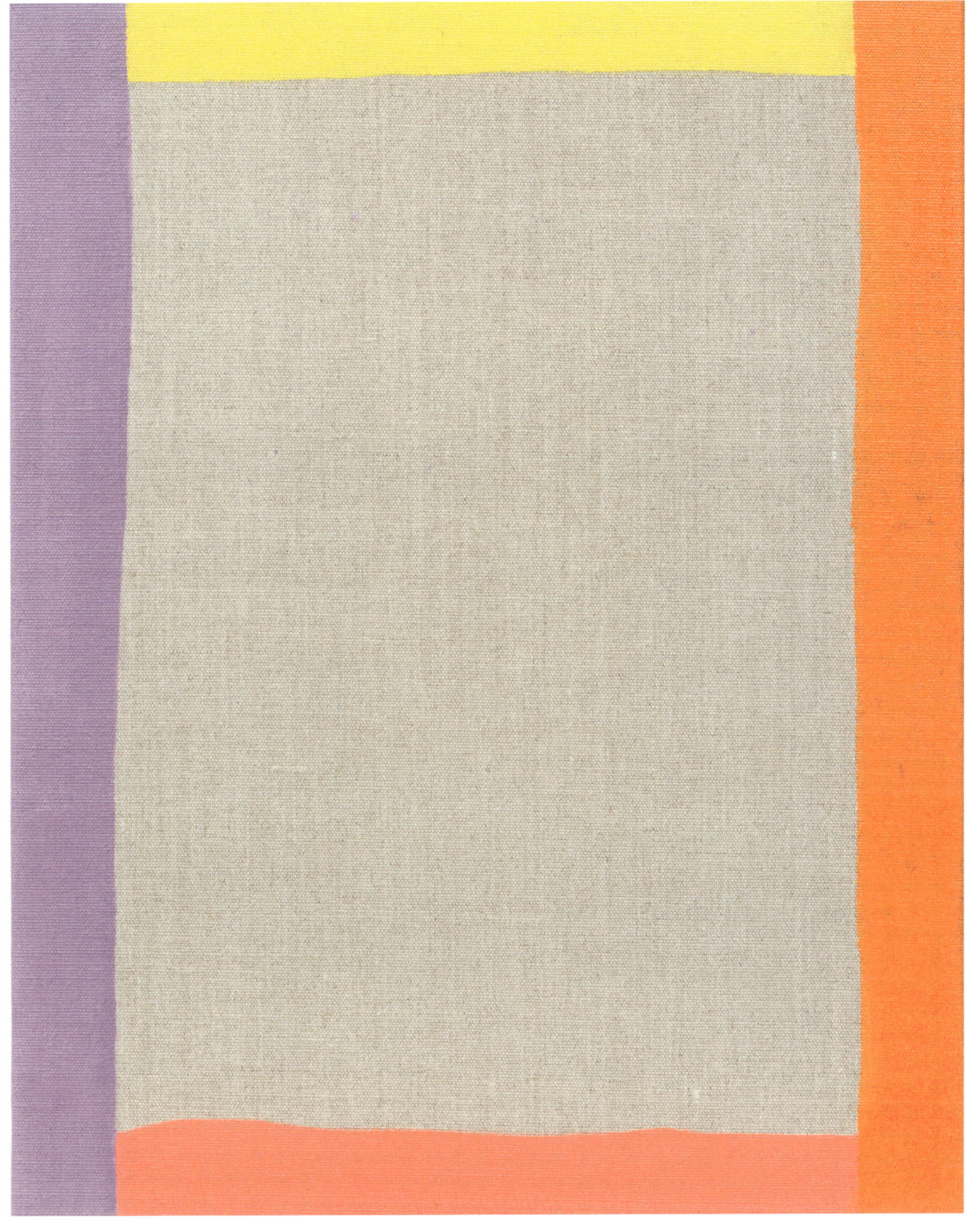

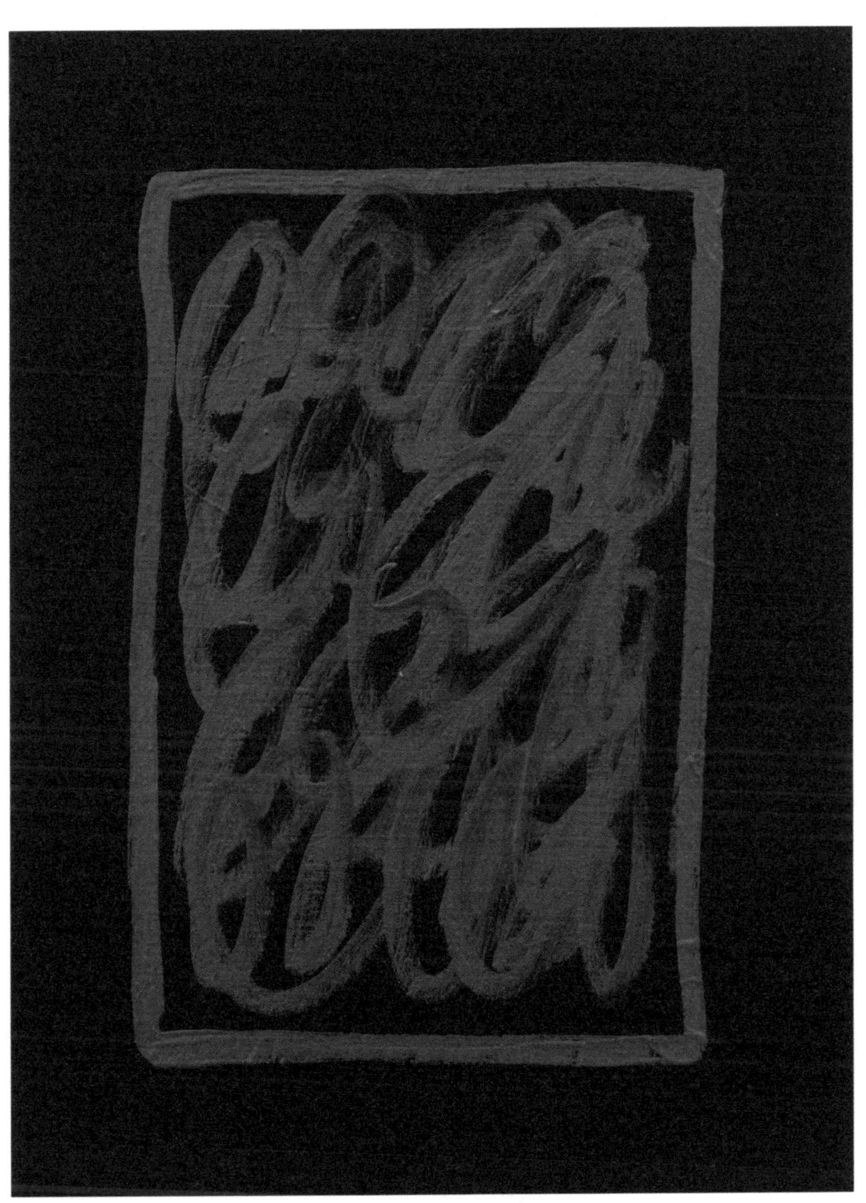

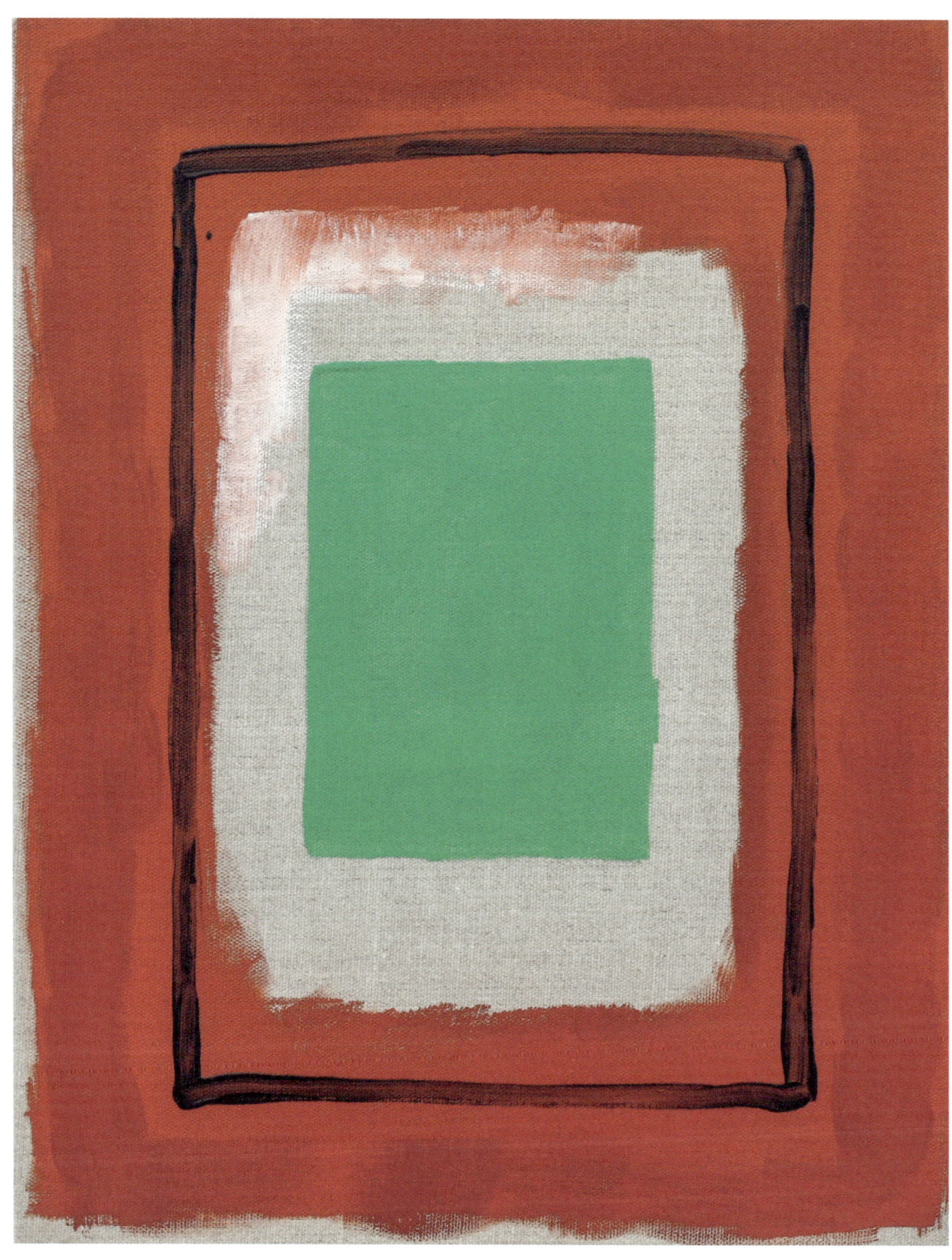

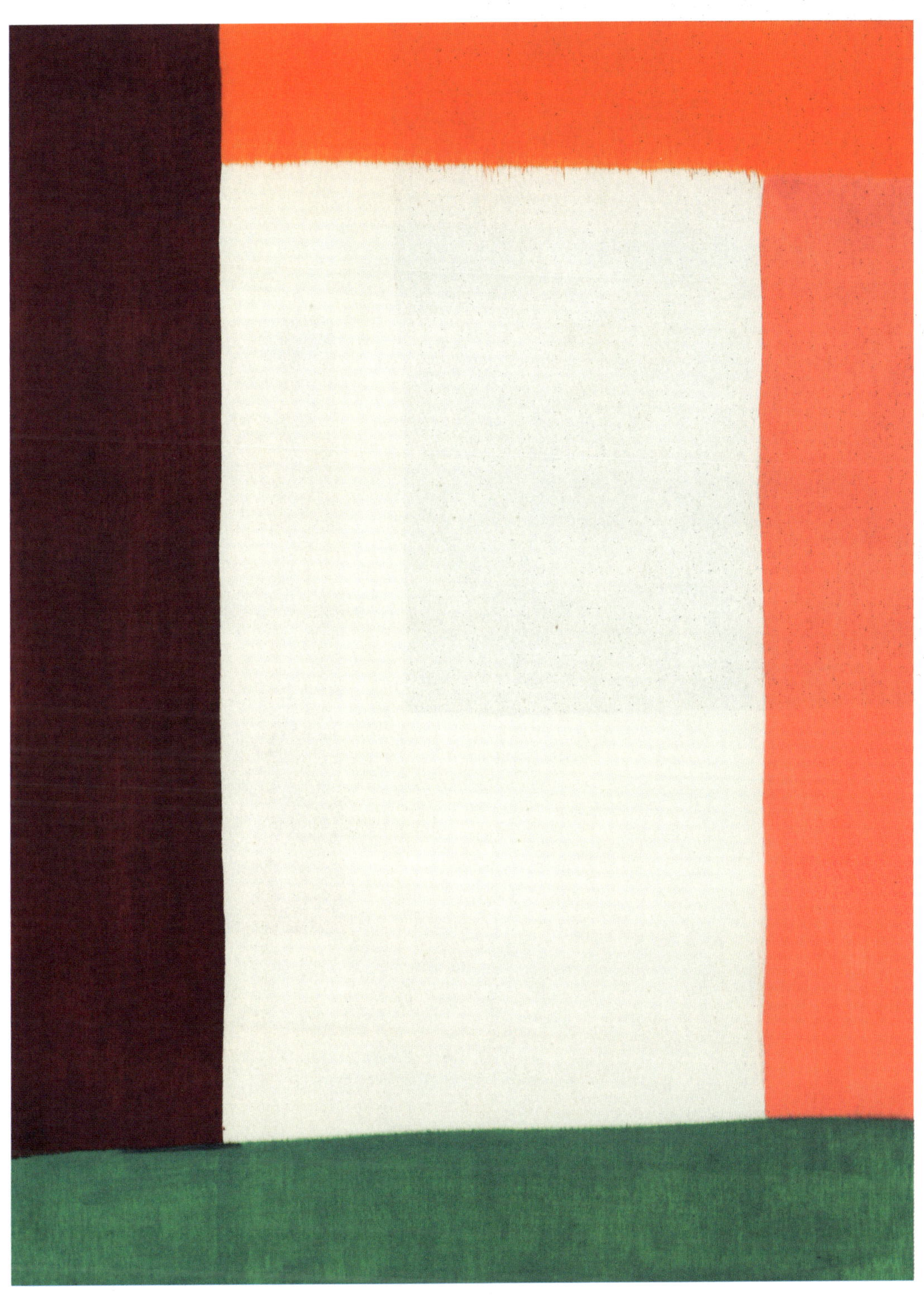

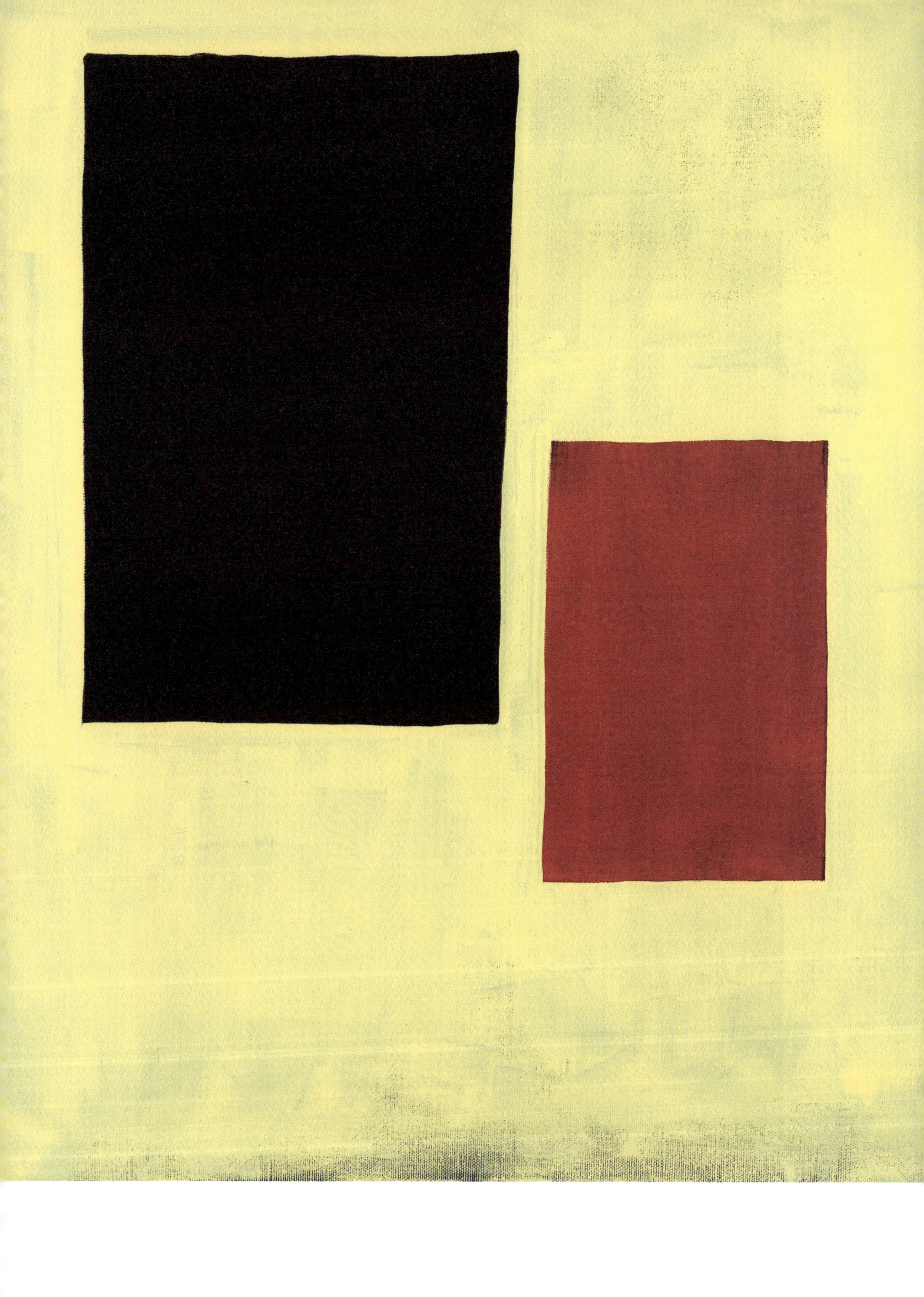

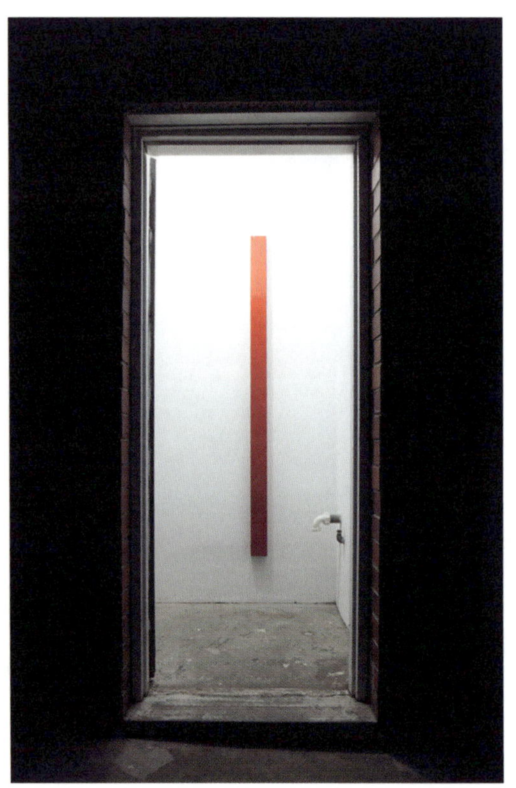

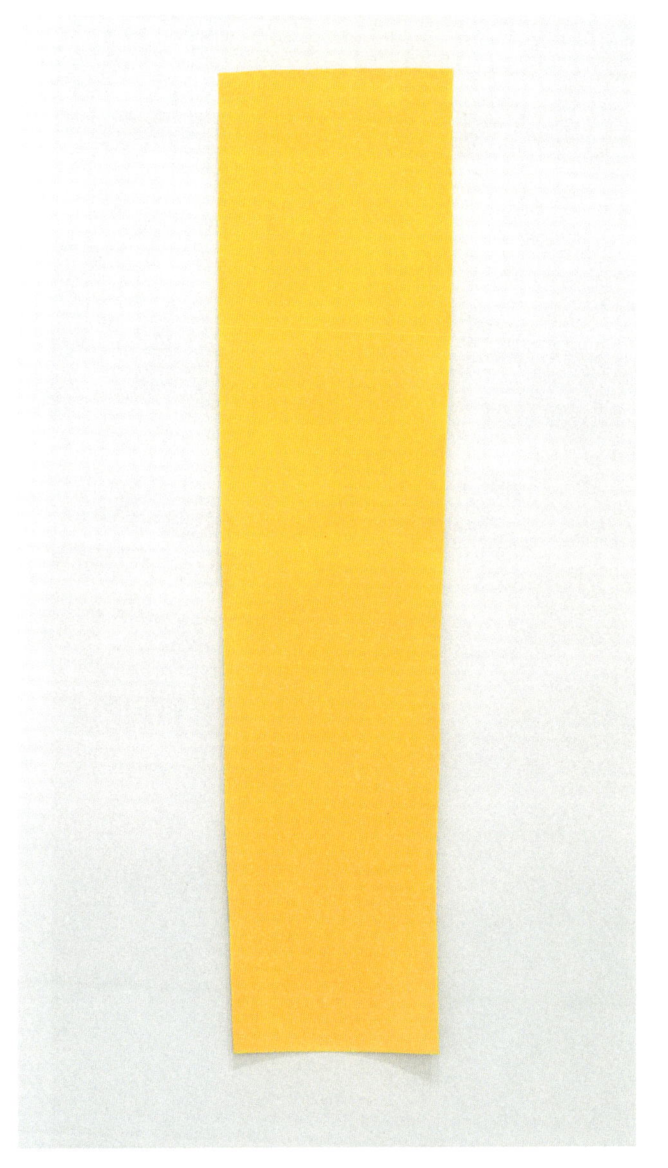

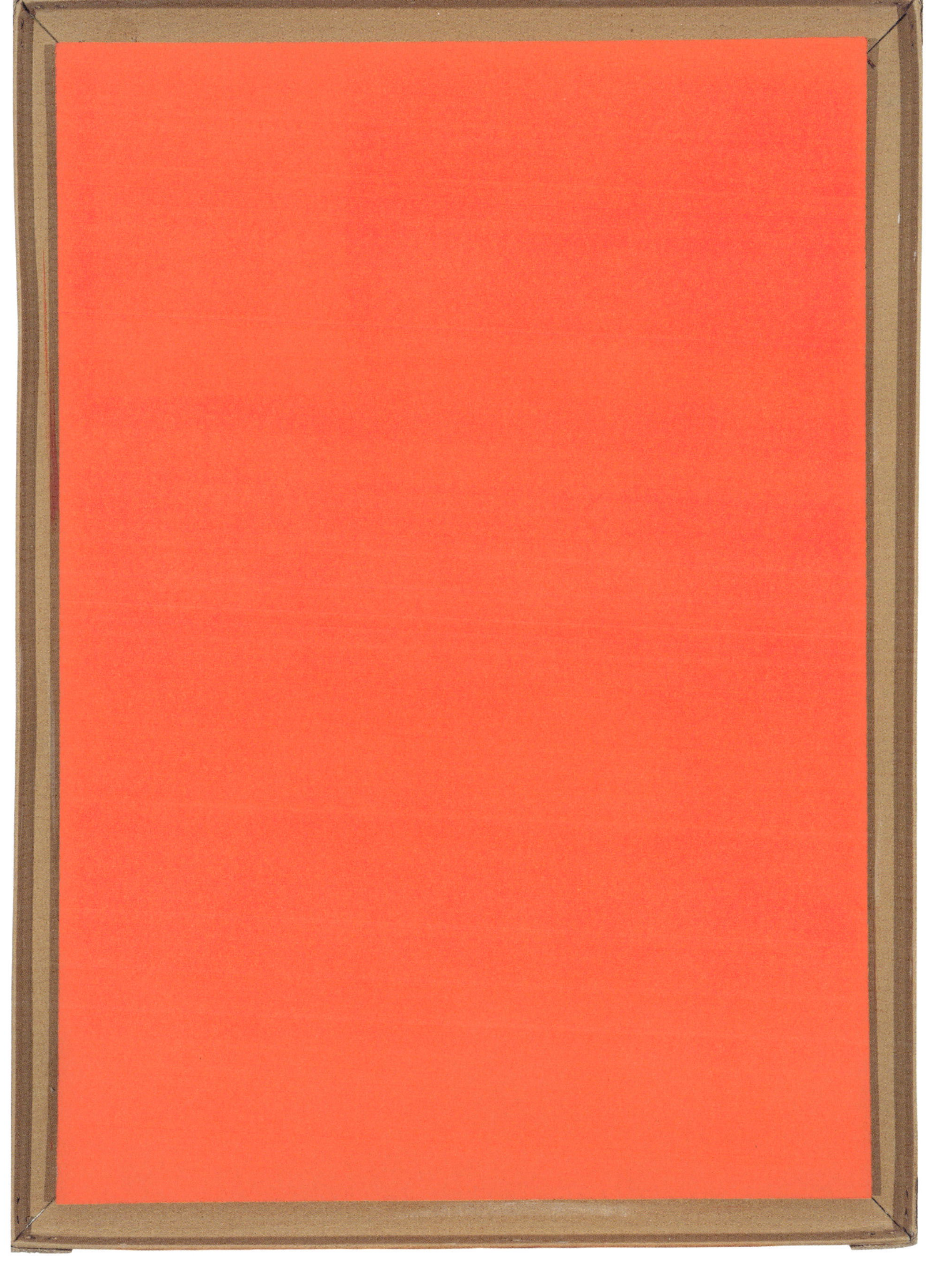

FROM THE MOVEMENT

TOWARD REVOLUTION

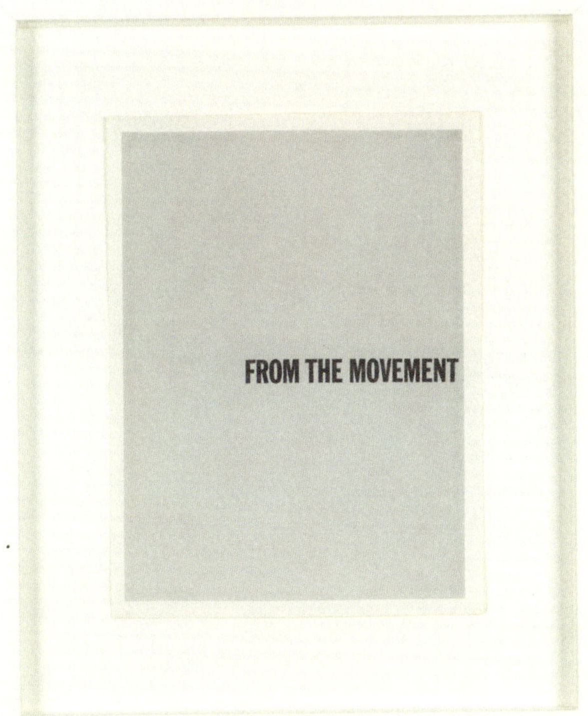
FROM THE MOVEMENT

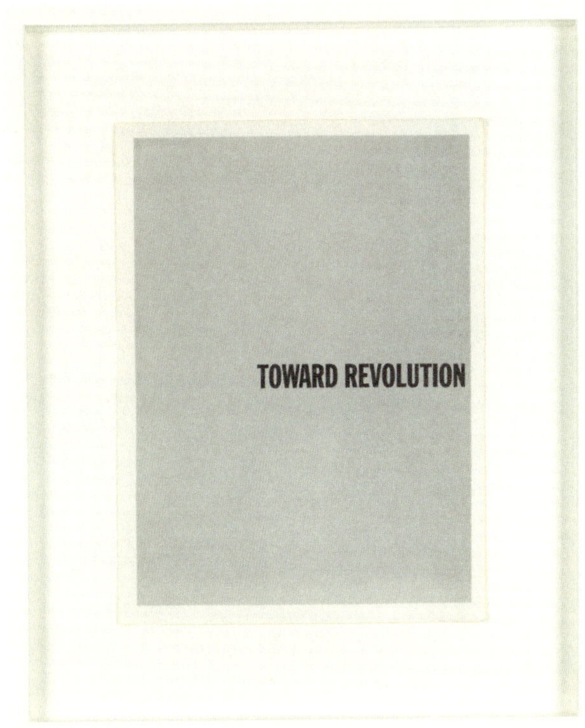
TOWARD REVOLUTION

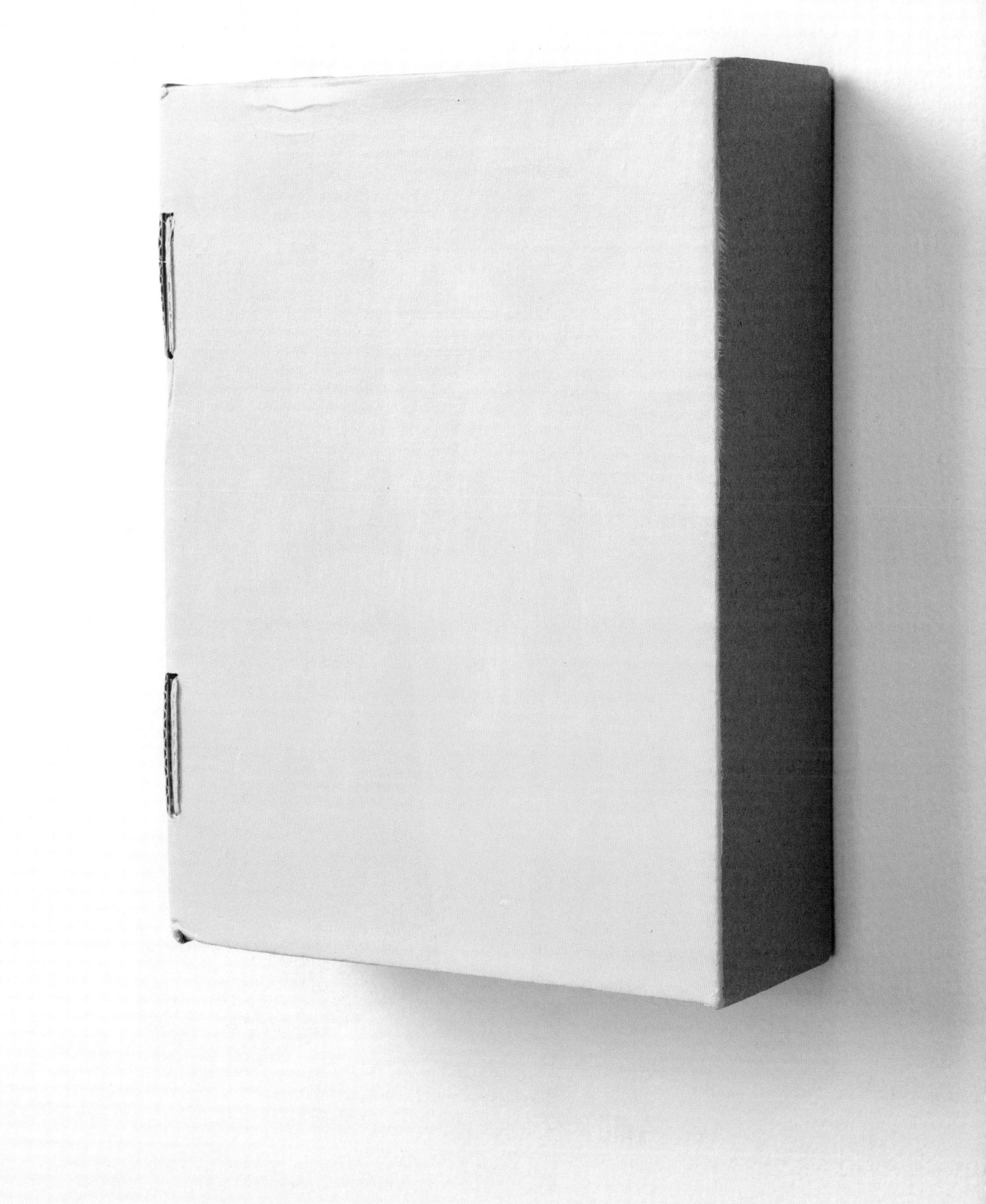

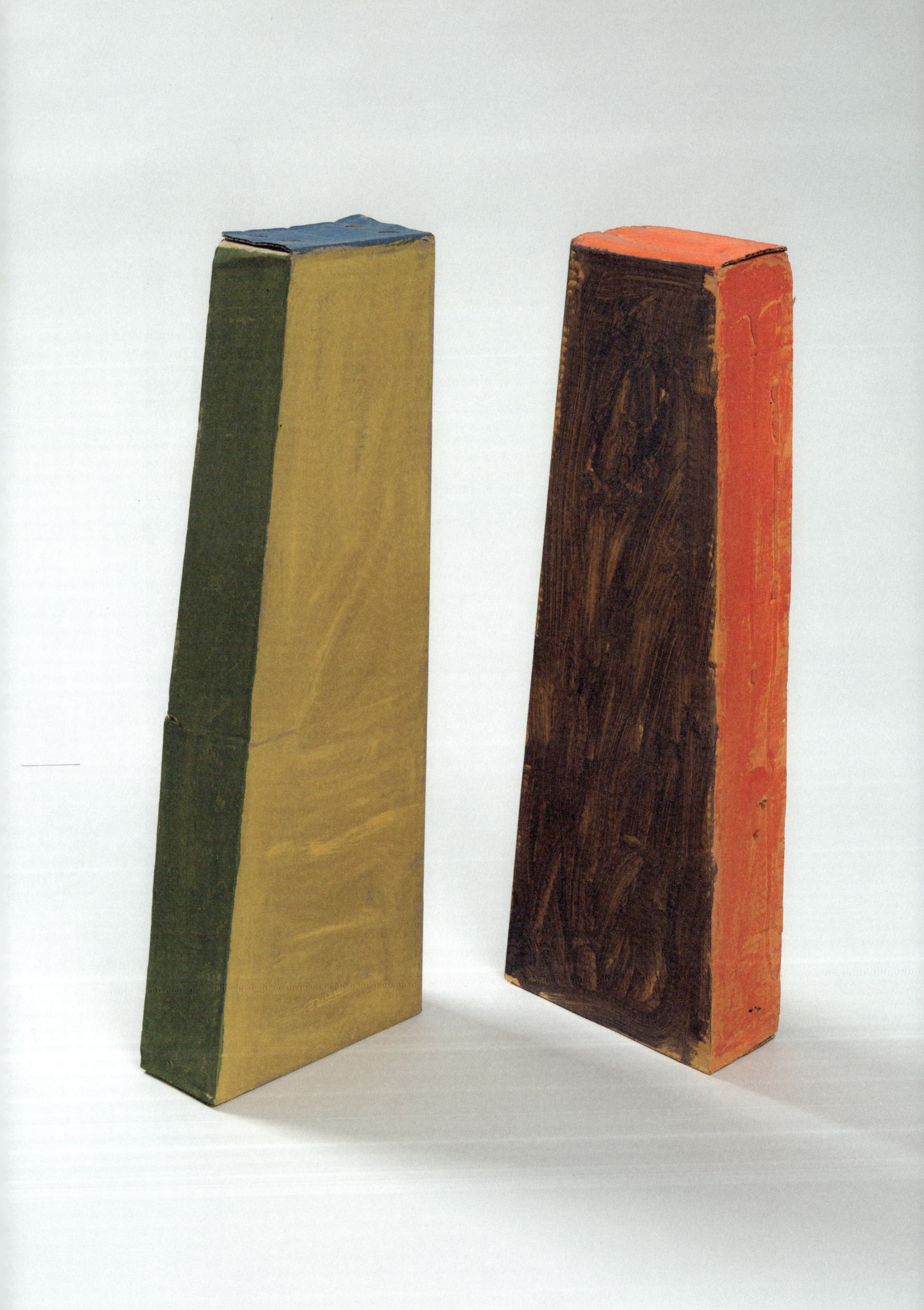

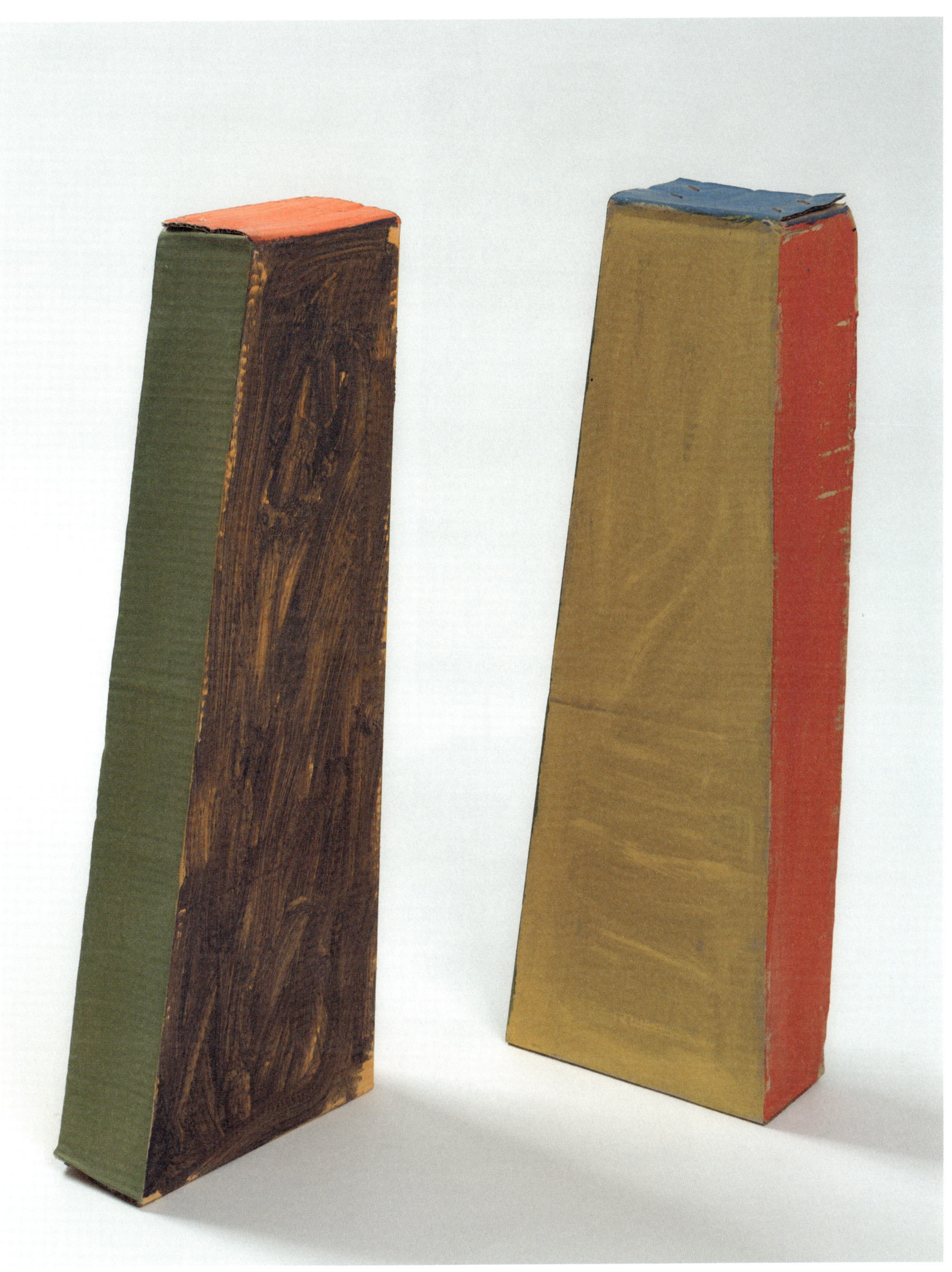

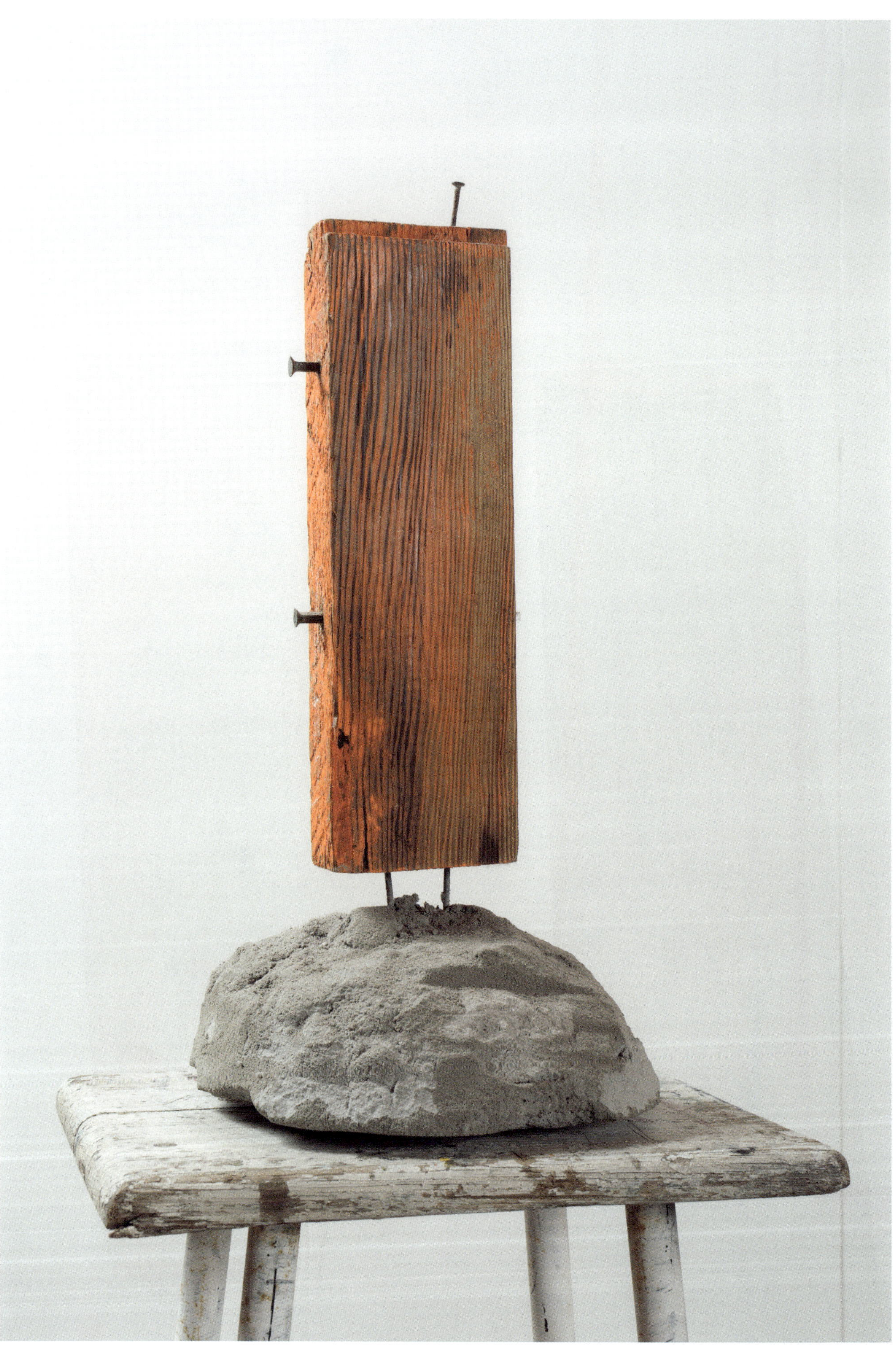

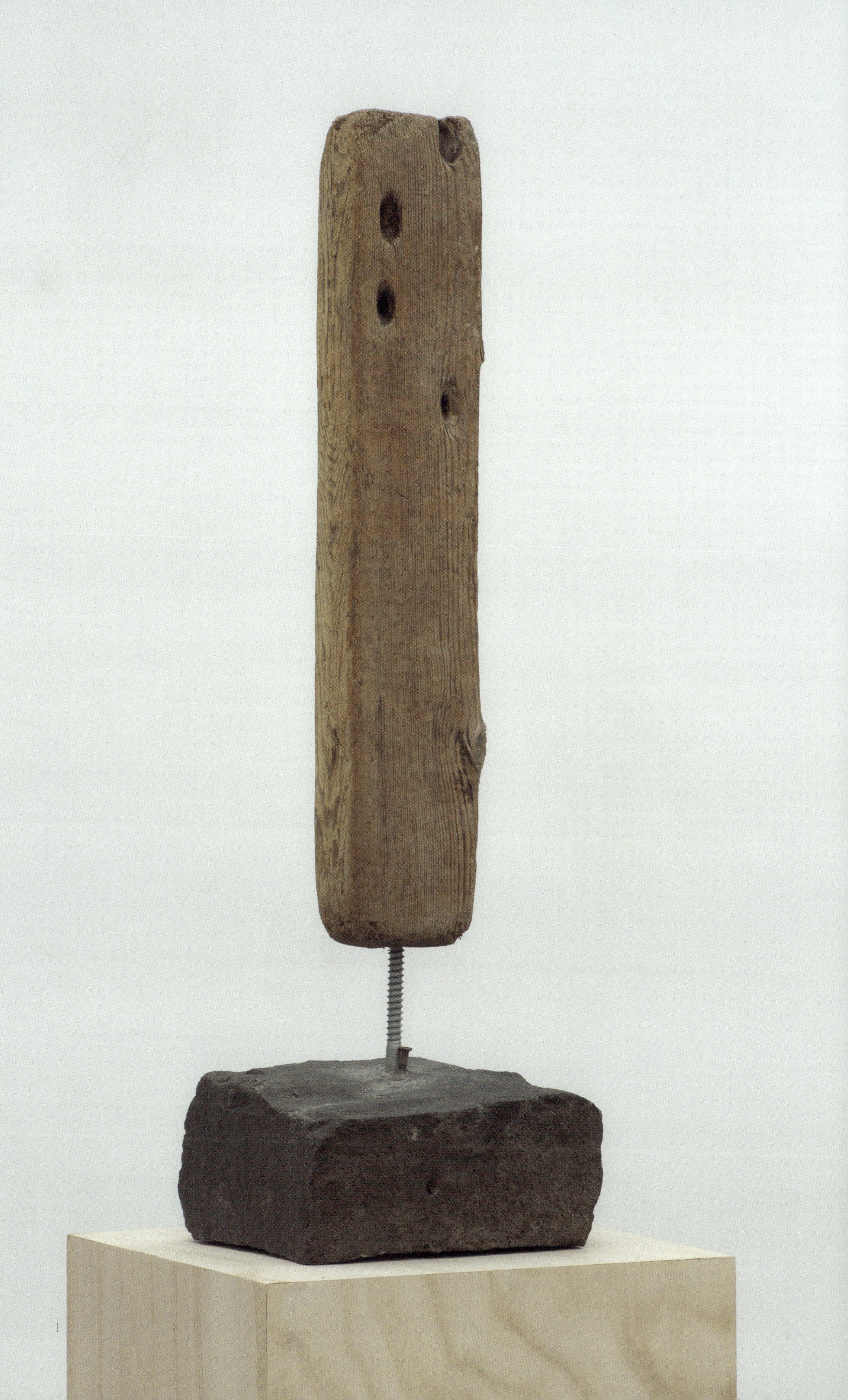

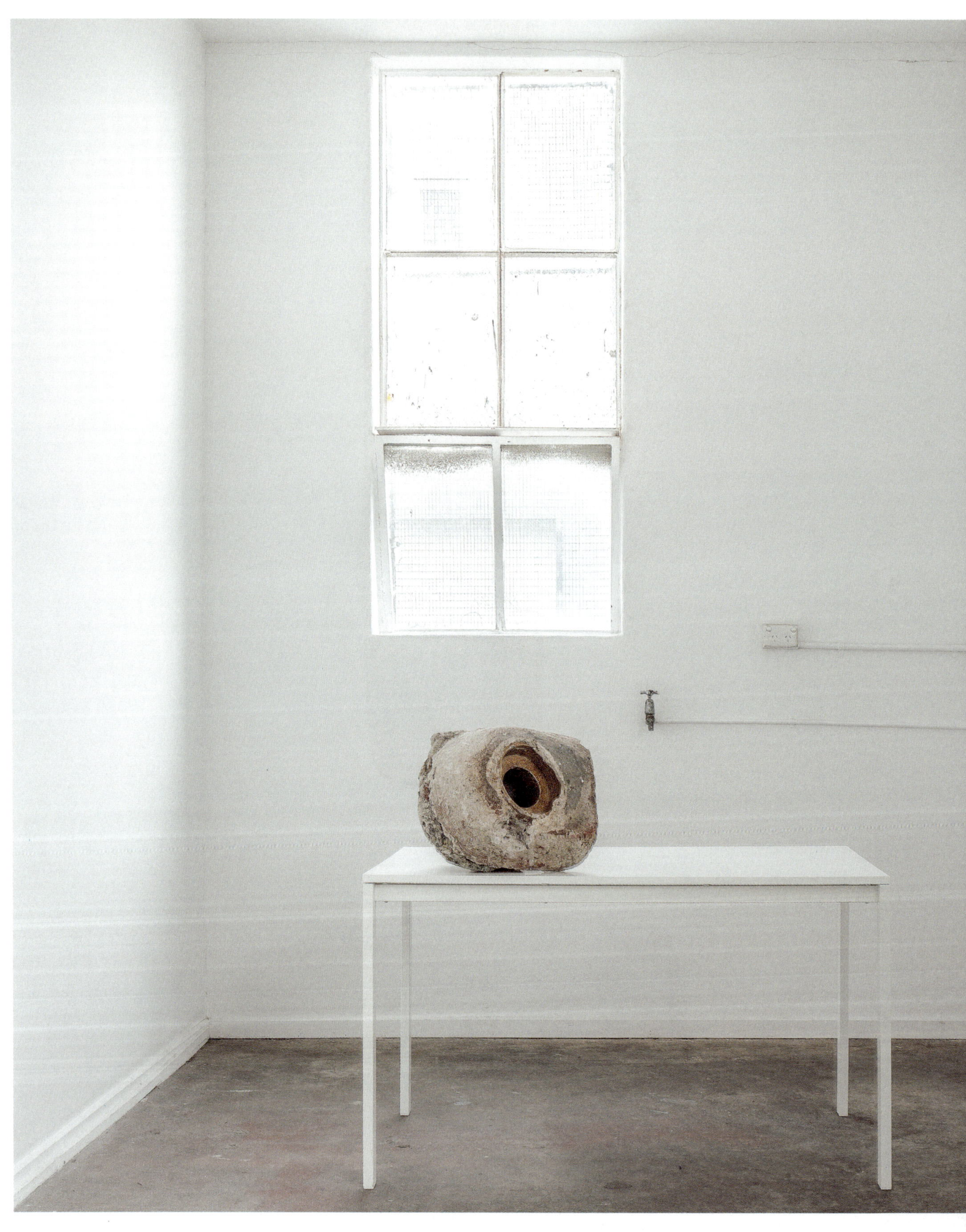

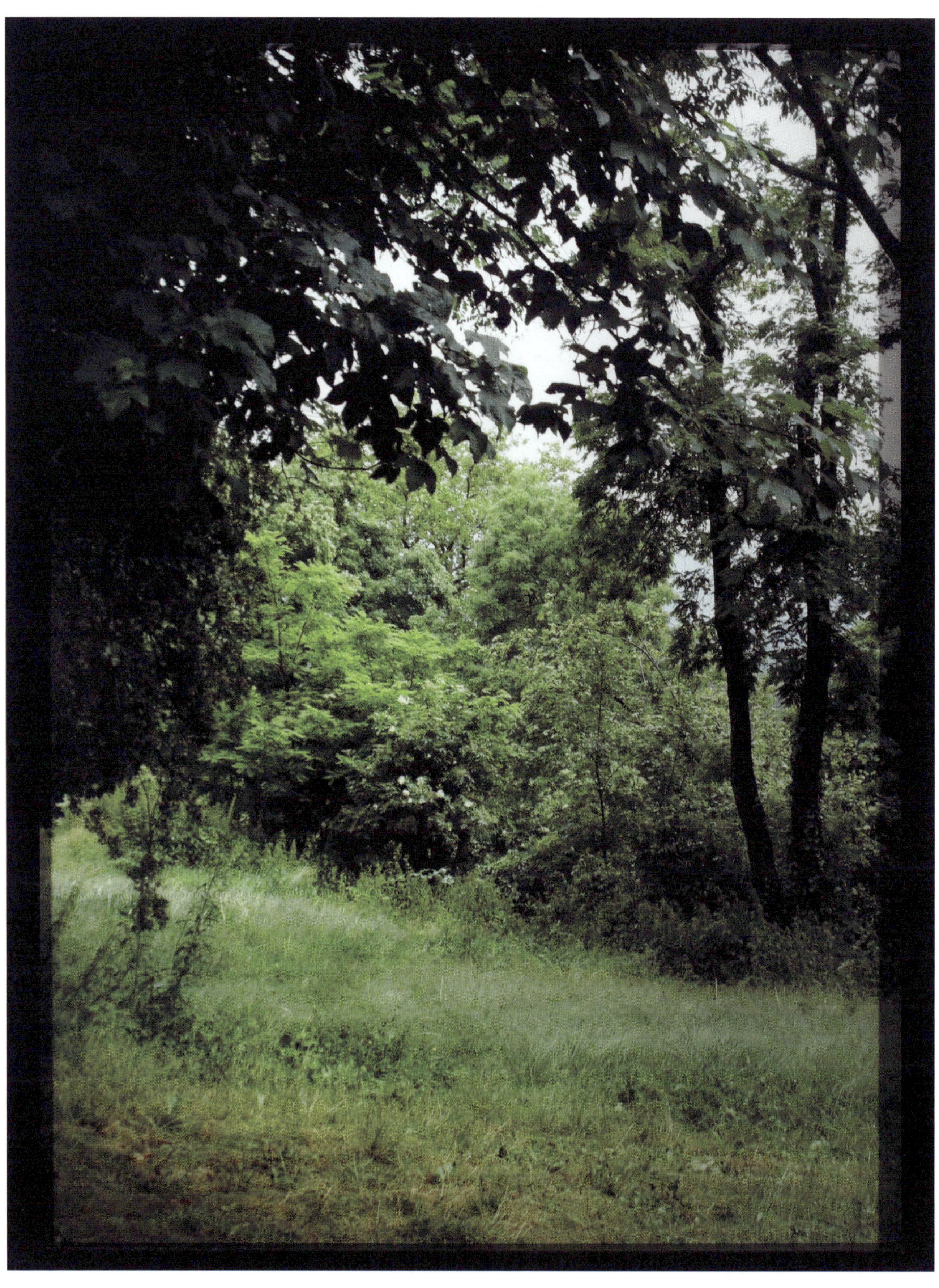

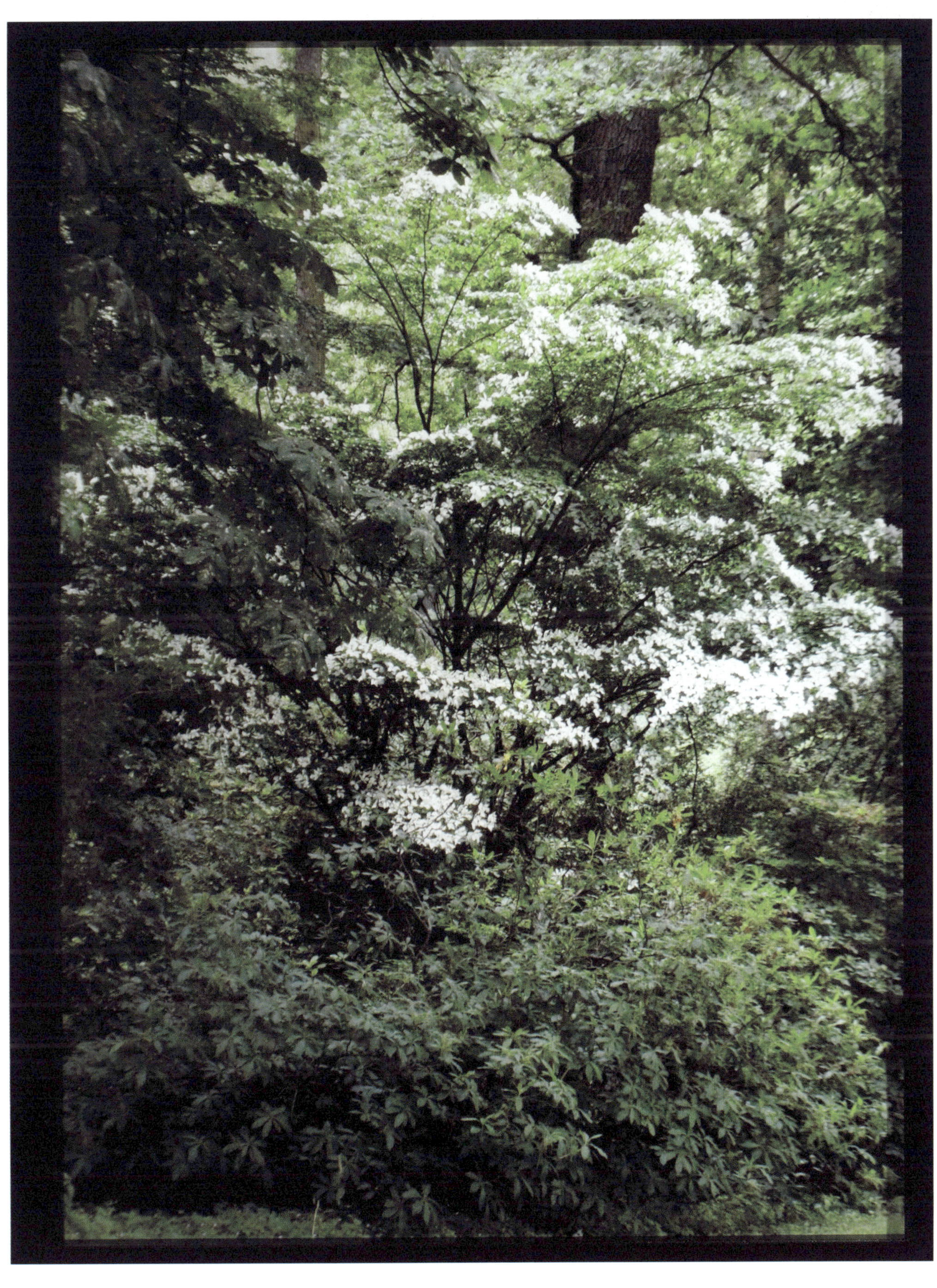

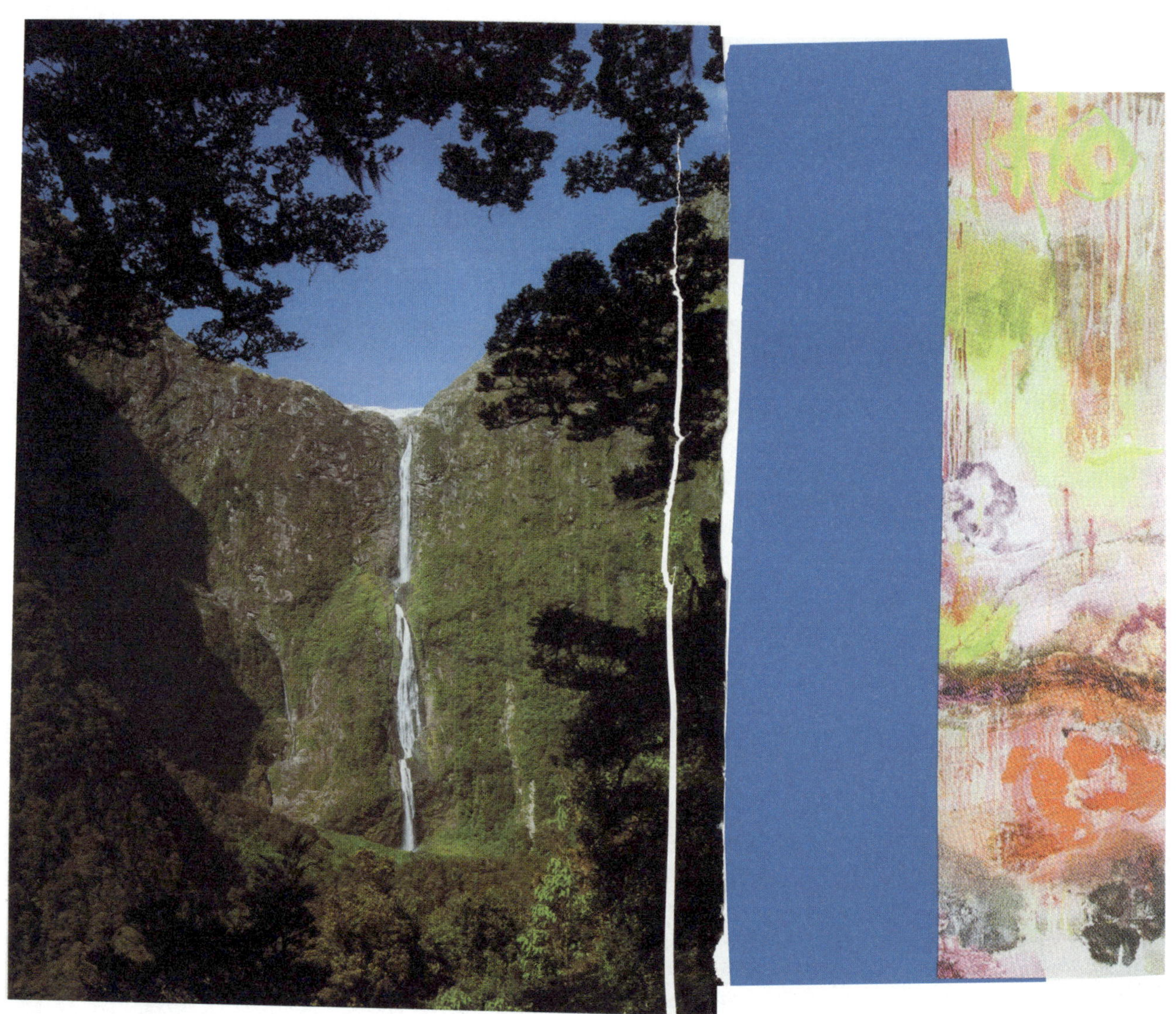

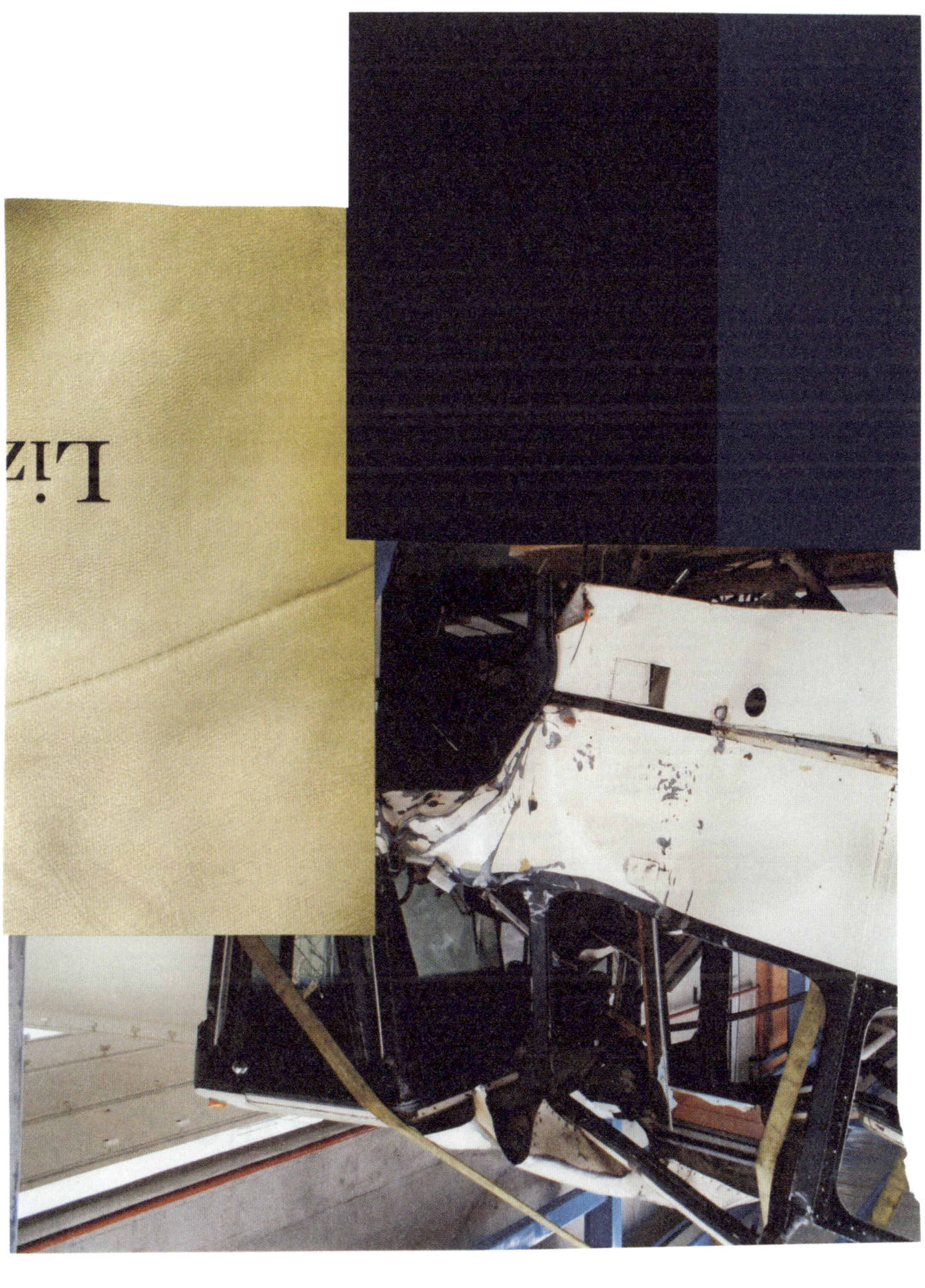

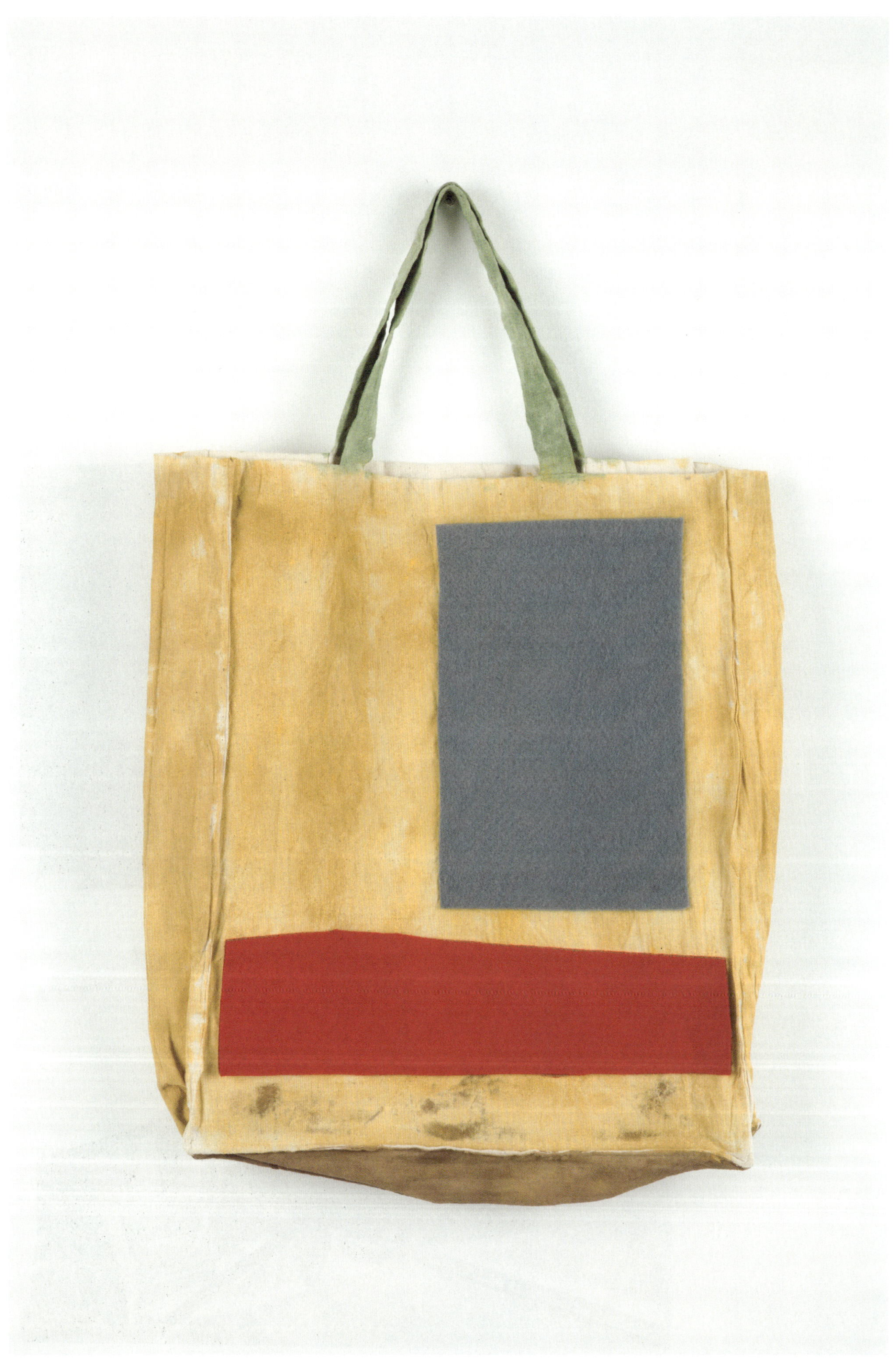

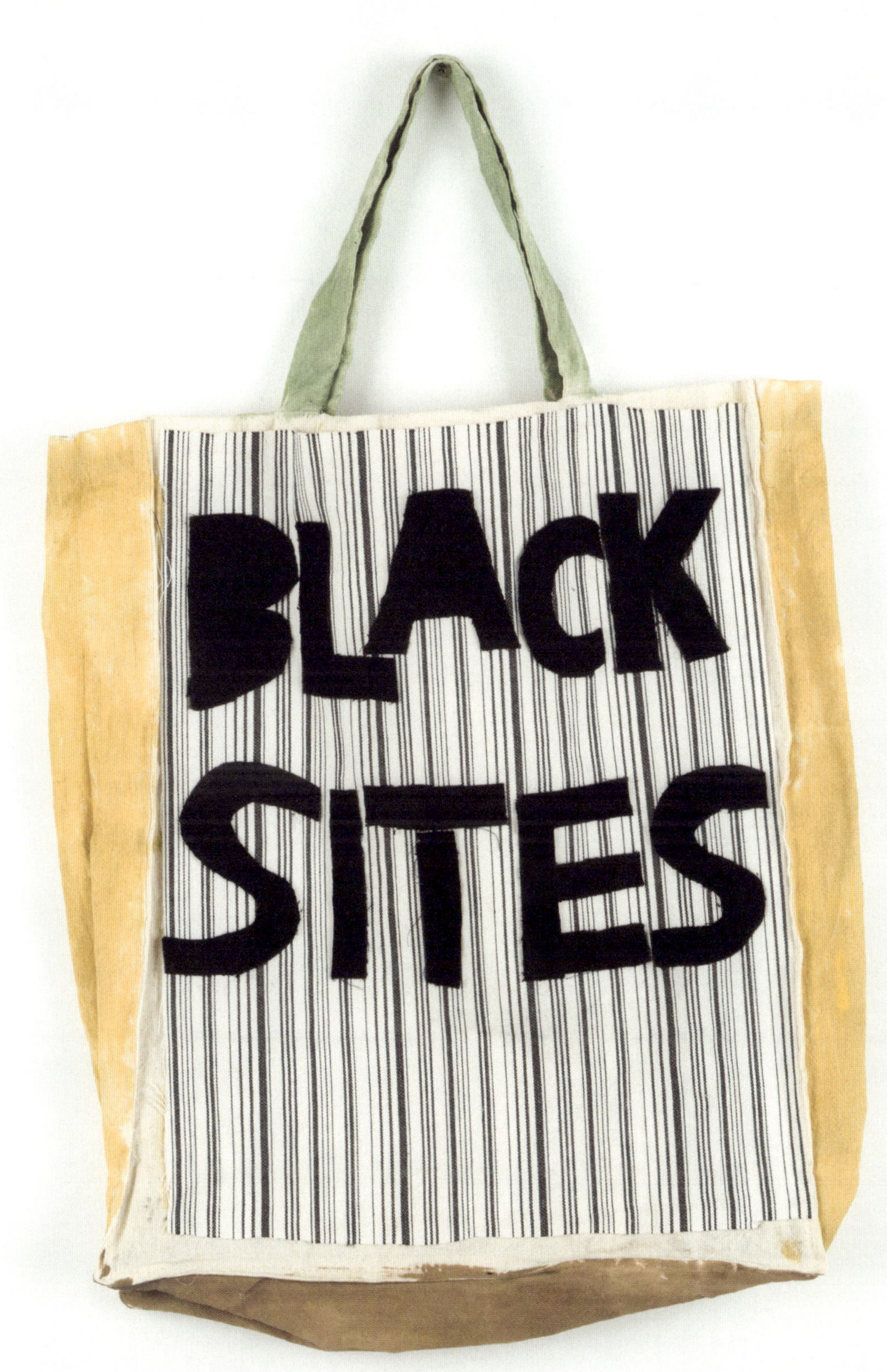
BLACK
SITES

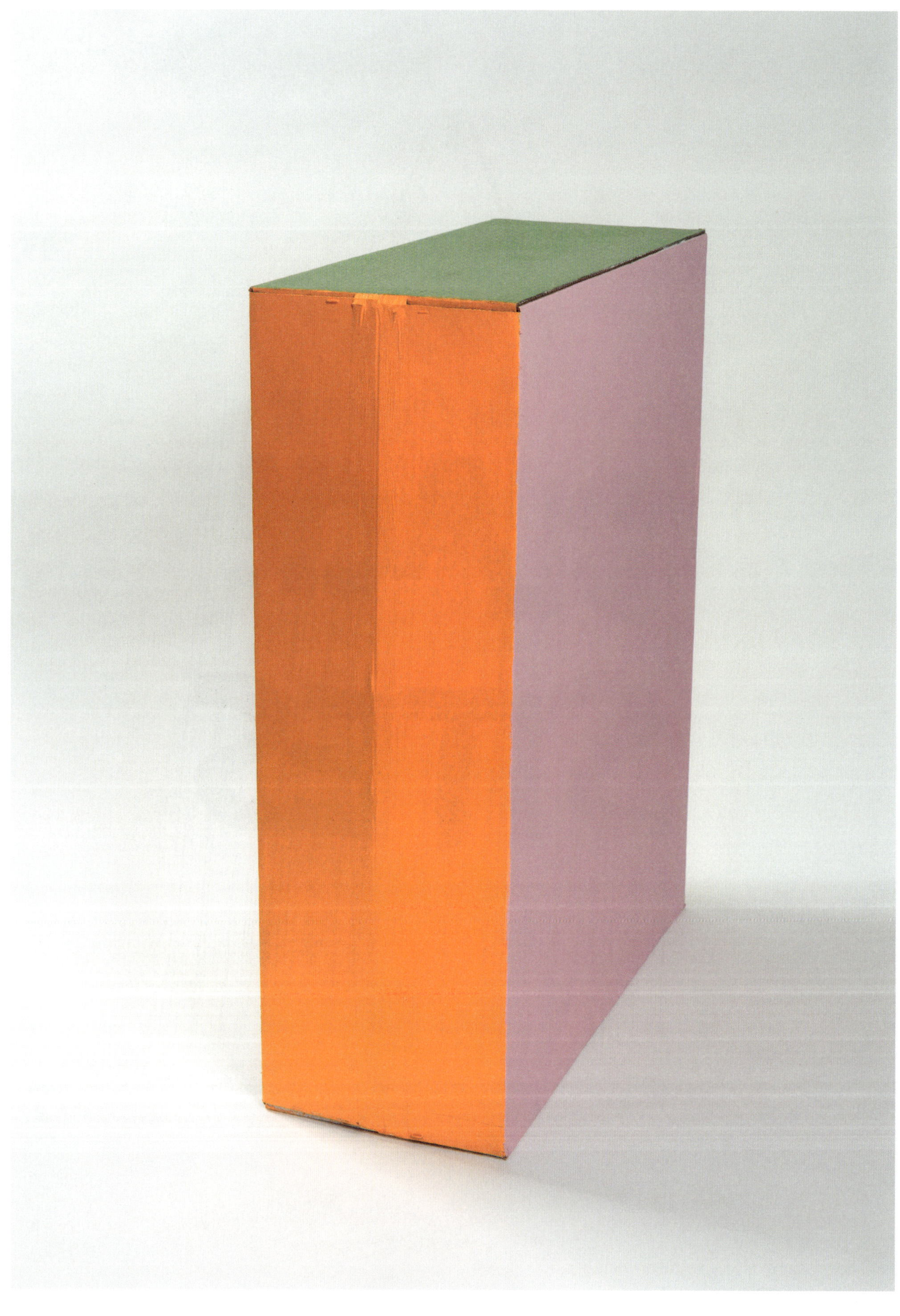

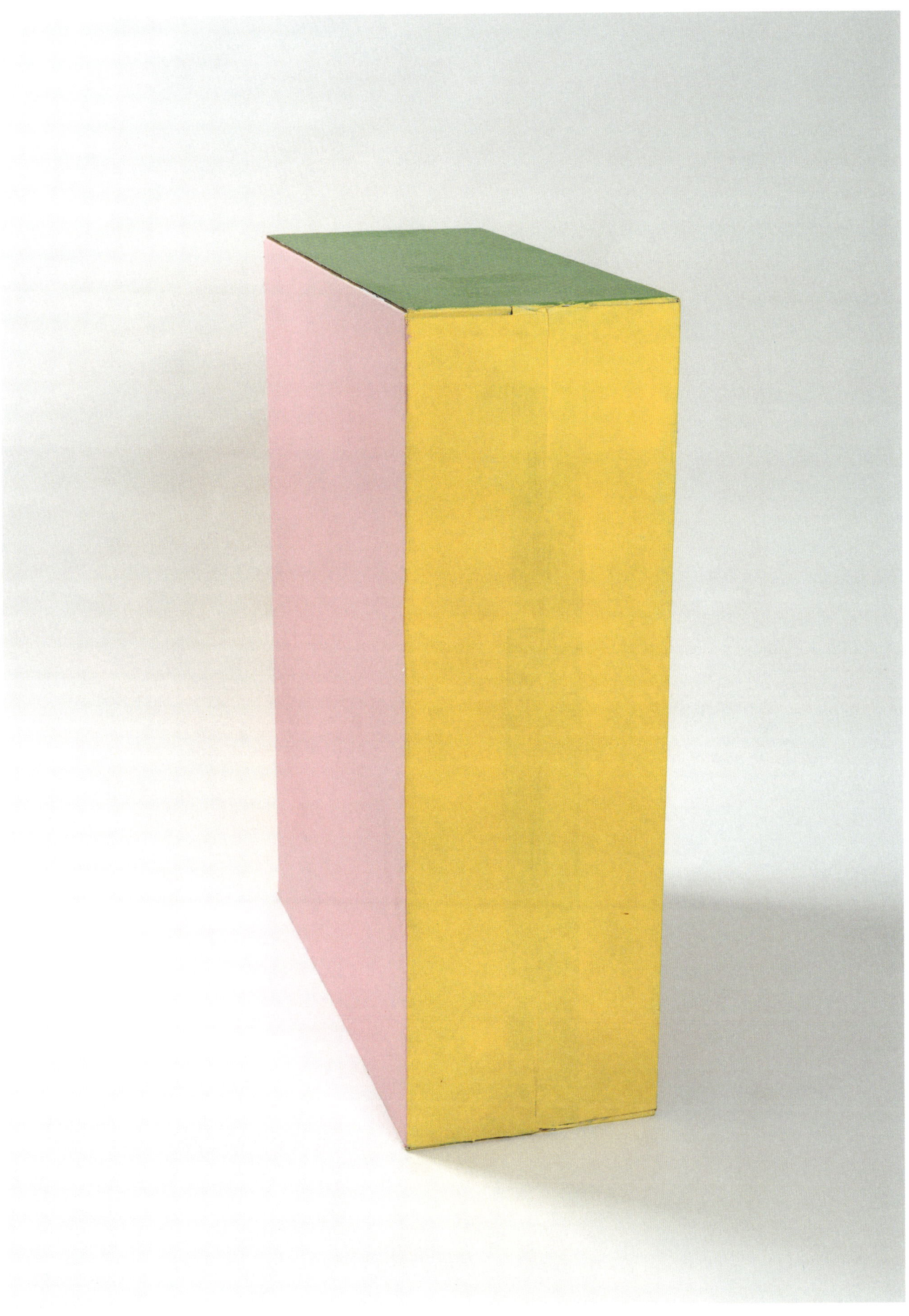

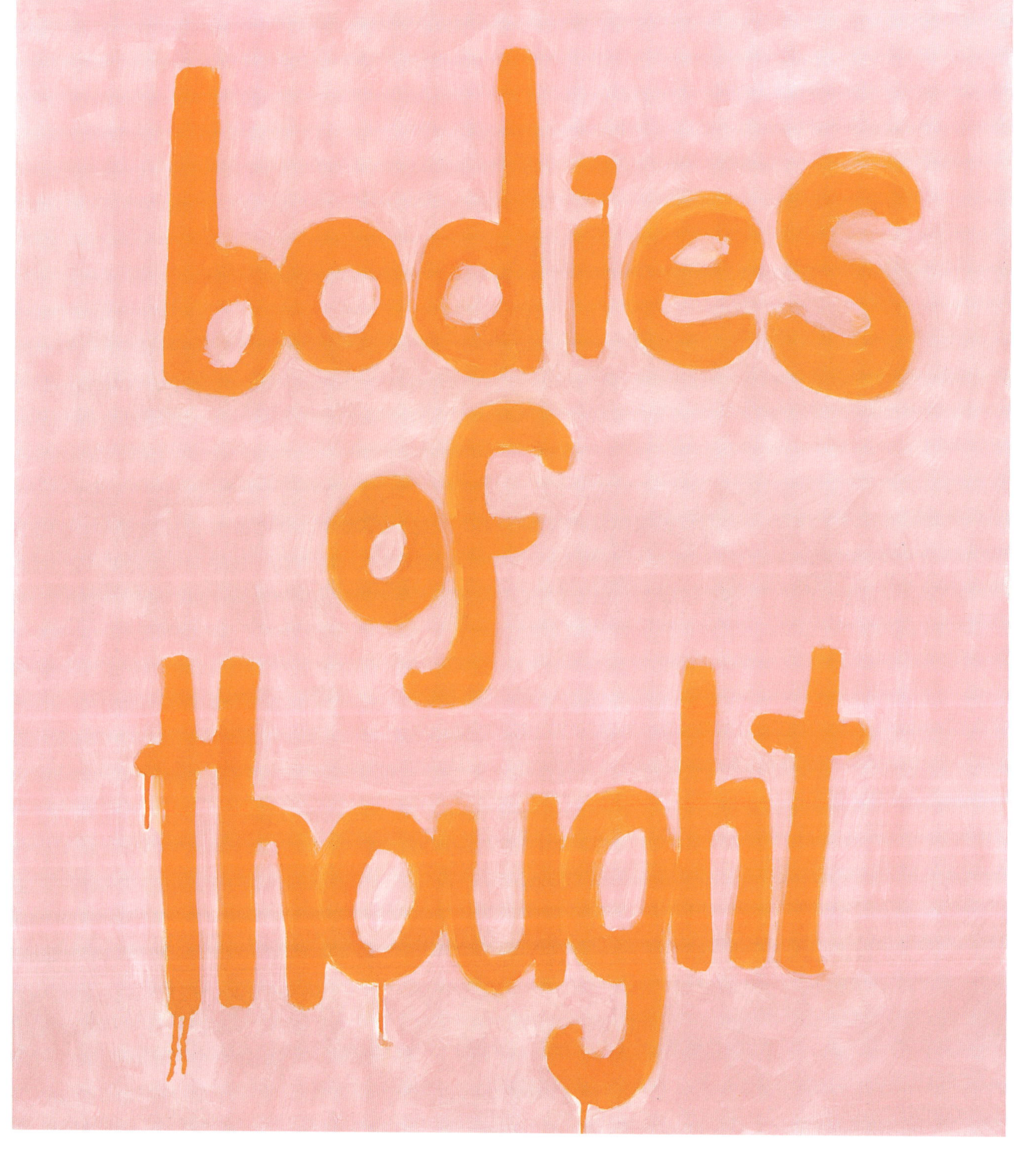
bodies
of
thought

THE TRUE
COLLECTOR
LOOKS FOR
THE WORK
THAT IS
UNFINISHED

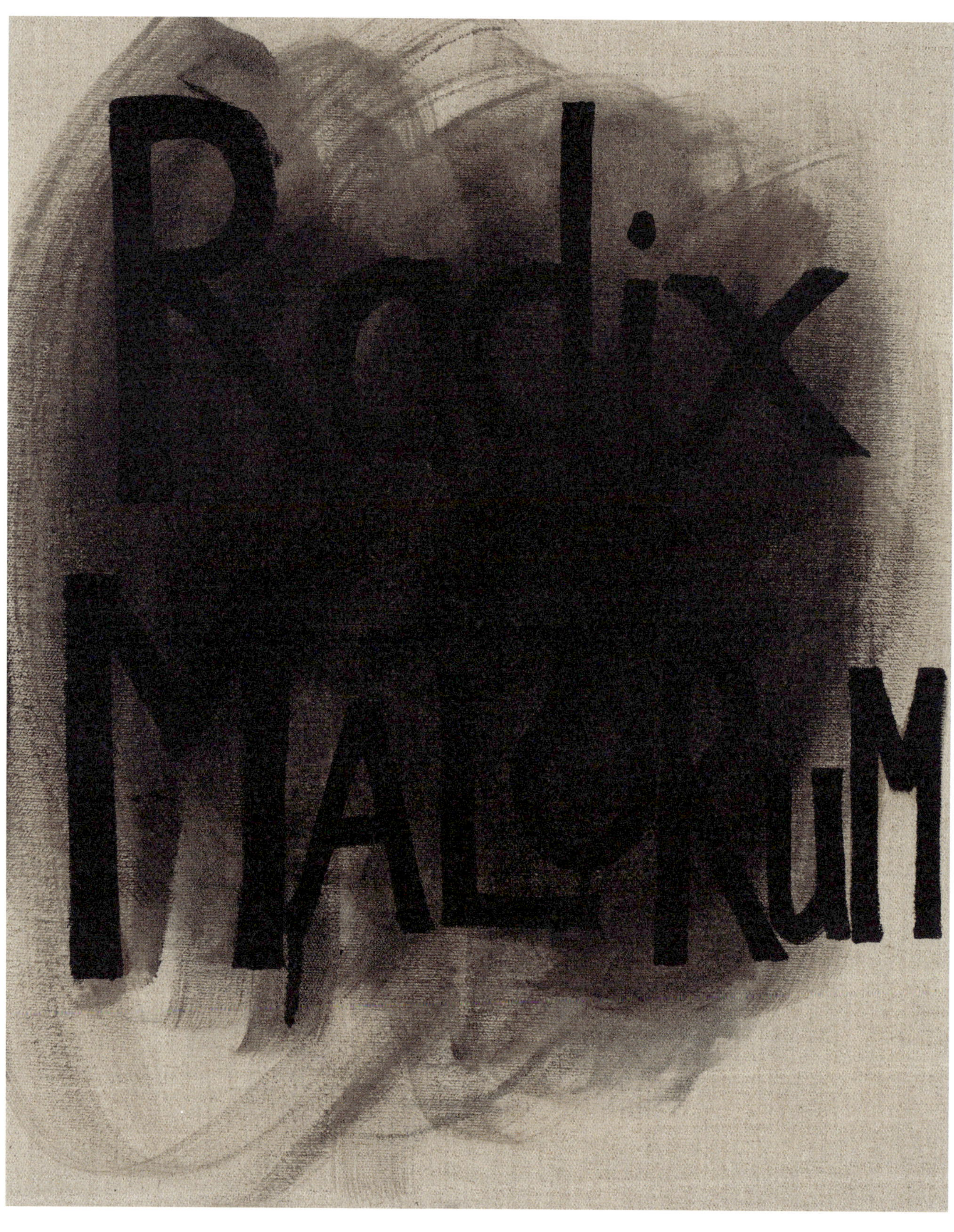
Radix
MALORuM

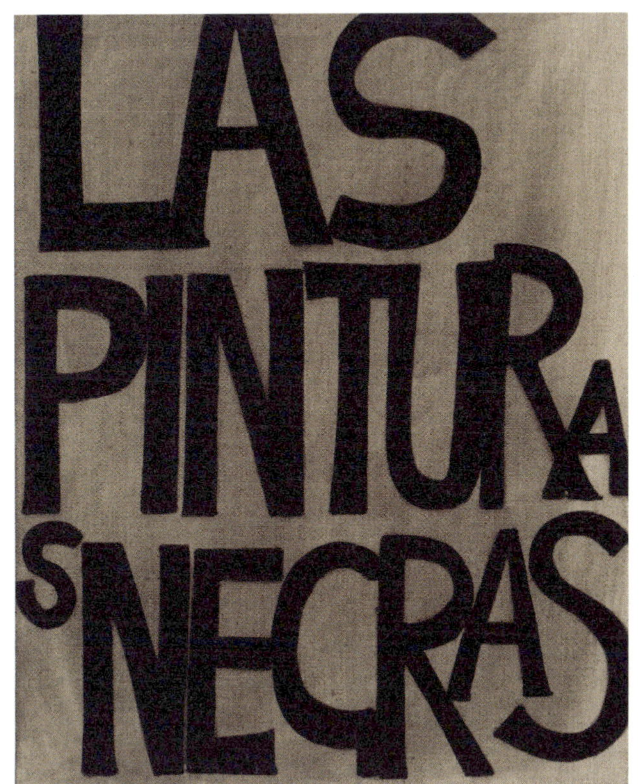
LAS
PINTURA
S NEGRAS

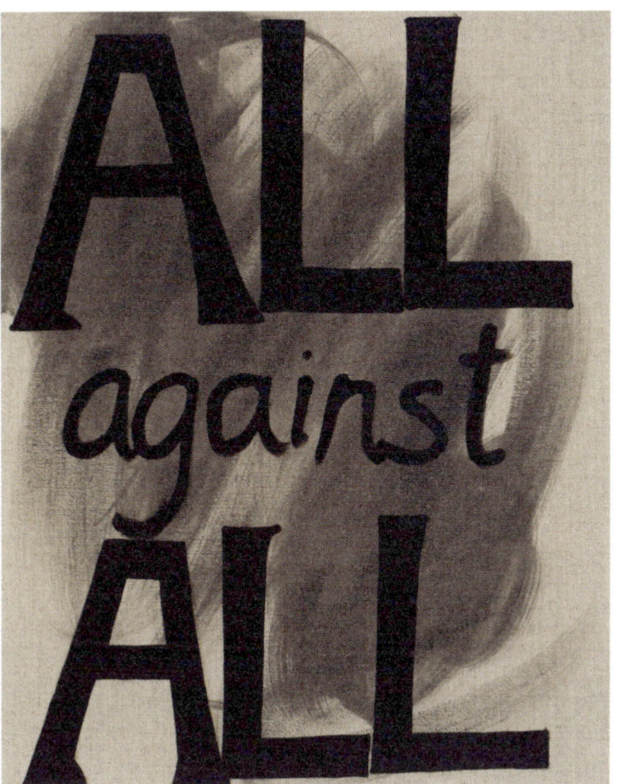
ALL
against
ALL

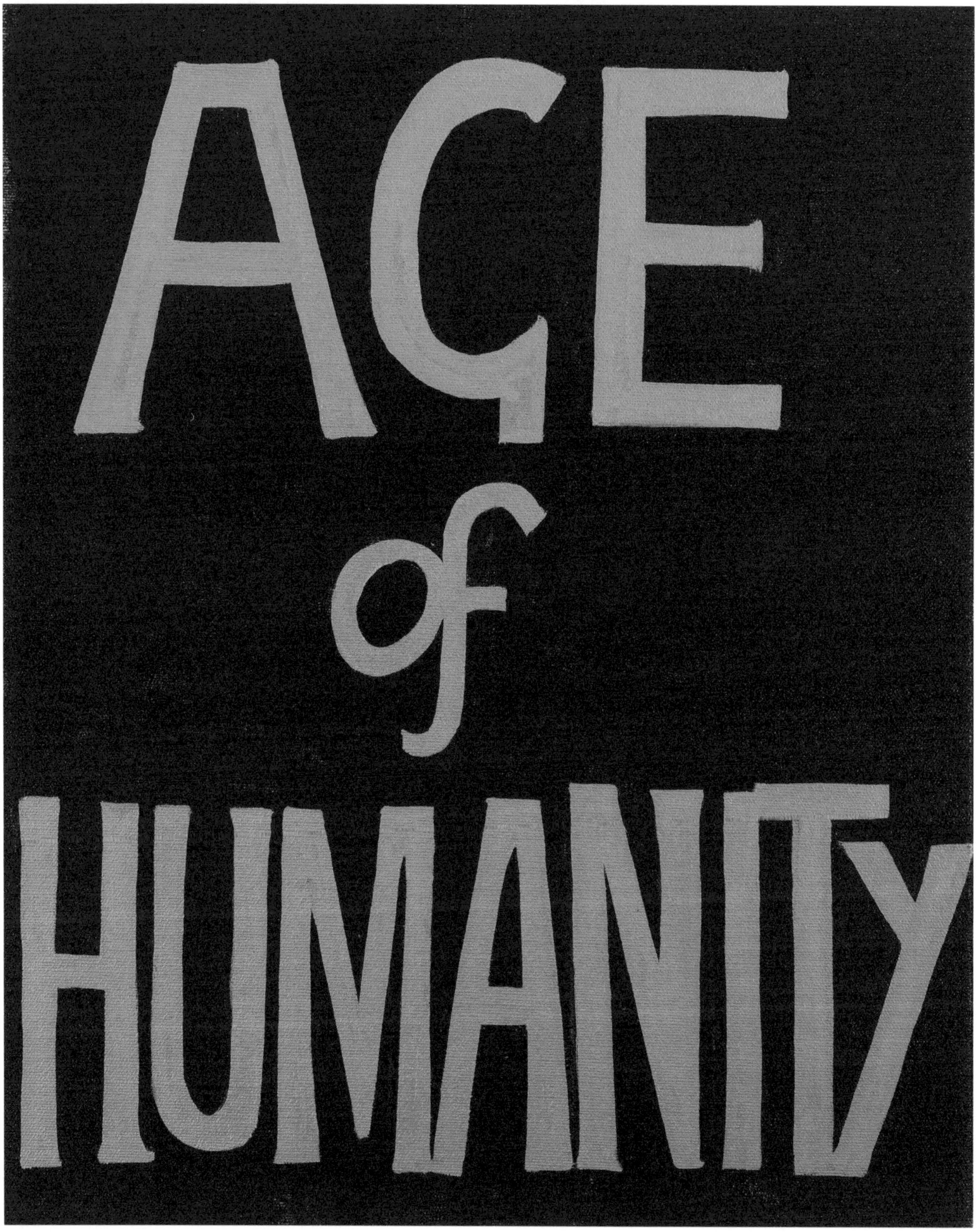

AGE
of
HUMANITY

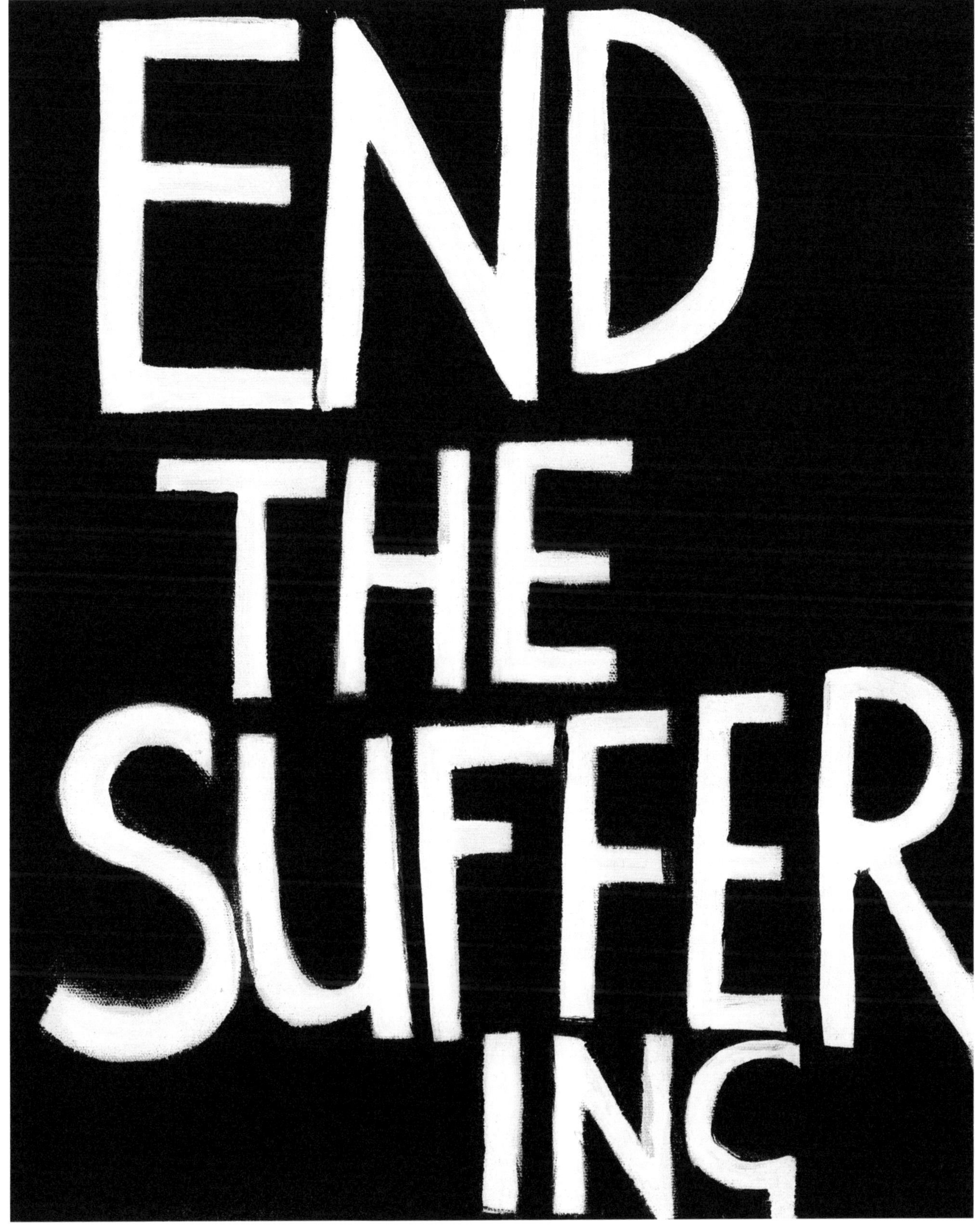
END
THE
SUFFER
ING

Elizabeth Newman
Still makin' history…

Published by Neon Parc and Discipline.
neonparc.com.au
discipline.net.au

Edited by Helen Hughes and Francis Plagne
Text by Francis Plagne
"Elizabeth Newman: Abstraction, Simulation, Obscuration" first published in *Discipline* 4 (2016): 35–40.
"Unknowns" first published in the catalogue of the exhibition *Elizabeth Newman: Un-titled* (Canberra: Drill Hall Gallery, 2021), 29–36.
Designed by Alexandra Margetic
Artwork photography by Christian Capurro, Simon Hewson
Darren Sylvester
Photograph editing by Aden Miller
Proofreading by Amy Stuart
Printed by Printon, Tallinn, Estonia
Edition of 500
Distributed in Australia by Manic Books

ISBN: 978-0-9945388-7-1

Acknowledgements
The publishers acknowledge the Wurundjeri people of the Kulin Nation as sovereign custodians of the land on which they live and work. Always was, always will be Aboriginal land.

The artist thanks Neon Parc and Darren Knight Gallery.

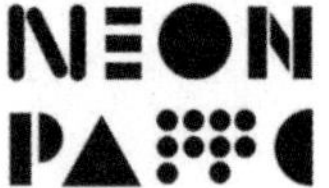